W9-BMQ-606

THOMSON

NELSON

ISBN 0-17-642269-2

Consists of:

Professional Selling: A Trust-Based Approach, Third Edition
Ingram/LaForge/Avila/
Schwepker Jr./Williams

ISBN 0-324-32103-1, © 2006

Tejal Govande

Contents

....

....

UNDERSTANDING YOUR BUYERS' NEEDS AND DREAMS IS THE KEY TO SUCCESS

David Laube is a securities principal at the Bloomington office of GCG Financial, where he works with a diverse client base including organizations, individuals, and families. Based on his 20-plus years of experience crafting innovative, effective solutions for clients' complicated financial problems, David emphasizes that customers do not simply buy products and features. Instead, they look for the greatest value in terms of the benefits and satisfaction brought to them by the features of a product. They make the decision to purchase through a purposeful decision process that begins with the recognition of needs and/or unfulfilled expectations. Like other top sales professionals, David is quick to explain that his success stems from an understanding that great salespeople do not sell, but rather serve as a counsel to the buyer to better understand the true nature of their problems and needs.

John and Laura Kent are typical of David's clients, illustrating the critical role today's sales professional plays in counseling buyers regarding unrecognized needs and assisting as a trusted partner in moving through the sequential stages of the buyer's purchase decision process. John and Laura truly believed their existing personal financial plan was working fine for them and their children. Their dual incomes of $165,000 produced adequate cash flow, they both participated in their respective companies' 401(k) plans, they were enrolled in their fringe benefit plans, and they received substantial tax refunds annually. Yet, on the advice and referral of a close friend of Laura's, they decided to seek professional guidance.

Little did the Kents realize that their plan was little more than a good start toward a comprehensive financial plan. After a preliminary meeting with veteran planner David Laube, CLU, CFS, ChFC, their eyes were opened further. The initial briefing revealed how little they actually knew about various planning strategies and options, not to mention the breadth of financial products available to them. They also quickly discovered that their "at-home, over-the dinner-table discussions" were sporadic and less communicative than they believed. Their major goals focused on retirement, family security in the event of any setback or tragedy, college funding for their two children, and creating an option plan to become self-employed and free of their stressful and often demanding corporate jobs.

During their second appointment, after deciding a fee-based plan would be more objective, they brought in their tax returns, investment contracts, wills, fringe benefit statements, life and health insurance contracts, and a roughly crafted budget. What they encountered, well beyond the mere contracts, were probing questions about their goals, objectives, dreams, and fears. Laube guided them through a one and one-half hour "discovery" session.

Emotionally, the Kents thought they were both on the "same page"; what the "discovery" appointment revealed to them was how differently they each viewed their financial plan along with their respective personal biases. Laube artfully led them through the differences and "pressure points" that their in-home discussions often avoided.

Financial planning, when done correctly, is a trust-based selling process. It is a series of coordinated steps leading to a comprehensive written plan with stated recommendations for implementation tied to the clients' goals, needs, and personal situation, yet anchored within the parameters of the clients' budget, risk-tolerance, tax bracket, time frames, and other variables. An effective planner listens closely and is

Objectives

After completing this module, you should be able to

1 Categorize primary types of buyers.

2 Discuss the distinguishing characteristics of business markets.

3 List the different steps in the business-to-business buying process.

4 Discuss the different types of buyer needs.

5 Describe how buyers evaluate suppliers and alternative sales offerings by using the multiattribute model of evaluation.

6 Explain the two-factor model that buyers use to evaluate the performance of sales offerings and develop satisfaction.

7 Explain the different types of purchasing decisions.

8 Describe the four communication styles and how salespeople must adapt and flex their own styles to maximize communication.

9 Explain the concept of buying teams and specify the different member roles.

59

a skilled and artful questioner. He utilizes a systematic process to uncover the clients' needs, wants, and objectives, plus their conscious and subconscious fears and emotional triggers. Once the plan was designed, planning strategies and financial products that utilize various companies' products were presented to the Kents in implementing their plan. Together with their advisor, they chose which recommendations to implement and began to follow a timeline to address the issues their plan encompassed.

The key to planning is understanding your clients' needs and dreams. This goes far beyond income, fringe benefits, and contracts they may hold—it encompasses attitudes, values, biases, dreams, and beliefs. Like any contemporary salesperson, educating the client and motivating the client to act—to implement the solution—are perhaps the financial consultant's greatest challenges.

David Laube's selling experience in assisting John and Laura Kent with their financial plan illustrates several fundamentals regarding buyer behavior. Principal among these fundamentals are (1) buyers do not buy products and features—they buy benefits and (2) purchase decisions result from a purposeful buying process that begins with the recognition of needs that are important to the buyer. As illustrated in the opening vignette, Laube recognizes that a family's financial plans are complicated. There are many needs that buyers are not initially aware of or are not easily recognized or anticipated. These unrecognized needs are opportunities for the salesperson to build and enhance added-value for the buyer while simultaneously generating a long-term buyer–seller relationship for valuable repeat business.

Source: Personal interview with David Laube, July 26, 2004.

Following a discussion on different types of buyers, this module develops a model of the buying process and the corresponding roles of the salesperson. Buyer activities characteristic to each step of the purchase decision process are explained and related to salesperson activities for effectively interacting with buyers. This is followed by an explanation of different types of purchasing decisions to which salespeople must respond. The influence of individual communication styles on selling effectiveness is also discussed. The growing incidence of multiple buying influences and buying teams is then demonstrated, along with their impact on selling strategy. Finally, emergent trends such as relationship strategies, supply-chain management, target pricing, and the growing importance of information and technology are discussed from the perspective of the salesperson.

TYPES OF BUYERS

Salespeople work and interact with many different types of buyers. These buyer types range from heavy industry and manufacturing operations to consumers making a purchase for their own use. These variants of customer types arise out of the unique buying situations they occupy. As a result, one type of buyer will have needs, motivations, and buying behavior that are very different from another type of buyer. Consider the different buying situations and the resulting needs of a corporate buyer for Footlocker compared with the athletic equipment buyer for a major university or Joe Smith, attorney at law and weekend warrior in the local YMCA's basketball league. As illustrated in Exhibit 3.1, each of these buyers may be looking for athletic shoes, but their buying needs are very different. To maximize selling effectiveness, salespeople must understand the type of buyer with whom they are working and respond to their specific needs, wants, and expectations.

The most common categorization of buyers splits them into either (1) **consumer markets** or (2) **business markets.** Consumers purchase goods and services for their own use or consumption and are highly influenced by peer group behavior, aesthetics, and personal taste. Business markets are composed of firms, institutions, and governments. These members of the business market acquire goods and services to use as inputs into their own manufacturing process (i.e., raw materials, component parts, and capital equipment), for use in their day-to-day operations (i.e., office supplies,

Different Needs of Different Athletic Shoe Buyers		**EXHIBIT 3.1**
	Buyer for Footlocker Shoe Stores	**University Athletic Equipment Buyer**	**Joe Smith—YMCA Weekend Warrior**

	Buyer for Footlocker Shoe Stores	**University Athletic Equipment Buyer**	**Joe Smith—YMCA Weekend Warrior**
Functional Needs	• Has the features customers want • Well constructed—minimizes returns • Offers point-of-sale displays for store use • Competitive pricing	• Individualized sole texture for different player performance needs • Perfect fit and size for each team member • Custom match with university colors • Size of supplier's payment to coach and school for using their shoes	• Offers the leading edge in shoe features • Prominent brand logo • Highest-priced shoes in the store
Situational Needs	• Can supply stores across North America • Ability to ship to individual stores on a just-in-time basis • Offers 90-day trade credit	• Ability to deliver on time • Provide supplier personnel for team fittings • Make contract payments to university and coach at beginning of season	• Right size in stock, ready to carry out • Takes Visa and MasterCard
Social Needs	• Invitation for buying team to attend trade show and supplier-sponsored reception	• Sponsor and distribute shoes at annual team shoe night to build enthusiasm • Include team and athletes in supplier brand promotions	• Offers user-group newsletter to upscale customers • Periodic mailings for new products and incentives to purchase
Psychological Needs	• Assurance that shoes will sell at retail • Brand name with strong market appeal • Option to return unsold goods for credit	• Brand name consistent with players' self-images • The entire team will accept and be enthusiastic toward product decision • Belief that the overall contract is best for the university, team, and coaches	• Reinforces customer's self-image as an innovator • Product will deliver the promised performance • One of only a few people having purchased this style of shoe
Knowledge Needs	• Level of quality—how the shoe is constructed • How the new features impact performance • What makes the shoe unique and superior to competitive offerings • Product training and materials for sales staff	• What makes the shoe unique and superior to competitive offerings • Supporting information and assurance that the contracted payments to university and coaches are superior to competitive offerings	• What makes the shoe unique and superior to competitive offerings • Assurance that everybody on the court will not be wearing the same shoe

professional services, insurance), or for resale to their own customers. Business customers tend to stress overall value as the cornerstone for purchase decisions.

Distinguishing Characteristics of Business Markets

Although there are similarities between consumer and business buying behaviors, business markets tend to be much more complex and possess several characteristics that are in sharp contrast to those of the consumer market. These distinguishing characteristics are described in the following sections.

Concentrated Demand

Business markets typically exhibit high levels of concentration in which a small number of large buyers account for most of the purchases. The fact that business buyers tend to be larger in size but fewer in numbers can greatly impact a salesperson's selling plans and performance. For example, a salesperson selling high-grade industrial silicon for use in manufacturing computer chips will find that his or her fate rests on acquiring and nurturing the business of one or more of the four or five dominant chip makers around the world. For example, Intel remains the dominant leader in this industry achieving a sales level that is three times that of the second, third, or fourth largest manufacturers. The concentration and size gaps are even more evident after the top four companies. In manufacturing positions 5 through 10, the average company's sales approximate only one-tenth of the industry leader's production.

Derived Demand

Derived demand denotes that the demand in business markets is closely associated with the demand for consumer goods. When the consumer demand for new cars and trucks increases, the demand for rolled steel also goes up. Of course, when the demand for consumer products goes down, so goes the related demand in business markets. The most effective salespeople identify and monitor the consumer markets that are related to their business customers so they can better anticipate shifts in demand and assist their buyers in staying ahead of the demand shifts rather than being caught with too much, too little, or even the wrong inventory. Republic Gypsum's salespeople accurately forecast a boom in residential construction and the pressure it would put on the supply of sheetrock wallboard. Working closely with their key customers, order quantities and shipping dates were revised to prevent those customers from being caught with inadequate inventories to supply the expanded demand. This gave those customers a significant competitive advantage over their competitors who were surprised and suddenly out of stock.

Higher Levels of Demand Fluctuation

Closely related to the derived demand characteristic, the demand for goods and services in the business market is more volatile than that of the consumer market. In economics, this is referred to as the **acceleration principle**. As demand increases (or decreases) in the consumer market, the business market reacts by accelerating the buildup (or reduction) of inventories and increasing (or decreasing) plant capacity. A good example would be the rapidly growing demand for tri-mode wireless phones with advanced capabilities such as voice-activated dialing and vision-enabled access to the Internet and Web on enhanced full-color screens. In response to higher consumer demand, wholesalers and retailers are increasing their inventories of these advanced phones while decreasing the number of single-mode voice-only devices they carry. In response, manufacturers have shifted their production away from the voice-only wireless phones to increase their production of the more advanced Internet-capable models. Salespeople are the source of valuable information and knowledge enabling their customers to anticipate these fluctuations and assisting them in developing more effective marketing strategies. As a result, both the buying and selling organizations realize mutual positive benefits.

Purchasing Professionals

Buyers in the business markets are trained as purchasing agents. The process of identifying suppliers and sourcing goods and services is their job. This results in a more professional and rational approach to purchasing. As a result, salespeople must possess increased levels of knowledge and expertise to provide customers with a richer and more detailed assortment of application, performance, and technical data.

Multiple Buying Influences

Reflecting the increased complexity of many business purchases, groups of individuals within the buying firm often work together as a buying team or center. As a result, salespeople often work simultaneously with several individuals during a sales call and even different sets of buyers during different sales calls. Buying team members come from different areas of expertise and play different roles in the purchasing process. To be effective, the salesperson must first identify, then understand and respond to, the role and key buying motives of each member.

Close Buyer–Seller Relationships

The smaller customer base and increased usage of supply chain management, characterized by buyers becoming highly involved in organizing and administering logistical processes and actively managing a reduced set of suppliers, has resulted in buyers and sellers becoming much more interdependent than ever before. This increased interdependence and desire to reduce risk of the unknown has led to an emphasis on developing long-term buyer–seller relationships characterized by increased levels of buyer–seller interaction and higher levels of service expectations by buyers. "Professional Selling in the 21st Century: It's No Longer All About Lowest Price"[1] describes the emerging change in buyers' expectations from a price emphasis to relationships and problem-solving solutions. This shift requires salespeople to change their focus from quickly selling the buyer and closing the current transaction and, in its place, adapt a longer-term perspective emphasizing continuing multiple exchanges into the future. This perspective often includes making multiple sales calls to develop a better understanding of the buyer's needs and then responding to those needs with a sales offering that solves the buyer's needs and enhances the buyer–seller relationship in favor of future interactions.

THE BUYING PROCESS

Buyers in both the consumer and business marketplace undergo a conscious and logical process in making purchase decisions. As depicted in Figure 3.1, the sequential and interrelated phases of the **business buyers' purchase process** begin with (1) *recognition of the problem or need*, (2) *determination of the characteristics of the item and the quantity needed*, (3) *description of the characteristics of the item and quantity needed*, (4) *search for and qualification of potential sources*, (5) *acquisition and analysis of proposals*, (6) *evaluation of proposals and selection of suppliers*, (7) *selection of an order routine*, and (8) *performance feedback and evaluation*.

PROFESSIONAL SELLING IN THE 21ST CENTURY

It's No Longer All About Lowest Price

Results from the Quality Insurance Congress (QIC) and the Risk and Insurance Management Society's (RIMS) series of "*Voice of the Customer*" research studies describe the tremendous changes in buyers' needs and expectations that are reshaping the commercial property and casualty insurance market.

These changes reflect a radically changed business environment and buying motives. No longer is lowest price the primary consideration in the insurance purchase decision. Certainly, price must be in line with the total value received. But today, business buyers of property and casualty insurance emphasize the importance of long-term *partnerships, mutual trust, and innovative solutions in their evaluation and choice of vendors. The RIMS-QIC Quality Scorecard research program documents this shift in buyer expectations and identifies the four primary supplier performance expectations impacting customer satisfaction and loyalty to suppliers as the following:*

1. *Identifying customer needs and creating innovative solutions.*
2. *Building internal and external partnerships.*
3. *Generating and maintaining trust and reliability.*
4. *Engaging in two-way interactive communications.*

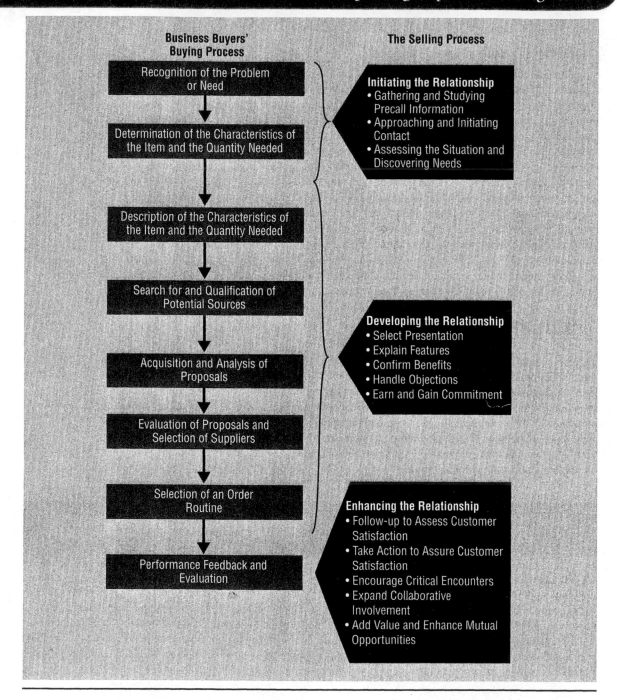

FIGURE 3.1   Comparison of Buying Decision Process Phases and Corresponding Steps in the Selling Process

Depending upon the nature of the buying organization and the buying situation, the buying process may be highly formalized or simply a rough approximation of what actually occurs. The decision process employed by General Motors for the acquisition of a new organization-wide computer system will be highly formalized and purposefully reflect each of the previously described decision phases. Compared to General Motors, the decision process of Bloomington Bookkeeping, a single office and four-person operation, could be expected to use a less formalized approach in working through their buying decision process for a computer system. In the decision to replenish stock office supplies, both of the organizations are likely to use a much less formalized routine—but still, a routine that reflects the different decision phases.

As further illustrated by Figure 3.1, there is a close correspondence between the phases of the buyer's decision process and the selling activities of the salesperson. It is important that salespeople understand and make use of the interrelationships between the phases of the buying process and selling activities. Effective use of these interrelationships offers salespeople numerous opportunities to interact with buyers in a way that guides the shaping of product specifications and the selection of sources while facilitating the purchase decision.

Phase One—Recognition of the Problem or Need: The Needs Gap

Needs are the result of a gap between buyers' **desired states** and their **actual states**. Consequently, need recognition results from an individual cognitively and emotionally processing information relevant to his or her actual state of being and comparing it to the desired state of being. As illustrated in Figure 3.2, any perceived difference, or **needs gap**, between these two states activates the motivation or drive to fill the gap and reach the desired state. For example, the SnowRunner Company's daily production capacity is limited to 1,000 molded skimobile body housings. Their research indicates that increasing capacity to 1,250 units per day would result in significant reductions in per-unit costs and allow them to enter additional geographic markets—both moves that would have significant and positive impacts on financial performance. The perceived need to expand production activates a corresponding motivation to search for information regarding alternative solutions and acquire the capability to increase production by 250 units.

However, if there is no gap, then there is no need and no active buying motive. It is common for salespeople to find themselves working with buyers who, for one reason or another, do not perceive a needs gap to be present. Possibly they do not have the right information or lack full understanding of the situation and the existence of options better than their current state. It is also possible that their understanding of the actual state might be incomplete or mistaken. For example, SnowRunner's buyers might not understand the cost reduction possibilities and increased market potential that could result from increased capacity. As a result, they perceive no need to increase production—the desired state is the same as their actual state. Similarly, the buyers might be functioning with incomplete information regarding the company's actual state of reduced production capacity due to SnowRunner's existing molding machines requiring increased downtime for maintenance. Properly realized, this lowering of the actual state would result in a needs gap. Successful salespeople position themselves to assist buyers in identifying and understanding needs as a result of their broader expertise and knowledge regarding product use and application.

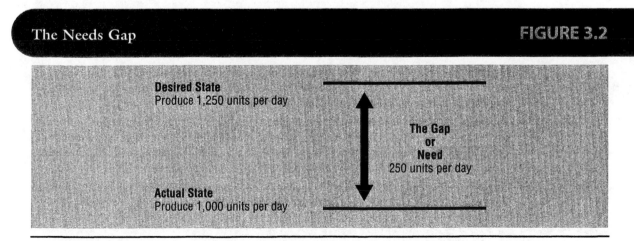

The Needs Gap   **FIGURE 3.2**

Desired State
Produce 1,250 units per day

**The Gap
or
Need**
250 units per day

Actual State
Produce 1,000 units per day

The needs gap is the difference between the buyer's perceived desired state and the buyer's perceived actual state.

Salespeople can also present buyers with information and opportunities that effectively raise the desired state, generate a need, and trigger the purchase decision process. Top-performing salespeople understand the importance of assisting their buyers in forming realistic perceptions of the actual state and the desired state. In this manner, the salesperson can continue to serve as a non-manipulative consultant to the buyer while affecting buying motives that yield mutual benefits to all parties. However, it should be noted that the persuasive power of assisting the buyer in determining and comparing desired and actual states can also be misused and lead to unethical and manipulative selling behaviors such as those exhibited in "An Ethical Dilemma."

AN ETHICAL DILEMMA

Ed Taylor is a senior salesperson for a national firm selling business automation equipment to retail and service companies. Ed has just been given the responsibility to mentor and help train a recently hired salesperson. Ed and the new salesperson have spent the day calling on new prospects and working through the company's fact-finder guide—a questioning sequence designed to collect information for profiling the prospective organization and its business automation needs. When they returned to the office, the salesperson asked Ed to show him how to analyze and use the customer information so that it would provide an understanding of which automation systems would be best for the particular customer's situation and needs. In response, Ed explained that, ". . . it is not necessary to detail the customer's needs. It's much more effective in terms of getting the sale to simply go through the information and find pieces to illustrate to the customer why they need the system that we want to sell them. That allows us to sell the systems that carry the highest sales commission." Ed commented further, "It might not be the optimum system for the specific customer, but it will work. And as long as you use some of the customer's information and feed it back to them, they think you have customized a system for them and will make the purchase. They're happy and you get the bigger commission—that's a win-win, right?" What do you think about Ed's preferred way of using customer information to make the sale? What problems might result from Ed's selling methodology?

Types of Buyer Needs

The total number of potential customer needs is infinite and sometimes difficult for salespeople to grasp and understand on a customer-by-customer basis. Consequently, many salespeople find it helpful to group customer needs into one of five basic types or categories that focus on the buying situation and the benefits to be provided by the product or service being chosen.[2] These five general types of buyer needs are described as follows:

- **Situational needs** are the specific needs that are contingent on, and often a result of, conditions related to the specific environment, time, and place (e.g., emergency car repair while traveling out of town, a piece of customized production equipment to fulfill a customer's specific situational requirements, or providing for quick initial shipment to meet a buyer's out-of-stock status).

- **Functional needs** represent the need for a specific core task or function to be performed—the functional purpose of a specific product or service. The need for a sales offering to do what it is supposed to do (e.g., alcohol disinfects, switches open and close to control some flow, the flow control valve is accurate and reliable).

- **Social needs** comprise the need for acceptance from and association with others—a desire to belong to some reference group. For example, a product or service might be associated with some specific and desired affinity group or segment (e.g., Polo clothing is associated with upper-income, successful people; ISO 9000 Certification is associated with high-quality vendors; leading e-commerce Web sites include discussion groups to build a sense of community).

- **Psychological needs** reflect the desire for feelings of assurance and risk reduction, as well as positive emotions and feelings such as success, joy, excitement, and stimulation (e.g., a Mont Blanc pen generates a feeling of success; effective training programs create a sense of self-control and determination; selection and use of well-known, high-quality brands provides assurance to buyers and organizations alike).

- **Knowledge needs** represent the desire for personal development, information, and knowledge to increase thought and understanding as to how and why things happen (e.g., product information, newsletters, brochures, along with training and user support group meetings/conferences provide current information on products and topics of interest).

Categorizing buyer needs by type can assist the salesperson in bringing order to what could otherwise be a confusing and endless mix of needs and expectations. Organizing the buyer's different needs into their basic types can help salespeople in several ways. First, as illustrated by Exhibit 3.1 and the example worksheet in Exhibit 3.2, the basic types can serve as a checklist or worksheet to ensure that no significant problems or needs have been overlooked in the process of needs discovery. Organizing what at first might appear to be different needs and problems into their common types also helps the salesperson to better understand the nature of the buyer's needs along with the interrelationships and commonalties between them. In turn, this enhanced understanding and the framework

Example Worksheet for Organizing Buyer Needs and Benefit-Based Solutions   **EXHIBIT 3.2**

Primary Buyer:	Bart Waits
Buying Organization:	SouthWest Metal Stampings
Primary Industry:	Stamped metal parts and sub-components

Basic Type of Need	Buyer's Specific Needs
Buyer's Situational Needs	• Requires an 18 percent increase in production to meet increased sales • On-hand inventory will not meet production/delivery schedule • Tight cash flow pending initial deliveries and receipt of payment
Buyer's Functional Needs	• Equipment to provide effective and efficient increase in production • Expedited delivery and installation in six weeks or less • Equipment financing extending payments beyond initial receipts
Buyer's Social Needs	• Expansion in production transforms them into Top 10 in industry • Belonging to user group of companies using this equipment • Feeling that they are an important customer of the supplier
Buyer's Knowledge Needs	• Confidence that selected equipment will meet needs and do job • Assurance that seller can complete installation in six weeks • Saving face—to believe borrowing for equipment is common • Evidence that this is the right choice • Understanding new technology used by the selected equipment • Training program for production employees and maintenance staff

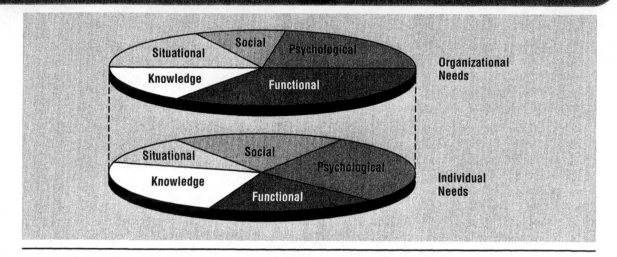

Business buyers' needs are a combination of the buyers' individual needs and the organization's needs.

of basic types combine to serve as a guide for salespeople in generating and then demonstrating value-added solutions in response to specific needs of the buyer.

As previously discussed, the specific circumstances or types of solution benefits that a buyer is seeking should determine a salesperson's strategy for working with that buyer. Consequently, it should be noted that the needs of business buyers tend to be more complex than consumers' needs. Like consumers, organizational buyers are people and are influenced by the same functional, social, psychological, knowledge, and situational experiences and forces that affect and shape individual needs. However, in addition to those individual needs, organizational buyers must also satisfy the needs and requirements of the organization for which they work. As depicted by Figure 3.3, these organizational needs overlay and interact with the needs of the individual. To maximize selling effectiveness in the organizational or business-to-business market, salespeople must generate solutions addressing both the individual and organizational needs of business buyers.

Phase Two—Determination of the Characteristics of the Item and the Quantity Needed

Coincident to recognizing a need or problem is the motivation and drive to resolve it by undertaking a search for additional information leading to possible solutions. This particular phase of the buying process involves the consideration and study of the overall situation to understand what is required in the form of a preferred solution. This begins to establish the general characteristics and quantities necessary to resolve the need or problem. Consultative salespeople use their knowledge and expertise at this point to assist the buyer in analyzing and interpreting the problem situation and needs. Salespeople offer valuable knowledge of problem situations and solution options that buyers typically perceive as beneficial.

Phase Three—Description of the Characteristics of the Item and the Quantity Needed

Using the desired characteristics and quantities developed in the previous phase as a starting point, buyers translate that general information into detailed specifications describing exactly what is expected and required. The determination of detailed specifications serves several purposes. First, detailed specifications guide supplier firms in developing their proposals. Second, these specifications provide the buyer a framework for evaluating, comparing, and choosing among the proposed solutions. Post-purchase specifications serve as a standard for evaluation to ensure that the buying firm receives the required product features and quantities. Trust-based buyer–seller relationships allow salespeople to work closely with buyers and collaboratively assist them in establishing the detailed specifications of the preferred solutions.

Phase Four—Search For and Qualification of Potential Sources

Next, buyers must locate and qualify potential suppliers capable of providing the preferred solution. Although buyers certainly utilize information provided by salespeople to identify qualified suppliers, there is an abundance of information available from other sources such as trade associations, product source directories, trade shows, the Internet, advertising, and word of mouth. Once identified, potential suppliers are qualified on their ability to consistently perform and deliver at the level of quality and quantity required. Due to the large number of information sources available to buyers researching potential suppliers, one of the most important tasks in personal selling is to win the position of one of those information sources and keep buyers informed about the salesperson's company, its new products, and solution capabilities.

Phase Five—Acquisition and Analysis of Proposals

Based on the detailed specifications, **requests for proposals** (known in the trade as an **RFP**) are developed and distributed to the qualified potential suppliers. Based on the RFP, qualified suppliers develop and submit proposals to provide the products as specified. Salespeople play a critical and influential role in this stage of the buying process by developing and presenting the proposed solution to the buyers. In this role, the salesperson is responsible for presenting the proposed features and benefits in such a manner that the proposed solution is evaluated as providing higher levels of benefits and value to the buyer than other competing proposals. Consequently, it is imperative that salespeople understand the basic evaluation procedures used by buyers in comparing alternative and competitive proposals so they can be more proficient in demonstrating the superiority of their solution over the competition.

Procedures for Evaluating Suppliers and Products

Purchase decisions are based on the buyers' comparative evaluations of suppliers and the products and services they propose for satisfying the buyers' needs. Some buyers may look for the sales offering that receives the highest rating on the one characteristic they perceive as being most important. Others may prefer the sales offering that achieves some acceptable assessment score across each and every attribute desired by the buyer. However, research into how purchase decisions are made suggests that most buyers use a compensatory, **multiattribute model** incorporating weighted averages across desired characteristics.[3] These weighted averages incorporate (1) assessments of how well the product or supplier performs in meeting each of the specified characteristics and (2) the relative importance of each specified characteristic.

Assessment of Product or Supplier Performance

The first step in applying the multiattribute model is to objectively rate how well each characteristic of the competing products or suppliers meets the buyers' needs. Let's use the example of General Motors (GM) evaluating adhesives for use in manufacturing. The buyers have narrowed the alternatives to products proposed by three suppliers: BondIt #302, AdCo #45, and StikFast #217. As illustrated in Exhibit 3.3, the GM buying team has assessed the competitive products according to how well they perform on certain important attributes. These assessments are converted to scores as depicted in Exhibit 3.4, with scores ranging from 1 (very poor performance) to 10 (excellent performance).

EXHIBIT 3.3   Important Product Information

Characteristics	BondIt #302	AdCo #45	StikFast #217
Ease of application	Excellent	Good	Very good
Bonding time	8 minutes	10 minutes	12 minutes
Durability	10 years	12 years	15 years
Reliability	Very good	Excellent	Good
Non-toxic	Very good	Excellent	Very good
Quoted price	$28 per gal.	$22 per gal.	$26 per gal.
Shelf-life in storage	6 months	4 months	4 months
Service factors	Good	Very good	Excellent

As illustrated, no single product is consistently outstanding across each of the eight identified characteristics. Although BondIt #302 is easy to apply and uses the buyer's current equipment, it is also more expensive and has the shortest durability time in the field. StikFast #217 also scores well for ease of application, and it has superior durability. However, it has the longest bonding time and could negatively influence production time.

Accounting for Relative Importance of Each Characteristic

To properly compare these performance differences, each score must be weighted by the characteristic's perceived importance. In the adhesive example, importance weights are assigned on a scale of 1 (relatively unimportant) to 10 (very important). As illustrated in Exhibit 3.5, multiplying each performance score by the corresponding attribute's importance weight results in a weighted average that can be totaled to calculate an overall rating for each product. The product or supplier having the highest comparative rating is typically the product selected for purchase. In this example, AdCo has the highest overall evaluation totaling 468 points compared with BondIt's 430 points and StikFast's 446 points.

Employing Buyer Evaluation Procedures to Enhance Selling Strategies

Understanding evaluation procedures and gaining insight as to how a specific buyer or team of buyers is evaluating suppliers and proposals is vital for the salesperson to be effective and requires the integration of several bases of knowledge. First, information gathered prior to the sales call must be combined with an effective needs-discovery dialogue with the buyer(s) to delineate the buyers' needs and the nature of the desired solution. This establishes the most likely criteria for evaluation. Further discussion between the buyer and seller can begin to establish the importance the buyers place on each of the different performance criteria and often yields information as to what suppliers and products are being considered. Using this information and the salesperson's knowledge of how their products compare with competitors' offerings allows the salesperson to complete a likely facsimile

EXHIBIT 3.4   Product Performance Scores

Characteristics	BondIt #302	AdCo #45	StikFast #217
Ease of application	10	5	8
Bonding time	8	6	4
Durability	6	8	9
Reliability	8	10	5
Non-toxic	8	10	8
Quoted price	5	9	7
Shelf-life in storage	9	6	6
Service factors	5	8	10

Weighted Averages for Performance Times Importance and Overall Evaluation Scores									EXHIBIT 3.5

Characteristics	BondIt #302			AdCo #45			StikFast #217		
	P	I	P×I	P	I	P×I	P	I	P×I
Ease of application	10	8	80	5	8	40	8	8	72
Bonding time	8	6	48	6	6	36	4	6	24
Durability	6	9	54	8	9	72	9	9	81
Reliability	8	7	56	10	7	70	5	7	35
Non-toxic	8	6	48	10	6	60	8	6	48
Quoted price	5	10	50	9	10	90	7	10	70
Shelf-life in storage	9	6	54	6	6	36	6	6	36
Service factors	5	8	40	8	8	64	10	8	80
Overall evaluation score			430			468			446

of the buyers' evaluation. With this enhanced level of preparation and understanding, the salesperson can plan, create, and deliver a more effective presentation using the five fundamental strategies that are inherent within the evaluation procedures used by buyers.

- *Modify the Product Offering Being Proposed.* Oftentimes, in the course of preparing or delivering a presentation, it becomes apparent that the product offering will not maximize the buyer's evaluation score in comparison with a competitor's offering. In this case, the strategy would be to modify or change the product to one that better meets the buyer's overall needs and thus would receive a higher evaluation. For example, by developing a better understanding of the adhesive buyer's perceived importance of certain characteristics, the BondIt salesperson could offer a different adhesive formulation that is not as easy to apply (low perceived importance) but offers improved durability (perceived high importance) and more competitive price (perceived high importance).

- *Alter the Buyer's Beliefs about the Proposed Offering.* Provide information and support to alter the buyer's beliefs as to where the proposed product stands on certain attributes. This is a recommended strategy for cases in which the buyer underestimates the true qualities of the proposed product. However, if the buyer's perceptions are correct, this strategy would encourage exaggerated and overstated claims by the salesperson and should be avoided. In the instance of BondIt #302's low evaluation score, the salesperson could offer the buyer information and evidence that the product's durability and service factors actually perform much better than the buyer initially believed. By working with the buyer to develop a more realistic perception of the product's performance, BondIt #302 could become the buyer's preferred choice.

- *Alter the Buyer's Beliefs about the Competitor's Offering.* For a variety of reasons, buyers often mistakenly believe that a competitor's offering has higher level attributes or qualities than it actually does. In such an instance, the salesperson can provide information to evidence a more accurate picture of the competitor's attributes. This has been referred to as **competitive depositioning** and is carried out by openly comparing (not simply degrading) the competing offering's attributes, advantages, and weaknesses. As an illustration, the BondIt salesperson might demonstrate the *total* cost for each of the three product alternatives, including quoted price, ease of application, and bonding time. BondIt is much easier to apply and has a faster bonding time. Consequently, less of it must be applied for each application, which results in a significantly lower total cost and a much improved evaluation score.

- *Alter the Importance Weights.* In this strategy, the salesperson uses information to emphasize and thus increase the importance of certain attributes on which the product offering is exceptionally strong. In the case of attributes on which the offering might be short, the strategy would be to de-emphasize their importance. Continuing the adhesive purchase decision, BondIt's salesperson might offer information to influence the buyer's importance rating for ease of application and storage shelf-life—two characteristics in which BondIt is much stronger than the two competitors.

- *Call Attention to Neglected Attributes.* In the case in which it becomes apparent that significant attributes may have been neglected or overlooked, the salesperson can increase the buyer's evaluation of the proposed offering by pointing out the attribute that was missed. For instance, the BondIt #302 adhesive dries to an invisible, transparent, and semi-flexible adhesive compared with the two competitors, which cure to a light gray color that could detract from the final product in cases in which the adhesive flowed out of the joint. The appearance of the final product is a significant concern, and this neglected attribute could substantially influence the comparative evaluations.

Phase Six—Evaluation of Proposals and Selection of Suppliers

The buying decision is the outcome of the buyer's evaluation of the various proposals acquired from potential suppliers. Typically, further negotiations will be conducted with the selected supplier(s) for the purpose of establishing the final terms regarding product characteristics, pricing, and delivery. Salespeople play a central role in gaining the buyer's commitment to the purchase decision and in the subsequent negotiations of the final terms.

Phase Seven—Selection of an Order Routine

Once the supplier(s) has been selected, details associated with the purchase decision must be settled. These details include delivery quantities, locations, and times along with return policies and the routine for re-orders associated with the purchase. For cases in which the purchase requires multiple deliveries over a period of time, the routine for placing subsequent orders and making deliveries must be set out and understood. Is the order routine standardized on the basis of a prearranged time schedule, or is the salesperson expected to monitor usage and inventories in order to place orders and schedule shipments? Will orders be placed automatically through the use of electronic data interchange or the Internet? Regardless of the nature of the order routine, the salesperson plays a critical role in facilitating communication, completing ordering procedures, and settling the final details.

Phase Eight—Performance Feedback and Evaluation

The final phase in the buying process is the evaluation of performance and feedback shared among all parties for the purpose of improving future performance and enhancing buyer–seller relationships. Research supports that salespeople's customer interaction activities and communication at this stage of the buying process become the primary determinants of customer satisfaction and buyer loyalty. Consequently, it is critical that salespeople continue working with buyers after the sale. The salesperson's follow-up activities provide the critical points of contact between the buyer and seller in order to assure consistent performance, respond to and take care of problems, maximize customer satisfaction, and further enhance buyer–seller relationships.

Understanding Post-Purchase Evaluation and the Formation of Satisfaction

Research shows that buyers evaluate their experience with a product purchase on the basis of product characteristics that fall into a **two-factor model of evaluation** as depicted in Figure 3.4.[4] The first category, **functional attributes**, refers to the features and characteristics that are related to *what* the product actually does or is expected to do—its functional characteristics. These functional characteristics have also been referred to as **"must-have attributes,"** features of the core product that are taken for granted by the customer. These are the attributes that must be present for the supplier or product to even be included among those being considered for purchase. Consequently, they tend

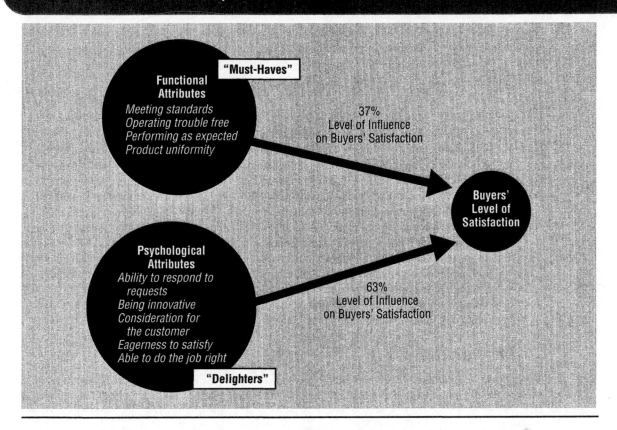

The Two-Factor Model of Buyer Evaluation   FIGURE 3.4

Buyers evaluate Functional Attributes and Psychological Attributes of a sales offering to assess overall performance and satisfaction.

to be fairly common across the set of suppliers and products being considered for purchase by a buyer. Characteristics such as reliability, durability, conformance to specifications, competitive pricing, and performance are illustrative of functional attributes.

Psychological attributes make up the second general category. This category refers to *how* things are carried out and done between the buyer and seller. These supplier and market offering characteristics are described as the **"delighter attributes"**—the augmented features and characteristics included in the total market offering that go beyond buyer expectations and have a significant positive impact on customer satisfaction. The psychological or delighter characteristics are not perceived as being universal features across the evoked set of suppliers and market offerings being considered. Rather, these are the differentiators between the competitors. The competence, attitudes, and behaviors of supplier personnel with whom the buyer has contact, as well as the salesperson's trustworthiness, consideration for the customer, responsiveness, ability to recover when there is a problem, and innovativeness in providing solutions are exemplary psychological attributes.

The Growing Importance of Salespeople in Buyer's Post-Purchase Evaluation

Understanding the differential impact of functional (must-haves) and psychological (delighters) attributes is important for salespeople. Functional attributes possess a close correspondence to the technical and more tangible product attributes whereas the psychological attributes are similar to the interpersonal communication and behaviors of salespeople and other personnel having contact with customers. Numerous research studies across a variety of industries evidences psychological attributes as having up to two times more influence on buyer satisfaction and loyalty than functional attributes. This observation underscores special implications for salespeople, as it is their interpersonal communication and behaviors—what they do—that make up the psychological attributes. Although both categories of product characteristics are important and have significant influences on buyer satisfaction, the activities and behaviors of the salesperson as she or he interacts with the buyer have more impact on that buyer's evaluation than the features of the product or service itself.

TYPES OF PURCHASING DECISIONS

Buyers are learners in that purchase decisions are not isolated behaviors. Buyer behavior and purchase decisions are based on the relevant knowledge that buyers have accumulated from multiple sources to assist them in making the proper choice. Internally, buyers reflect on past experiences as guides for making purchase decisions. When sufficient knowledge from past experiences is not available, buyers access external sources of information: secondary sources of information (e.g., trade journals, product test reports, advertising) and other individuals the buyer perceives as being trustworthy and knowledgeable in a given area.

The level of experience and knowledge a buyer or buying organization possesses relevant to a given purchasing decision is a primary determinant of the time and resources the buyer will allocate to that purchasing decision. The level of a buyer's existing experience and knowledge has been used to categorize buyer behavior into three types of purchasing decisions: straight rebuys, modified rebuys, and new tasks. As summarized in Exhibit 3.6, selling strategies should reflect the differences in buyer behaviors and decision-making characteristic of each type of buying decision.

Straight Rebuys

If past experiences with a product resulted in high levels of satisfaction, buyers tend to purchase the same product from the same sources. Comparable with a routine repurchase in which nothing has changed, the **straight rebuy decision** is often the result of a long-term purchase agreement. Needs have been predetermined with the corresponding specifications, pricing, and shipping requirements already established by a blanket purchase order or annual purchase agreement. Ordering is automatic and often computerized by using electronic data interchange (EDI) and e-commerce (Internet, intranet, and extranet). Mitsubishi Motor Manufacturing of America uses a large number of straight rebuy decisions in its acquisition of component parts. Beginning as a primary supplier of automotive glass components, Vuteq has developed a strong relationship with Mitsubishi Motor Manufacturing of America over a period of several years. As a result, Vuteq's business has steadily increased and now includes door trim, fuel tanks, and mirrors in addition to window glass. These components are purchased as straight rebuys by using EDI, allowing Vuteq to deliver these components to Mitsubishi on a minute-to-minute basis, matching ongoing production. .

EXHIBIT 3.6   Three Types of Buying Decisions

	Decision Type		
	Straight Rebuy	**Modified Rebuy**	**New Task**
Newness of problem or need	Low	Medium	High
Information requirements	Minimal	Moderate	Maximum
Information search	Minimal	Limited	Extensive
Consideration of new alternatives	None	Limited	Extensive
Multiple buying influences	Very small	Moderate	Large
Financial risks	Low	Moderate	High

Buyers allocate little, if any, time and resources to this form of purchase decision. The primary emphasis is on receipt of the products and their continued satisfactory performance. With most of the purchasing process automated, straight rebuy decisions are little more than record keeping that is often handled by clerical staff in the purchasing office.

For the in-supplier (a current supplier), straight rebuys offer the advantage of reduced levels of potential competition. Rather than becoming complacent, however, in-salespeople must continually monitor the competitive environment for advances in product capabilities or changes in price structures. They should also follow up on deliveries and interact with users as well as decision makers to make sure that product and performance continue to receive strong and positive evaluations.

Straight rebuy decisions present a major challenge to the out-salesperson. Buyers are satisfied with the products and services from current suppliers and see no need to change. This is a classic case where the buyer perceives no difference or needs gap between their actual and desired state. Consequently, there is no active buying motive to which the out-salesperson can respond. In this case, out-salespeople are typically presented with two strategy choices. First, they can continue to make contact with the buyer so that when there is a change in the buying situation or if the current supplier makes a mistake, they are there to respond. Second, they can provide information and evidence relevant to either the desired or actual states so that the buyer will perceive a needs gap. For example, Vuteq's competitors will find it most difficult to gain this portion of Mitsubishi's business by offering similar or equal products and systems. However, a competitor might adopt future advances in technology that would enable them to offer significant added value over and beyond that being offered by Vuteq. Effectively communicating and demonstrating their advanced capabilities holds the potential for raising the desired state and thus producing a needs gap favoring their solution over Vuteq's existing sales offering.

New Tasks

The purchase decision characterized as a new task decision occurs when the buyer is purchasing a product or service for the first time. As illustrated in Figure 3.5, new task purchase decisions are located at the opposite end of the continuum from the straight rebuy and typify situations in which buyers have no experience or knowledge on which to rely. Consequently, they undertake an extensive purchase decision and search for information designed to identify and compare alternative solutions. Reflecting the extensive nature of this type of purchase decision, multiple members of the buying team are usually involved. As a result, the salesperson will be working with several different individuals rather than a single buyer. Mitsubishi buyers and suppliers were presented with new task decisions when the new Mitsubishi four-wheel-drive sport utility vehicle was moving from design to production. Moving from their historical two-wheel-drive to four-wheel-drive powerlines and transmissions presented a variety of new needs and problems.

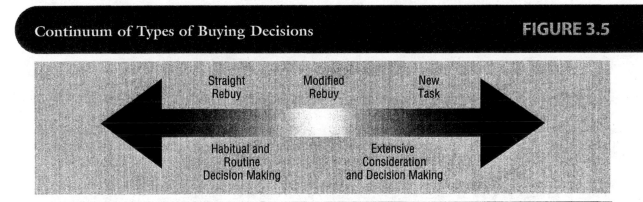

Continuum of Types of Buying Decisions   FIGURE 3.5

Straight Rebuy — Modified Rebuy — New Task

Habitual and Routine Decision Making — Extensive Consideration and Decision Making

Relevant to a new task purchasing decision, there is no in- or out-supplier. Further, the buyer is aware of the existing needs gap. With no prior experience in dealing with this particular need, buyers are often eager for information and expertise that will assist them in effectively resolving the perceived needs gap. Selling strategies for new task decisions should include collaborating with the buyer in a number of ways. First, the salesperson can provide expertise in fully developing and understanding the need. The salesperson's extensive experience and base of knowledge is also valuable to the buyer in terms of specifying and evaluating potential solutions. Finally, top salespeople will assist the buyer in making a purchase decision and provide extensive follow-up to ensure long-term satisfaction. By implementing this type of a consultative strategy, the salesperson establishes a relationship with the buyer and gains considerable competitive advantage.

Modified Rebuys

Modified rebuy decisions occupy a middle position on the continuum between straight rebuys and new tasks. In these cases, the buyer has experience in purchasing the product in the past but is interested in acquiring additional information regarding alternative products and/or suppliers. As there is more familiarity with the decision, there is less uncertainty and perceived risk than for new task decisions. The modified rebuy typically occurs as the result of changing conditions or needs. Perhaps the buyer wishes to consider new suppliers for current purchase needs or new products offered by existing suppliers. Continuing the example of buyer–seller experiences at Mitsubishi, the company's recent decision to reexamine their methods and sources for training and education corresponds to the characteristics of a modified rebuy decision. Since its beginning, Mitsubishi Motor Manufacturing of America has used a mix of company trainers, community colleges, and universities to provide education and training to employees. Desiring more coordination across its training programs, the company has requested proposals for the development and continued management of a corporate university from a variety of suppliers, including several current as well as new sources.

Often a buyer enters into a modified rebuy type of purchase decision to simply check the competitiveness of existing suppliers in terms of the product offering and pricing levels. Consequently, in-salespeople will emphasize how well their product has performed in resolving the needs gap. Out-salespeople will use strategies similar to those undertaken in the straight rebuy. These strategies are designed to alter the relative positions of the desired and actual state in a way that creates a perceived gap and influences buyers to rethink and reevaluate their current buying patterns and suppliers.

UNDERSTANDING COMMUNICATION STYLES

Verbal and nonverbal messages can also provide salespeople with important cues regarding buyers' personalities and communication styles. Experienced salespeople emphasize the importance of reading and responding to customer communication styles. Effectively sensing and interpreting customers' communication styles allows salespeople to adapt their own interaction behaviors in a way that facilitates buyer–seller communication and enhances relationship formation. Most sales training programs use a two-by-two matrix as a basis for categorizing **communication styles** into four primary types.[5] As illustrated by Figure 3.6, the four styles are based on two determinant dimensions: assertiveness and responsiveness.

> *Assertiveness*—**Assertiveness** refers to the degree to which a person holds opinions about issues and attempts to dominate or control situations by directing the thoughts and actions of others. Highly assertive individuals tend to be fast paced, opinionated, and quick to speak out and take confrontational positions. Low-assertive individuals tend to exhibit a slower pace. They typically hold back, let others take charge, and are slow and deliberate in their communication and actions.

> *Responsiveness*—**Responsiveness** points to the level of feelings and sociability an individual openly displays. Highly responsive individuals are relationship

Comparison of the Principal Characteristics of Assertiveness and Responsiveness

FIGURE 3.6

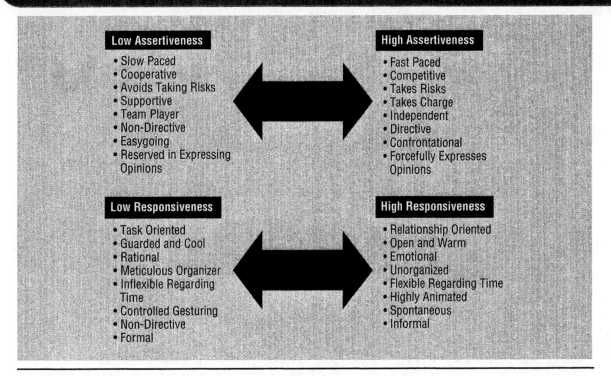

Low Assertiveness
- Slow Paced
- Cooperative
- Avoids Taking Risks
- Supportive
- Team Player
- Non-Directive
- Easygoing
- Reserved in Expressing Opinions

High Assertiveness
- Fast Paced
- Competitive
- Takes Risks
- Takes Charge
- Independent
- Directive
- Confrontational
- Forcefully Expresses Opinions

Low Responsiveness
- Task Oriented
- Guarded and Cool
- Rational
- Meticulous Organizer
- Inflexible Regarding Time
- Controlled Gesturing
- Non-Directive
- Formal

High Responsiveness
- Relationship Oriented
- Open and Warm
- Emotional
- Unorganized
- Flexible Regarding Time
- Highly Animated
- Spontaneous
- Informal

Most sales training programs use a two-by-two matrix as a basis for categorizing communication styles into four primary types. The four styles are based on two dimensions: assertiveness and responsiveness.

oriented and openly emotional. They readily express their feelings and tend to be personable, friendly, and informal. However, low-responsive individuals tend to be task oriented and very controlled in their display of emotions. They tend to be impersonal in dealing with others, with an emphasis on formality and self-discipline.

The actual levels of assertiveness and responsiveness will vary from one individual to another on a continuum ranging from high to low. An individual may be located anywhere along the particular continuum, and where the individual is located determines the degree to which he or she possesses and demonstrates the particular behaviors associated with that dimension. The following figures illustrate the range of behaviors commonly associated with each dimension.

Overlaying the assertiveness and responsiveness dimensions produces a four-quadrant matrix as illustrated in Figure 3.7. The four quadrants characterize an individual as exhibiting one of four different communication styles on the basis of his or her demonstrated levels of assertiveness and responsiveness. *Amiables* are high on responsiveness but low on assertiveness. *Expressives* are defined as high on both responsiveness and assertiveness. *Drivers* are low on responsiveness but high on assertiveness. *Analyticals* are characterized as being low on assertiveness as well as responsiveness. A salesperson's skill in properly classifying customers can provide valuable cues regarding customer attitudes and behaviors. In turn, these cues allow the salesperson to be more effective by adapting his or her communication and responses to better fit the customer's style.

Amiables—Developing and maintaining close personal relationships is important to **amiables**. Easy-going and cooperative, they are often characterized as friendly backslappers due to their preference for belonging to groups and their

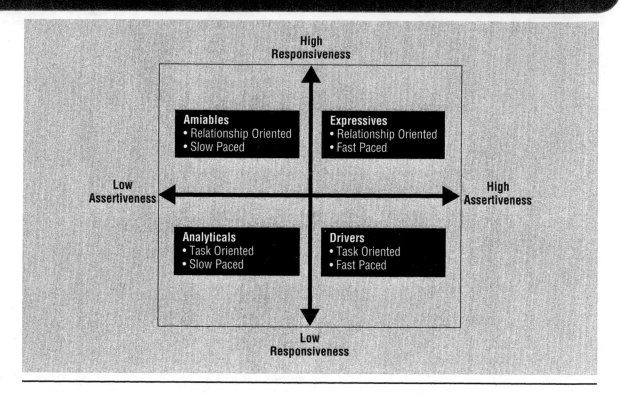

FIGURE 3.7

Communication Styles Matrix

The four quadrants characterize an individual as one of four different communication styles on the basis of his or her demonstrated levels of assertiveness and responsiveness. A salesperson's skill in properly classifying customers can provide valuable cues regarding customer attitudes and behaviors.

sincere interest in other people—their hobbies, interests, families, and mutual friends. With a natural propensity for talking and socializing, they have little or no desire to control others but rather prefer building consensus. Amiables are not risk takers and need to feel safe in making a decision. Somewhat undisciplined with regard to time, amiables appear to be slow and deliberate in their actions. They avoid conflict and tend to be more concerned with opinions—what others think—than with details and facts. When confronted or attacked, amiables tend to submit. In working with an amiable customer, salespeople should remember that their priority "must-have" is to be liked and their fundamental "want" is for attention.

Expressives—**Expressives** are animated and highly communicative. Although very competitive by nature, they also exhibit warm personalities and value building close relationships with others. In fact, they dislike being alone and readily seek out others. Expressives are extroverted and are highly uninhibited in their communication. When confronted or crossed, they will attack. Enthusiastic and stimulating, they seem to talk in terms of people rather than things and have a ready opinion on everything. Yet, they remain open-minded and changeable. Expressives are fast paced in their decision making and behavior and prefer the big picture rather than getting bogged down in details. As a result, they are very spontaneous, unconcerned with time schedules, and not especially organized in their daily lives. They are creative, comfortable operating on intuition, and demonstrate a willingness to take risks. The two keys for expressives that salespeople must keep in mind are the "must-have" of never being hurt emotionally and their underlying "want" is attention.

Drivers—Sometimes referred to as the director or dictator style, **drivers** are hard and detached from relationships with others. Described as being cool, tough, and competitive in their relationships, drivers are independent and willing to run over others to get their preferred results. As they seek out and openly demonstrate power and control over people and situations, they are difficult to get close to and appear to treat people as things. Drivers are extremely formal, businesslike, and impatient, with a penchant for time and organization. They are highly opinionated, impatient, and quick to share those opinions with those around them. When attacked or confronted, drivers will dictate. Drivers exhibit a low tolerance for taking advice, tend to be risk takers, and favor making their own decisions. Although they are highly task oriented, drivers prefer to ignore facts and figures and instead rely on their own gut feelings in making decisions—after all, they do know it all. When working with drivers, salespeople should remember that this style's "must-have" is winning and their fundamental "want" is results.

Analyticals—The descriptive name for this style is derived from their penchant for gathering and analyzing facts and details before making a decision. **Analyticals** are meticulous and disciplined in everything they do. Logical and very controlled, they are systematic problem solvers and thus very deliberate and slower in pace. In stressful situations and confrontations, analyticals tend to withdraw. Many times, they appear to be nit-picky about everything around them. They do not readily let their feelings hang out nor are they spontaneous in their behaviors. As a result, they are often seen as being cool and aloof. Analyticals shy away from personal relationships and avoid taking risks. Time and personal schedules are close to being a religious ritual for the analytical. The two fundamentals that salespeople must keep in mind when working with this style are the "must-have" of being right and the underlying "want" for analytical activities.

MASTERING COMMUNICATION STYLE FLEXING

In addition to sensing and interpreting the customer's communication style, salespeople must also be aware of their own personal style. Mismatched and possibly clashing styles can be dysfunctional and present significant barriers to communication and relationship building. To minimize possible negative effects stemming from mismatched styles, salespeople can flex their own style to facilitate effective communication. For example, an expressive salesperson calling on an analytical buyer would find considerable differences in both pace and relationship/task orientation that could hinder the selling process unless adjustments are made. Flexing his or her own style to better match that of the buyer enhances communication. In terms of our example, the salesperson would need to make adjustments by slowing down his or her natural pace, reining in the level of spontaneity and animation, and increasing task orientation by offering more detailed information and analysis.

Adapting to buyers by flexing their own communication style has been found to have a positive impact on salespeople's performance and the quality of buyer–seller relationships. Nevertheless, flexing should not be interpreted as meaning an exact match between a salesperson's style and that of a customer. Not only is it not required, exact matches could even be detrimental. For example, a buyer and seller with matching expressive styles could easily discover that the entire sales call regressed to little more than a personal discussion with nothing of substance being accomplished. However, a buyer and seller matched as drivers could find it difficult, if not impossible, to reach a decision that was mutually beneficial. Rather than matching the buyer's style, flexing infers that the salesperson should adjust to the needs and preferences of the buyer to maximize effectiveness. Growmark, an international agricultural product and service organization, teaches their salespeople to flex throughout their interaction with a buyer by studying different behaviors a salesperson might demonstrate with each style of buyer (see Exhibit 3.7).[6]

EXHIBIT 3.7   Recommended Flexing Behaviors for Different Communication Styles

Selling Task or Objective	Selling to the Analytical	Selling to the Driver	Selling to the Amiable	Selling to the Expressive
Setting an Appointment	• Send a business letter specifying details about yourself and the company. • Follow the letter with a phone call to confirm expectations and set appointment.	• Drivers may not take time to read your letter. • Contact them by phone first and follow up with a letter. • Keep call businesslike and to the point by identifying yourself, explain the business problem addressed by your product, and ask for appointment. • Letter should simply confirm time and date of appointment and include materials the driver might review prior to the meeting.	• Send a letter with a personal touch stating who you are and why you are contacting the Amiable. • Letter should include your experience working with clients the prospect knows by reputation or experience, your reliability and follow-through, and the quality of your product/service. • Follow letter with a personal phone call. • Take time to be friendly, open, sincere, and to establish trust in the relationship.	• Generally, a phone call is most appropriate. • Make your call open and friendly, stressing quick benefits, personal service, your experience, and your company's experience with its products and services. • If you send a letter, make it short and personal, stressing who you are, how you know of the Expressive, and what you are interested in talking about.
Opening the Call	• Provide background information about you and the company. • Approach in an advisory capacity acknowledging buyer's expertise. • Show evidence that you have done your homework on buyer's situation. • Offer evidence of providing previous solutions. • Be conscious of how you are using buyer's time.	• Listen and focus on driver's ideas and objectives. • Provide knowledge and insight relevant to driver's specific business problems. • Be personable but reserved and relatively formal. • Present factual evidence that establishes the business problem and resulting outcome. • Maintain a quick pace. Drivers value punctuality and efficient use of time.	• Engage in informal conversation before getting down to business. • Demonstrate that you are personally interested in the Amiable's work and personal goals. • You will have to earn the right to learn more personally about the Amiable. • Demonstrate your product/service knowledge by referencing a common acquaintance with whom you've done business.	• Quickly describe the purpose of your call and establish credibility—you must earn the right to develop a business relationship with the Expressive. • Share stories about people you both know. • Share information the Expressive would perceive as exclusive. • Share your feelings and enthusiasm for the Expressive's ideas and goals. • Once the Expressive has confidence in your competence, take time to develop an open and trusting personal relationship.

(continued)

EXHIBIT 3.7 Recommended Flexing Behaviors for Different Communication Styles—*Continued*

Selling Task or Objective	Selling to the Analytical	Selling to the Driver	Selling to the Amiable	Selling to the Expressive
Gathering Information	• Ask specific, fact-finding questions in a systematic manner. • Establish comprehensive exchange of information. • Encourage buyer to discuss ideas while focusing on factual information. • Be thorough and unhurried—listen. • Explain that you are in alignment with their thinking and can support their objectives.	• Ask, don't tell. Ask fact-finding questions leading to what the driver values and rewards. • Make line of questioning consistent with your call objective. • Follow up on requests for information immediately. • Support the buyer's beliefs; indicate how you can positively affect goals. • Clarify the driver's expectations.	• Create a cooperative atmosphere with an open exchange of information and feelings. • Amiables tend to understate their objectives, so you may need to probe for details and specifics about their goals. • Listen responsively. Give ample amounts of verbal and nonverbal feedback. • Verify whether there are unresolved budget or cost justification issues. • Find out who else will contribute to the buying decision. • Summarize what you believe to be the Amiable's key ideas and feelings.	• Begin by finding out the Expressive's perception of the situation and vision of the ideal outcome. • Identify other people who should contribute to analysis and planning. • Listen, then respond with plenty of verbal and non-verbal feedback that supports the Expressive's beliefs. • Question carefully the critical data you'll need. • Keep the discussion focused and moving toward a result. • If the Expressive shows limited interest in specifics, summarize what has been discussed and begin to suggest ways to move the vision toward reality.
Reinforcing the Need to Change	• Use their records to supply information. • Use a logical approach. • Illustrate with dollars and cents.	• Be fast-paced and business-like. Be sure of your figures. Show the Driver the bottom line. Appeal to rational thinking and avoid appeal to emotions.	• Address emotional needs in line with safety and comfort needs. • Use the Amiable's own figures rather than your own. • Do not push!	• Support the Expressive's ideas and goals. • Work toward his/her esteem needs. • Supply data from people seen as leaders to the Expressive.

(continued)

EXHIBIT 3.7   Recommended Flexing Behaviors for Different Communication Styles—*Continued*

Selling Task or Objective	Selling to the Analytical	Selling to the Driver	Selling to the Amiable	Selling to the Expressive
Providing the Sales Story	• Provide detailed written proposal as part of presentation. • Include strongest cost-benefit justifications. • Support with third-party data. • Be reserved and decisive but not aggressive. • Limit emotional or testimonial appeals. • Recommend specific course of action. • Give buyer chance to review all documents related to purchase and delivery.	• Present your recommendation so that the driver can compare alternative solutions and their probable outcomes. • Provide documented options. • Offer the best quality given the cost limitations. • Be specific and factual without overwhelming the driver with details. • Appeal to esteem and independence needs. • Reinforce the driver's preference for acting in a forthright manner. • Summarize content quickly, then let Driver choose a course of action.	• Define clearly in writing and make sure the Amiable understands: • What you can do to support the Amiable's personal goals; • What you will contribute and what the Amiable needs to contribute; and • The support resources you intend to commit to the project. • Provide a clear solution to the Amiable's problem with maximum assurances that this is the best solution and that there is no need to consider others. • Ask the Amiable to involve other decision makers. • Satisfy needs by showing how your solution is best now and will be best in the future and support it with references and third-party evidence. • Use testimonials from perceived experts and others close to the Amiable.	• Provide specific solutions to the Expressive's ideas—in writing. • Build confidence that you have the necessary facts, but do not overwhelm the Expressive with details. • Do not rush the discussion. Spend time developing ways to implement ideas. • Appeal to personal esteem needs. • Try to get commitments to action in writing.
Asking for the Commitment	• Ask for commitment in a low-key but direct manner. • Expect to negotiate changes. • Pay special attention to pricing issues. • Work for commitment now to avoid Analytical's tendency to delay decisions.	• Ask for the order directly. • Put your offer in clear factual terms. • Offer options and alternatives. • Be prepared to negotiate changes and concessions.	• Ask for the order indirectly—do not push. • Emphasize the guarantees that offer protection to the Amiable. • Do not corner the Amiables, they want a way out if things go wrong.	• When you have enough information to understand the need and have tested the appropriateness of the recommendation, assume the sale and ask for the order in a casual and informal way.

(continued)

EXHIBIT 3.7   Recommended Flexing Behaviors for Different Communication Styles—*Continued*

Selling Task or Objective	Selling to the Analytical	Selling to the Driver	Selling to the Amiable	Selling to the Expressive

Asking for the Commitment (continued)	• Cite data supporting company's service records.
	• Respond to objections by emphasizing the Analytical's buying principles and objectivity.
		• Drivers sometimes attach conditions to a sale.
		• Offer the Driver time to consider the options.
		• Anticipate objections in advance and come prepared with facts.
		• Respond to objections based on Driver's values and priorities.
			• Guard against "buyer's remorse"—get a commitment even if you have to base it on a contingency.
			• Stress your personal involvement after the sale.
			• Encourage the Amiable to involve others in the final purchase decision.
			• Welcome objections and be patient and thorough in responding to them.
			• When responding to objections:
			  • Describe financial justification;
			  • Refer to experts or others the Amiable respects; and
			  • Keep in mind how the Amiable feels about and will be affected by the purchase decision.
				• When the opportunity presents itself, offer incentives to encourage the purchase.
				• Do not confuse the issue by presenting too many options or choices.
				• Get a definite commitment. Be sure the Expressive understands the decision to purchase.
				• Save the details until after you have a firm buying decision. The Expressive believes it is the salesperson's job to handle details.
				• In handling objections:
				  • Describe what others have done to get over that hurdle;
				  • Respond to the Expressive's enthusiasm for their goals;
				  • Deal with how the recommendation meets with this buyer's options;
				  • Restate benefits that focus on the satisfaction a buying decision will bring.

(continued)

EXHIBIT 3.7 Recommended Flexing Behaviors for Different Communication Styles—*Continued*

Selling Task or Objective	Selling to the Analytical	Selling to the Driver	Selling to the Amiable	Selling to the Expressive

Providing Follow-up	• Provide detailed implementation plan.
	• Maintain regular contact.
	• Check to confirm satisfactory and on-schedule delivery.
		• Set up communication process with the Driver that encourages quick exchange of information about checkpoints and milestones.
		• Make sure you have a contingency plan to responsively implement corrections and incorporate changes.
		• Make sure there are no surprises.
			• Immediately after the purchase decision is made, make a follow-up appointment.
			• Initiate and maintain frequent contacts providing services such as:
			  • Periodic progress reports on installation;
			  • Arrangements for service and training;
			  • Introduction of new products and services; and
			  • Listening carefully to concerns, even those that seem trivial.
				• As soon as the order is signed, reaffirm the schedule for delivery and your personal relationship with the buyer, and introduce the implementation person or team.
				• A social situation such as a lunch can be a very effective opportunity for following up on business with this buyer.
				• Work toward becoming an ongoing member of the buyer's team.
				• In case of any complaints, handle them yourself. Never refer them to another in your organization without the buyer's assent.

Study and compare the flexing behaviors that Growmark recommends their sales-people demonstrate while working with each different buyer communication style. Note the differences in recommended salesperson behavior and rationalize them in terms of the specific characteristics of each buyer's style. Overlaying and integrating these two sets of information will enhance the understanding of how to flex to different buyers and why that form of flexing is recommended.

It is not always possible to gain much information about a buyer's communication style, especially if the buyer is new. If this is the case, it may be more appropriate to assume the buyer is an analytical-driver and prepare for this style. If the buyer proves to be close to an amiable-expressive, then the salesperson can easily adapt. It is much more difficult to prepare for the amiable-expressive and then switch to an analytical-driver style.

MULTIPLE BUYING INFLUENCES

A single individual typically makes routine purchase decisions such as straight rebuys and simpler modified rebuys. However, the more complex modified rebuy and new task purchase decisions often involve the joint decisions of multiple participants within a buying center or team. **Buying teams** (also referred to as **buying centers**) incorporate the expertise and multiple buying influences of people from different departments throughout the organization. As the object of the purchase decision changes, the makeup of the buying team may also change to maximize the relevant expertise of team members. The organization's size, as well as the nature and volume of the products being purchased, will influence the actual number and makeup of buying teams. The different members of a buying team will often have varied goals reflecting their individual needs and those of their different departments. Buying team members are described in terms of their roles and responsibilities within the team.[7]

- *Initiators*—**Initiators** are individuals within the organization who identify a need or perhaps realize that the acquisition of a product might solve a need or problem.
- *Influencers*—Individuals who guide the decision process by making recommendations and expressing preferences are referred to as **influencers**. These are often technical or engineering personnel.
- *Users*—**Users** are the individuals within the organization who will actually use the product being purchased. They evaluate a product on the basis of how it will affect their own job performance. Users often serve as initiators and influencers.
- *Deciders*—The ultimate responsibility for determining which product or service will be purchased rests with the role of **deciders**. Although buyers may also be deciders, it is not unusual for different people to fill these roles.
- *Purchasers*—**Purchasers** have responsibility for negotiating final terms of purchase with suppliers and executing the actual purchase or acquisition.
- *Gatekeepers*—Members who are in the position to control the flow of information to and between vendors and other buying center members are referred to as **gatekeepers**.

Although each of these influencer types will not necessarily be present on all buying teams, the use of buying teams incorporating some or all of these multiple influences has increased in recent years. One example of multiple buying influences is offered in the recent experience of an Executive Jet International salesperson selling a Gulfstream V corporate jet to a Chicago-based pharmaceutical company. Stretching over a period of six months, the salesperson worked with a variety of individuals serving different roles within the buying organization:

- *Initiator:* The initiator of the purchase process was the chief operating officer of the corporation who found that the recent corporate expansions had outgrown the effective service range of the organization's existing aircraft. Beyond pointing out the need and thus initiating the search, this individual would also be highly involved in the final choice based on her personal experiences and perceived needs of the company.
- *Influencers:* Two different employee groups acted as the primary influencers. First were the corporate pilots who contributed a readily available and extensive background

of knowledge and experience with a variety of aircraft types. Also playing a key influencer role were members from the capital budgeting group in the finance department. Although concerned with documented performance capabilities, they also provided inputs and assessments of the different alternatives using their capital investment models.

- *Users:* The users provided some of the most dynamic inputs, as they were anxious to make the transition to a higher performance aircraft to enhance their own efficiency and performance in working at marketing/sales offices and plants that now stretched over the continents of North and South America. Primary players in this group included the vice presidents for marketing and for production/operations in addition to the corporate pilots who would be flying the plane.

- *Deciders:* Based on the contribution and inputs of each member of the buying team, the ultimate decision would be made by the chief executive officer. Primarily traveling by commercial carriers, her role as decider was based more on her position within the firm rather than her use of the chosen alternative. As the organization's highest operating officer, she was in a position to move freely among all members of the buying team and make the decision on overall merits rather than personal feelings or desires.

- *Purchaser:* Responsibility for making the actual purchase, negotiating the final terms, and completing all the required paperwork followed the typical lines of authority and was the responsibility of the corporate purchasing department with the director of purchasing actually assuming the immediate contact role. The purchasing office typically handles purchasing contracts and is staffed to draw up, complete, and file the related registrations and legal documents.

- *Gatekeepers:* This purchase decision actually involved two different gatekeepers within the customer organization: the executive assistant to the chief operating officer and an assistant purchasing officer. The positioning of these gatekeepers facilitated the salesperson's exchange of information and ability to keep in contact with the various members of the buying team. The COO's executive assistant moved easily among the various executives influencing the decision and was able to make appointments with the right people at the right times. However, the assistant purchasing officer was directly involved with the coordination of each member and bringing their various inputs into one summary document for the CEO. The salesperson's positive dealings and good relationships with each of the gatekeepers played a significant role in Executive Jet getting the sale.

A classic and all-too-common mistake among salespeople is to make repetitive calls on a purchasing manager over a period of several months only to discover that a buying team actually exists and that the ultimate decision will be made by someone other than the purchasing manager. Salespeople must gather information to discover who is in the buying team, their individual roles, and which members are the most influential. This information might be collected from account history files, people inside the salesperson's organization who are familiar with the account sources within the client organization, and even other salespeople. A salesperson should work with all members of the buying team and be careful to properly address their varied needs and objectives. Nevertheless, circumstances sometimes prevent a salesperson from working with all members of the team, and it is important that they reach those that are most influential.

CURRENT DEVELOPMENTS IN PURCHASING

Today's business organizations are undergoing profound change in response to ever-increasing competition and rapid changes in the business environment. The worldwide spread of technology has resulted in intense and increasingly global competition that is highly dynamic in nature. Accelerating rates of change have fragmented what were once mass markets into more micro and niche markets composed of more knowledgeable and demanding customers with ever-increasing expectations. In response, traditional purchasing practices are also rapidly changing.

Increasing Use of Information Technology

Buyers and sellers alike are increasingly using technology to enhance the effectiveness and efficiency of the purchasing process. Business-to-business e-commerce is growing at a rate exceeding 33 percent a year. Although EDI over private networks has been in use for some time, nearly all the current growth has been in Internet-based transactions.

Information technology electronically links buyers and sellers for direct and immediate communication and transmission of information and data. Transactional exchanges such as straight rebuy decisions can now be automated with Internet- and World Wide Web-enabled programs tracking sales at the point of purchase and capturing the data for real-time inventory control and order placing. By cutting order and shipping times, overall cycle times are reduced, mistakes minimized, and working capital invested in inventories is made available for more productive applications. Further, the automation of these routine transactions allows buyers and salespeople to devote more time to new tasks, complex sales, and post-sale service and relationship-building activities. In addition to facilitating exchange transactions, applications integrating the Internet are also being used to distribute product and company information along with training courses and materials. Several companies have begun publishing their product catalogs online as a replacement for the reams of product brochures salespeople have traditionally had to carry with them. The online catalogs can be easily updated without the expense of obsolete brochures and can be selectively downloaded by salespeople to create customized presentations and proposals.

Relationship Emphasis on Cooperation and Collaboration

More than ever before, the business decisions made by one company directly affect decisions in other companies. Business in today's fast-paced and dynamic marketplace demands continuous and increased levels of interactivity between organizations. As illustrated in "An Ethical Dilemma," more and more buying organizations are adapting by emphasizing longer-term relationships with fewer suppliers to forge stronger and more enduring bonds with a select group of highly capable, trustworthy, and committed suppliers.[8]

Rather than competing to win benefits at the expense of one another, leading organizations are discovering that it is possible for all parties to reduce their risk and increase

AN ETHICAL DILEMMA

As a key account manager for B&J Chemicals, Jay Wright has developed strong relationships with each of the 21 accounts comprising his client list. These clients include Industrial Stampings, a large metal forming company whose purchases have steadily increased and that now accounts for 32 percent of Jay's annual sales—his largest customer. Consistent with industry practice, and within the limits prescribed by B&J's policy manual, Jay occasionally provides gifts to buyers at his accounts as reminders of his and B&J's appreciation for their continuing business. Last week Jay had taken Industrial Stampings' head buyer, an avid golfer, out for a day of golf at one of Milwaukee's best, private golf clubs. After Jay hit a great drive off the eighth tee, the buyer started admiring Jay's new driver. Purchased only a few days earlier at the cost of $500, the TaylorMade Model r7 driver was indeed among the most technologically advanced drivers on the market. At Jay's insistence, the buyer borrowed the club and drove a solid shot from the ninth tee box. The buyer handed the club back to Jay with many positive exclamations including that he could not wait to get one for himself. Upon hearing that comment and thinking how it would further strengthen the account relationship, Jay tossed the driver back to the buyer saying, ". . . it seems to work well for you. Go ahead and put it in your bag! Just remember to think of me when you use it in the future." What do you think about Jay's latest relationship-building effort? How would you have handled this situation if you were in Jay's shoes?

the level of benefits each receives by sharing information and coordinating activities, resources, and capabilities.[9] These longer-term buyer–seller relationships are based on the mutual benefits received by and the interdependence between all parties in this value network. In addition to being keenly aware of changing customer needs, collaborative relationships require salespeople to work closely with buyers to foster honest and open two-way communication and develop the mutual understanding required to create the desired solutions. Further, salespeople must consistently demonstrate that they are dependable and acting in the buyer's best interests.

Supply Chain Management

Having realized that their success or failure is inextricably linked to other firms in the value network, many organizations are implementing **supply chain management** across an extended network of suppliers and customers. Beyond a buyer–seller relationship, supply chain management emphasizes the strategic coordination and integration of purchasing with other functions within the buying organization as well as external organizations including customers, customers' customers, suppliers, and suppliers' suppliers.[10] Salespeople must focus on coordinating their efforts with all parties in the network—end users and suppliers alike—and effectively work to add value for all members of the network. As described in "Professional Selling in the 21st Century: Enhancing Value for the Customer Through the Use of Information Technology," CDW has effectively employed the innovative use of information technology to enhance continuing customer purchase experiences and generate significant benefits for CDW and the company's customers.

Increased Outsourcing

Broader business involvement and expanded integration between organizations is a natural evolution as buyers and suppliers become increasingly confident of the other's performance capabilities and commitment to the relationship. These expanded agreements often involve **outsourcing** to a supplier certain activities that were previously performed by the buying

---

PROFESSIONAL SELLING IN THE 21ST CENTURY

Enhancing Value for the Customer Through the Use of Information Technology

CDW rates among the top companies employing information technology to enhance customer purchasing experiences and maximize added value benefits for both CDW and its customers. Jennifer Klein of CDW discusses this innovative use of information technology.

Here at CDW we use the technology that we sell and we have been consistently recognized as an innovator for integrating information technology into a wide range of business practices. As evidence of the effectiveness of the company's use of technology in the selling process, CDW achieved the number 6 ranking in Selling Power *magazine's "Top 15 Most Effective Sales Forces." In January 2004, the company was recognized with the number 11 ranking in* Fortune *magazine's annual "100 Best Companies*

to Work For" listing. Prestigious honors such as these show that we don't simply use technology for technology's sake. Rather, we use technology to automate our systems and translate the efficiencies into savings and increased levels of service for our customers. Our information technology systems allow customers to benefit from one-on-one relationships with highly trained, knowledgeable account managers; telephone and online purchasing; custom configurations; and lifetime phone and online technical support— benefits that are unmatched by any of our competitors. These benefits are further extended through our CDW@work system, which provides personalized Extranet services to our business customers and gives them 24 × 7 access to the company 365 days a year. Customer-centered technological innovations such as these provide high levels of added value for our customers and will continue to set us apart from the competition in the future.

organization. These activities are necessary for the day-to-day functioning of the buying organization but are not within the organization's core or distinct competencies. Outsourcing these activities allows the organization to focus on what it does best. However, these activities are typically among those in which the supplying organization specializes or even excels. As a result of the outsourcing agreement, the relationship gains strength and is further extended in such a way that all parties benefit over the long term. Outsourcing agreements place increased emphasis on the role of the salesperson to provide continuing follow-up activities to ensure customer satisfaction and nurture the buyer–seller relationship. Changes in customer needs must be continually monitored and factored into the supplier's market offering and outsourcing activities.

Target Pricing

Using information gathered from researching the marketplace, buyers establish a **target price** for their final products. For example, buyers determine the selling price for a new printing press should be $320,000. Next, they divide the press into its subsystems and parts to estimate what each part is worth in relation to the overall price. Using such a system, buyers might conclude that the maximum price they could pay for a lead roller platen would be $125 and then use this information when working with potential suppliers. In working with targeted pricing requirements, salespeople find they have two fundamental options. They can meet the required cost level, which often entails cutting their prices, or they can work with the buyer to better understand and possibly influence minimum performance specifications. Certain restrictive specifications might be relaxed as a tradeoff for lower pricing. For example, a salesperson might negotiate longer lead times, fewer or less complex design features, or less technical support in exchange for lower prices. The latter option requires salespeople to have a high level of knowledge regarding their products, organizational capabilities, and customer applications and needs. Just as important is the ability to create feasible options and effectively communicate them to the buyer.

Increased Importance of Knowledge and Creativity

The increased interdependence between buyer and seller organizations hinges on the salesperson's capabilities to serve as a problem solver in a dynamic and fast-changing business environment. Buyers depend on the salesperson to provide unique and value-added solutions to their changing problems and needs. To shape such innovative solutions, salespeople must have broad-based and comprehensive knowledge readily available and the ability to use that knowledge in creative ways. This includes knowledge of one's own products and capabilities, as well as the products and capabilities of competitors. More important, the salesperson must possess a thorough understanding of product applications and the needs of the customer to work with the buyer in generating innovative solutions.

SUMMARY

1. **Categorize primary types of buyers.** Buyers are classified according to their unique buying situations that influence their needs, motivations, and buying behavior. The most common categorization splits buyers into either consumer markets or business markets. Consumers purchase goods and services for their own use or consumption whereas members of the business market acquire goods and services to use them as inputs into manufacturing, for use in the course of doing business, or for resale. Business markets are further divided into firms, institutions, and governments.

2. **Discuss the distinguishing characteristics of business markets.** Business markets have numerous characteristics that distinguish them from consumer markets. Among the more common characteristics are consolidation, which has resulted in buyers being

fewer in number but larger in size; demand that is derived from the sale of consumer goods; more volatile demand levels; professional buyers; multiple buying influences from a team of buyers; and increased interdependence and relationships between buyers and sellers.

3. **List the different steps in the business-to-business buying process.** There are eight sequential and interrelated phases that make up the business buyers' decision process. This process begins with (1) recognition of the problem or need, (2) determination of the characteristics of the item and the quantity needed, (3) description of the characteristics of the item and quantity needed, (4) search for and qualification of potential sources, (5) acquisition and analysis of proposals, (6) evaluation of proposals and selection of suppliers, (7) selection of an order routine, and (8) performance feedback and evaluation.

4. **Discuss the different types of buyer needs.** Organizing what might appear to be an endless and confusing mixture of different needs and problems into their common types helps salespeople better understand the nature of the buyer's needs along with their interrelationships. In turn, salespeople are better able to generate and demonstrate value-added solutions that address the different needs. The five general types of buyer needs are described as follows:

   Situational Needs—Needs that are related to, or possibly the result of, the buyer's specific environment, time, and place.
   Functional Needs—The need for a specific core task or function to be performed— the need for a sales offering to do what it is supposed to do.
   Social Needs—The need for acceptance from and association with others—a desire to belong to some reference group.
   Psychological Needs—The desire for feelings of assurance and risk reduction, as well as positive emotions and feelings such as success, joy, excitement, and stimulation.
   Knowledge Needs—The desire for personal development and need for information and knowledge to increase thought and understanding as to how and why things happen.

5. **Describe how buyers evaluate suppliers and alternative sales offerings by using the multiattribute model of evaluation.** Purchase decisions are based on the buyer's comparative evaluation of how well they perceive a supplier or product compares on the basis of specific characteristics that the buyer judges as being important. Using the multiattribute model, buyers establish the attributes they perceive as important and evaluate the degree to which each of the specified attributes is present (or how well each performs) in a proposed solution. Each evaluation is then multiplied by the attribute's relative level of importance to calculate a weighted average for each attribute. These weighted averages are then totaled to derive an overall score for each supplier or product being compared. The product or supplier having the highest score is favored for purchase.

6. **Explain the two-factor model that buyers use to evaluate the performance of sales offerings and develop satisfaction.** The two-factor model is a special type of multiattribute model in which further analysis of the multiple characteristics results in two primary groupings of factors: functional attributes and psychological attributes. Functional attributes are the more tangible characteristics of a market offering whereas the psychological attributes are primarily composed of the interpersonal behaviors and activities between the buyer and seller. The psychological attributes have been repeatedly found to have higher levels of influence than functional attributes on customer satisfaction and repeat purchase.

7. **Explain the different types of purchasing decisions.** A buyer's level of experience relevant to a given purchasing situation is a primary determinant of the time and

resources that the buyer will allocate to a purchasing decision and can be used to categorize buyer behavior into three types of purchasing decisions: straight rebuys, modified rebuys, and new tasks.

Straight Rebuy. Comparable with a routine repurchase in which nothing has changed, the straight rebuy is often the result of past experience and satisfaction with buyers purchasing the same products from the same sources. Needs have been predetermined with specifications already established. Buyers allocate little, if any, time or resources to this form of purchase decision, and the primary emphasis is on continued satisfactory performance.

Modified Rebuy. Modified rebuys occupy the middle ground between straight rebuys and new tasks. The buyer has some level of experience with the product but is interested in acquiring additional information regarding alternative products and/or suppliers. The modified rebuy typically occurs as the result of changing conditions or needs. Perhaps the buyer wishes to consider new suppliers for current purchase needs or new products offered by existing suppliers.

New Task. New tasks decisions occur when a buyer is purchasing a product or service for the first time. With no experience or knowledge on which to rely, buyers undertake an extensive purchase decision and search for information designed to identify and compare alternative solutions. Reflecting the extensive nature of this type of purchase decision, multiple members of the buying center or group are usually involved. As a result, the salesperson often works with several different individuals rather than a single buyer.

8. **Describe the four communication styles and how salespeople must adapt and flex their own styles to maximize communication.** Based on high and low levels of two personal traits, assertiveness and responsiveness, communication styles can be categorized into four primary types:

   - Amiables are high on responsiveness and low on assertiveness.
   - Expressives are defined as high on both responsiveness and assertiveness.
   - Drivers are low on responsiveness but high on assertiveness.
   - Analyticals are characterized as low on assertiveness as well as responsiveness.

   Mismatched styles between a seller and buyer can be dysfunctional in terms of effective collaboration and present significant barriers for information exchange and relationship building. Differences in styles manifest themselves in the form of differences in preferred priorities (relationships versus task orientation) and favored pace (fast versus slow) of information exchange, socialization, and decision making. To minimize potential communication difficulties stemming from mismatched styles, salespeople should flex their personal styles to better fit the preferred priorities and pace of the buyer.

9. **Explain the concept of buying teams and specify the different member roles.** In the more complex modified rebuy and new task purchasing situations, purchase decisions typically involve the joint decisions of multiple participants working together as a buying team. Team members bring the expertise and knowledge from different functional departments within the buying organization. Team members may also change as the purchase decision changes. Team members are described by their roles within the team: initiators, influencers, users, deciders, purchasers, and gatekeepers.

UNDERSTANDING PROFESSIONAL SELLING TERMS

consumer markets	needs
business markets	desired states
derived demand	actual states
acceleration principle	needs gap
business buyers' purchase process	situational needs

functional needs	responsiveness
social needs	amiables
psychological needs	expressives
knowledge needs	drivers
requests for proposals (RFP)	analyticals
multiattribute model	style flexing
competitive depositioning	buying teams
two-factor model of evaluation	buying centers
functional attributes	initiators
must-have attributes	influencers
psychological attributes	users
delighter attributes	deciders
straight rebuy decisions	purchasers
new task decisions	gatekeepers
modified rebuy decisions	supply chain management
communication styles	outsourcing
assertiveness	target price

DEVELOPING PROFESSIONAL SELLING KNOWLEDGE

1. How might the following characteristic of business-to-business markets affect the relational selling activities of salespeople:

   - Larger, but fewer, buyers?
   - Derived demand?
   - Higher levels of demand fluctuation?

2. How do the three different types of purchasing decisions (straight rebuy, modified rebuy, new task) influence the time and effort a buyer might allocate to the different steps of the purchase decision process?

3. List and compare the probable functional, situational, psychological, social, and knowledge needs of (a) a large financial investment office and (b) a college student, who are both looking to purchase a new computer printer.

4. How might a salesperson work with and assist a business buyer in each step of the buying process:

   - Recognition of the problem or need
   - Determination of the characteristics of the item and the quantity needed
   - Description of the characteristics of the item and the quantity needed
   - Search for and qualification of potential sources
   - Acquisition and analysis of proposals
   - Evaluation of proposals and selection of suppliers
   - Selection of an order routine
   - Performance feedback and evaluation

5. Explain the role of functional attributes and psychological attributes in the post-purchase determination of customer satisfaction.

6. How might salespeople use their knowledge of the multiattribute evaluation model to plan and deliver their sales presentation to a buyer?

7. What are the implications for a salesperson if, when making a sales call, they discover that there is no needs gap present? Illustrate your answer with an example.

8. Why has knowledge and the capability to creatively apply that knowledge in creating unique solutions become so important for today's salesperson in the business-to-business marketplace?

9. Explain the concept of communication styles and how a salesperson might flex his or her own style to better match the style of a buyer. How would the salesperson's

behaviors and activities differ as he/she advances through the different stages of the selling process? Illustrate your answer with examples.

10. What are the implications of buying teams for a salesperson selling complex production equipment to a manufacturer firm? Develop an example to further explain and illustrate your answer.

BUILDING PROFESSIONAL SELLING SKILLS

1. Respond to each of the following buying situations by describing what you would do as (a) an in-salesperson and (b) an out-salesperson.

- *Straight Rebuy.* This is a buying situation in which the customer is basically reordering an item already in use. Little or nothing has changed in terms of product, price, delivery, the available sources of supply, or any other aspect. This is a low-risk situation involving little cognitive effort and requiring little information. The purchasing department or a clerical person is most often the key decision maker and buyer.

   (a) What do you need to do as an in-salesperson to keep this business?
       Explain: _____
       _____
       _____
       _____
       _____

   (b) What do you need to do as an out-salesperson to get your foot in the door and persuade this company to buy from you?
       Explain: _____
       _____
       _____
       _____
       _____

- *Modified Rebuy.* A buying situation in which the customer is already purchasing the item but some key aspect has changed. For example, there may be a proposed price change, a new competitive source of supply, a problem with delivery, a change in product specifications, or a newly available product or service. These are moderate-risk situations requiring greater effort and necessitating better information and information sources.

   (a) What do you need to do as an in-salesperson to keep this business?
       Explain: _____
       _____
       _____
       _____
       _____

   (b) What do you need to do as an out-salesperson to get your foot in the door and persuade this company to buy from you?
       Explain: _____
       _____
       _____
       _____
       _____

2. You are a salesperson for Accu-Press Corporation, a regional manufacturer of metal stamping tools used for the shaping (stamping) of small metal component parts. Accu-Press has just introduced a new line of tools featuring several breakthrough design features. The new equipment is faster and easier to use. Tests indicate that it can increase production by 15 percent over conventional tools while simultaneously reducing the rate of defective parts. You are calling on Federal Metal Stampings, a major supplier to the automotive industry, with the objective of selling them the new line of tools. Federal purchases their tools from two of your competitors, and you

have been calling on the buyer at Federal for the past six months. In the past, the buyer has seen no need to switch sources and has ended each call by telling you that they are satisfied with their current suppliers.

Describe how you might use the advanced capabilities of your new tool line to assist the buyer at Federal Metal Stampings to realize a needs gap and thus create an opportunity to sell them the new product.

_____

_____

_____

_____

_____

ROLE PLAY

Situation: Read Item 2.

Characters: Yourself, salesperson for Accu-Press Corporation; the buyer, director of purchasing for Federal Metal Stampings

Scene: *Location*—The office of the director of purchasing at Federal Metal Stampings. *Action*—As described, this is the most recent of several sales calls you have made to Federal Metal Stampings. Your objective for this sales call is to utilize the potential increased productivity your new line of tools offers the buyer in order to create a needs gap and thereby create an opportunity to sell them your new products.

Role play how you might create a needs gap for this buyer. Begin with the usual greeting and small talk that might typify a repeat sales call. Proceed to the point where you demonstrate the enhanced production capacity of your new tool line in a manner that will alter the buyer's desired state and create a needs gap that you might address.

Upon completion of the role play, address the following questions:

2a. How do the buyer's perceived actual and desired states of being impact and activate their recognition of a need?

2b. Other than the method role played in the assignment, in what other ways might the salesperson for Accu-Press influence the buyer's recognition of a needs gap?

3. Put yourself in the role of salesperson for National Computer Corporation. You are currently working to sell the College of Business at your university a large number of upgraded personal computers. These computers will be placed in staff and faculty offices for use with a variety of networking, word processing, spreadsheet, and statistical analysis applications. The committee responsible for the purchase decision includes two faculty members and the director of purchasing for the university. Based on your work with these members of the buying team, you have compiled the following list of buyers' expectations of the salesperson and supplier organization:

• Coordinate all aspects of the product/service mix to provide a total package.
• Provide counseling to the customer based on in-depth knowledge of the product, the market, and the customers' needs.
• Engage in problem solving with a high degree of proficiency so as to ensure satisfactory customer service over extended time periods.
• Demonstrate high ethical standards and be honest in all communication.
• Advocate the customer's best interests within the selling organization.
• Be imaginative in meeting the buyers' needs.
• Be well prepared for sales calls.
• Demonstrate a high level of dependability.

From the perspective of this buying scenario:

(a) Explain what each of these buyer expectations mean.
(b) Discuss the implications of each expectation and how it might influence your behavior.
(c) Give an example of how a salesperson might fulfill each buyer expectation.

1. Coordinate all aspects of the product/service mix to provide a total package.

   _____

   _____

   _____

2. Provide counseling to the customer based on in-depth knowledge of the product, the market, and the customer's needs.

   _____

   _____

   _____

3. Engage in problem solving with a high degree of proficiency so as to ensure satisfactory customer service over extended time periods.

   _____

   _____

   _____

   _____

4. Demonstrate high ethical standards and be honest in all communication.

   _____

   _____

   _____

   _____

5. Advocate the customer's best interests within the selling organization.

   _____

   _____

   _____

   _____

6. Be imaginative in meeting the buyer's needs.

   _____

   _____

   _____

7. Be well prepared for sales calls.

   _____

   _____

   _____

8. Demonstrate a high level of dependability.

   _____

   _____

   _____

4. Use the following Communication Styles Survey[11] to assess your communication style. First, complete the Assertiveness Scale and the Responsiveness Scale by circling the number that best represents your self-evaluation regarding each of the paired characteristics. Give your candid reaction—there is no right or wrong answer. After completing each set, complete the scoring as instructed and plot your scores on the grid chart.

Assertiveness Scale

I perceive myself as being:

Cooperative				Competitive
1	2	3	4	5
Submissive				Authoritarian
1	2	3	4	5
Accommodating				Domineering
1	2	3	4	5
Hesitant				Decisive
1	2	3	4	5
Reserved				Outgoing
1	2	3	4	5
Compromising				Insistent
1	2	3	4	5
Cautious				Risk-Taking
1	2	3	4	5
Patient				Hurried
1	2	3	4	5
Complacent				Influential
1	2	3	4	5
Quiet				Talkative
1	2	3	4	5
Shy				Bold
1	2	3	4	5
Supportive				Demanding
1	2	3	4	5
Relaxed				Tense
1	2	3	4	5
Restrained				Assertive
1	2	3	4	5

Scoring for Assertiveness Scale:
Add the circled numbers on this page and enter the sum here _____
Divide this sum by 14 to compute your Assertiveness Score and enter it here _____

Responsiveness Scale

I perceive myself as being:

Disciplined				Easy-Going
1	2	3	4	5
Controlled				Expressive
1	2	3	4	5
Serious				Light-Hearted
1	2	3	4	5
Methodical				Unstructured
1	2	3	4	5
Calculating				Spontaneous
1	2	3	4	5
Guarded				Open
1	2	3	4	5
Stalwart				Humorous
1	2	3	4	5
Aloof				Friendly
1	2	3	4	5
Formal				Casual
1	2	3	4	5
Reserved				Attention-Seeking
1	2	3	4	5
Cautious				Carefree
1	2	3	4	5
Conforming				Unconventional
1	2	3	4	5
Reticent				Dramatic
1	2	3	4	5
Restrained				Impulsive
1	2	3	4	5

Scoring for Responsiveness Scale:

Add the circled numbers on this page and enter the sum here _____

Divide this sum by 14 to compute your Responsiveness Score and enter it here _____

Use the grid chart on the next page to plot your Assertiveness Score and your Responsiveness Score to determine your individual communication style.

What is your communication style? _____

Do you feel this is an accurate portrayal of your style? Why or why not?

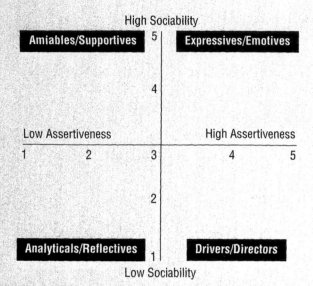

5. Based on your understanding of (a) interpersonal communication styles and (b) your personal communication style, respond to each of the following questions. These questions refer to how and why you would flex your style to better relate to buyers characterized by various communication styles.

(a) What preparations and style flexing would you make to better relate to and communicate with customers characterized as *Drivers/Directors*?

(b) What preparations and style flexing would you make to better relate to and communicate with customers characterized as *Analyticals/Reflectives*?

(c) What preparations and style flexing would you make to better relate to and communicate with customers characterized as *Expressives/Emotives*?

(d) What preparations and style flexing would you make to better relate to and communicate with customers characterized as *Amiables/Supportives*?

ROLE PLAY

6. **Situation:**   As a key account manager for Hirsch Production Controls, Jerry has developed a strong relationship with St. Louis-based Forrestor Manufacturing and the members of Forrestor's team of buyers. In place for several years now, this relationship has propelled Jerry into Hirsch's top salesperson and transformed Forrestor into Hirsch's best customer—accounting for some 20 percent of the company's business. Jerry has been working with one of Forrestor's competitors, Chicago-based Dorval Products for several months hoping to add them as a customer. As is typical in relationship selling, Jerry has had access to proprietary materials concerning Dorval's manufacturing processes and long-range planning.

Characters: Jerry, key account manager for Hirsch Production Controls; Clark Hughley, director of purchasing for Forrestor Manufacturing

Scene: *Location*—Clark Hughley's office at Forrestor Manufacturing. *Action*—Jerry is on a sales call discussing a new product relevant to Forrestor's production system. While there, Hughley begins asking Jerry about Dorval. It is apparent that Hughley wants to learn anything he can about Dorval's processes and a rumored plant expansion—proprietary or not, he keeps pushing Jerry for information.

Role play the situation that is playing out in Clark Hughley's office. Begin with the usual greeting and approach that might typify a longstanding relationship and proceed to the point where Hughley begins asking questions about Dorval's plans. Demonstrate how you would handle this situation in an ethical and professional manner.

Upon completion of the role play, address the following questions:

6a. Develop a list of five different ways that Jerry might handle this situation. Which one do you believe is the best option? Explain why you feel your choice is better than one of the other four options not selected.

6b. If you were Jerry, what would you do if Hughley continued to ask for information about Dorval? What if he hinted that your business with Forrestor might be in jeopardy if you did not come through with the desired information about Dorval?

7. Personality traits and temperament have been found to be important predictors of individuals' preferences and behaviors. One of the well-researched personality and temperament assessment scales has been made available for individuals to use as an online assessment of their own personality. This same Web site offers a large amount of information explaining the different categories of personality and temperament and how each category can predict certain tendencies in likes and dislikes, communication, and interpersonal behaviors.

Go to the Web site http://www.keirsey.com. Click on "Take the Keirsey Sorter." After reading the explanatory information, scroll down and click on "Take the Sorter." Complete the self-assessment and get your free individual temperament description. Return to the main keirsey.com page. Click on some of the icons found on this page and read about the different temperament styles and how they can predict an individual's behaviors.

Discussion Questions

7a. What are the different temperament styles identified by the Keirsey Sorter? What are key characteristics of each style?

7b. What was your indicated temperament category? How well do you feel it depicts the image you have of yourself? Why?

7c. Compare and contrast the Keirsey temperament styles with the communication style categories studied in the text.

7d. Having identified your temperament category, what implications might it have for you as a salesperson dealing with other people? What about working with people that are in different categories than you?

MAKING PROFESSIONAL SELLING DECISIONS

Case 3.1: Candoo Computer Corporation

Background

As a salesperson for Candoo Computer Corporation (CCC), you have just received a call from your regional manager regarding a program now under way at one of your key accounts, Farmland Companies. Farmland is a national insurance company with agency offices spread across the United States. The company is in the early stages of designing and specifying a computer system that will place a computer in each agency office. The system will allow each agency to develop, operate, and maintain its own customer database to provide better service to customers. In addition, by linking through the CCC mainframe, agencies, regional offices, and CCC headquarters will be networked for improved internal communications and access to the corporate database.

Current Situation

You have serviced this account for several years, and CCC equipment accounts for the biggest share of computers now in place at Farmland—some 35 to 40 percent of all units. As reflected in your share of this account's business, you and CCC have a good reputation and strong relationship with Farmland. In talking with Aimee Linn, your usual contact in the Farmland purchasing office, you have learned that this agency network system is the brainstorm and pet project of Mike Hughes, a very "hands-on" CEO. Consequently, the probability of the system becoming a reality is high. While faxing a complete set of hardware specs to you, Aimee has also let you know that, although Kerri Nicks, director of the Farmland MIS department, is actually heading up this project, the national agency sales director, Tim Long, is also very active in its design and requirement specification. His interest stems not only from wanting to make sure the system will do what is needed at the corporate, regional, and agency levels but also from the fact that he brainstormed and spearheaded a similar project two years ago that was never implemented. The previous effort did not have the blessing of Nicks in the MIS department, and it became a political football between the two departments. Each department wanted something different, and both sides accused the other of not knowing what it was doing. Primarily because the CEO has commanded that it will be done, both sides seem to be playing ball with each other this time.

Aimee did hint at one concern, however; although corporate is designing and specifying the system, each agency has to purchase its units out of its own funds. Although the agencies exclusively represent only Farmland Insurance products, each agency is owned by the general agent—not Farmland. Some of the agents are not convinced that the system is worth the projected price tag of $3,500 per system, and Farmland cannot force them to buy the systems.

As with other selling opportunities with Farmland, this has all the makings of a decision that will be made as a result of multiple inputs from an assortment of individuals across the company—a buying team of sorts. As the salesperson having primary responsibility for this account, how would you go about identifying the various members of the buying center? Using the worksheet provided, respond to the following activities.

Questions

1. Identify each member of the buying center and the role each participant plays, and estimate the amount of influence (low, medium, high, very high) each has on the final decision.
2. What are the major problems, needs, and expectations that you will need to address for each of these buying center members?

As you complete this assignment, remember that a single individual can perform multiple roles in the center. Furthermore, it is common to find more than one individual playing the same buying center role.

Situation:	Read Case 3.1.
Characters:	Yourself, salesperson for the Candoo Computer Corporation; Aimee Linn, purchasing manager for Farmland Companies; Kerri Nicks, director of MIS for Farmland Companies; Tim Long, national agency sales director for Farmland Companies; Mike Hughes, CEO for Farmland Companies
Scene 1:	*Location*—Aimee Linn's office at Farmland Companies. *Action*—You, as the Candoo Computer salesperson, are entering the first meeting with the Farmland buying team. Your goal for this first sales call is to establish rapport with each of the buying team members and identify the needs and expectations that will determine the purchases for this project. Identifying these needs and expectations is critical so that you can work with your own technology

ROLE PLAY

Worksheet for Identifying Buying Team Members and Roles			
Buying Team Role	**Team Member Playing This Role**	**Level of Influence**	**Team Member's Perceived Needs and Expectations**
Initiators			
Users			
Influencers			
Purchasers			
Deciders			
Gatekeepers			

support people and develop a customized system as a solution to Farmland's needs.

Join with a group of fellow students to role play this first sales call and demonstrate how you would (a) build rapport with the team members, (b) identify the needs and expectations the team members have for this information technology project, and (c) bridge the gap between the sales manager and the MIS director that seemed to kill the project once before.

Scene 2:   *Location*—Aimee Linn's office at Farmland Companies. *Action*— Based on the needs and expectations discovered in your first sales call, you have worked with your support team at Candoo Computers to develop a customized system meeting Farm-

land's primary needs. You are now making a follow-up sales call for the purpose of presenting your proposed system and making the sale.

Upon completion of the role play, address the following questions:

1. In what way would the different communication styles of the buying team members present complications in the critical stages of building rapport and discovering the buyers' needs and expectations?

2. How can a salesperson effectively build rapport with a team of different individuals that have large variations across their communication styles?

3. In a buying team situation, it is typical that certain needs will be championed by specific members while other members will be vocal in support of other needs the solution must address. How might a salesperson best present

the proposed package of features and benefits and recognize the relevant interests of the different buying team members?

4. What suggestions do you have for improving the presentation of the proposed solution and maximizing the positive involvement and buyin of the different team members?

Case 3.2: American Seating Company

Background

You are a salesperson for the American Seating Company (ASC) working with the Seattle Metropolitan Auditorium Authority to replace the seating as part of a major rejuvenation of the auditorium. The remodeling project is being done in response to several private theaters and two universities' entertainment centers that had begun to take major show bookings from the auditorium.

Current Situation

The buyers want the new auditorium seating to be as comfortable as possible and have specified units complete with arms and hinged seats/backs that allow the user to sit upright or slightly recline by leaning back 4 inches. The specifications also specify heavy frames, hardware, and linkage assemblies to yield an expected usable life of 10 years before requiring any form of service or replacement. However, these specifications increased the cost of the chairs by 13 percent. As a result, the buyers are now wanting a lower grade vinyl fabric in hopes of making up for some of the increased hardware costs.

With your expertise of chairs and fabrics, you have recommended the use of higher-grade nylon velvet rather than vinyl. The velvet will not only be much more comfortable but also more durable than the vinyl. Although both fabrics are equally moisture and stain resistant, the velvet comes with a guaranteed usable life of 10 years compared with the vinyl's 6-year guarantee.

Question

Use the multiattribute model of evaluation to develop a strategy for reselling the better-grade fabric as the best choice for the new auditorium seating.

ROLE PLAY

Situation:	Read Case 3.2.
Characters:	Yourself, salesperson for the American Seating Company; the buyer, purchasing manager for Seattle Metropolitan Auditorium Authority
Scene:	*Location*—Buyer's office at the Seattle Metropolitan Auditorium Authority. *Action*—You are presenting the chairs and seating equipment that your company is proposing to sell and install in line with the desired specifications outlined by the design architect and the management for the Seattle Metropolitan Auditorium Authority.

Demonstrate how you might present the advantages and benefits of the higher-grade nylon velvet over the lower-grade vinyl fabric and gain the buyer's commitment to use the better fabric on the seating that is purchased.

Upon completion of the role play, address the following questions:

1. What is the role of the salesperson in explaining and demonstrating that the longer-term added values of a solution with a higher initial cost can make it the lowest lifetime cost alternative?

2. What sales aids could assist the salesperson in demonstrating the longer-term added value and evidencing the greater benefits to the buyer?

CAPTURING THE POWER OF COLLABORATIVE COMMUNICATION

John Klich, a financial representative with the Northwestern Mutual Financial Network, believes the questions he asks of a prospective client during the initial meeting will determine his ability to develop a longstanding, mutually beneficial relationship with that person. In his first meeting with a prospect, called a factfinder, he seeks to understand everything about the client; their fears, their accomplishments; information they have never told anyone. In doing so, he asks a lot of "feeling" questions designed to have the prospect open up and express beliefs. John underscores that, "To be able to truly be a resource to someone, you need to have an intricate understanding of their goals, objectives, thoughts, and feelings. You cannot expect someone to open up until you start asking questions about why a belief or goal is important and to be genuinely interested in the answer." His little checkpoints throughout a meeting are when someone says "Good question. I have not thought of that before." But this does not necessarily guarantee a successful meeting. "Once someone has opened up to you it is important not to be judgmental on their situation. At the end of the day, I have to remember and respect the decisions people make are not mine. I can only point them in the right direction by educating them."

Managing expectations is another one of John's keys to success. In every meeting, he asks the client for their immediate and long-term expectations of him. He believes this is crucial in the financial services industry. "Conflict arises from unmet expectations. Having clear lines of communication and managing expectations are paramount to retaining clients for a long period of time. The reality is there are hundreds of thousands of people who do what I do." He is proud that many of his clients consider him their most trusted adviser, even in areas he does not work in directly. "Clients call me quite regularly seeking advice on areas outside my area of expertise. Although I refer them to someone who can better serve their needs, it still makes me feel good that they would think of me as someone who can help them."

John feels it is important to the service he gives his clients to promptly return their calls and answer their questions. His mission statement includes the following: It is my priority to offer them uncommon and superior service and to continue to add value to their lives.

One recent experience brings these principles to light. John scheduled a meeting with a young married couple that had done some prior planning with another advisor. They had recently had their first child and had experienced some significant life changes. After initial reluctance, the couple agreed to meet with John for a factfinder. During the meeting, John discovered that both the husband and wife had no life insurance and, despite good intentions, they had not yet established the appropriate accounts to save for their daughter's education. Furthermore, he learned that the previous advisor had not taken the time to ask the important questions; rather, he had just made assumptions about the clients' goals. John got a thorough understanding of what goals were important to the couple and how to address their desires. As a result, they accomplished their goals and John was able to establish himself

Objectives

After completing this module, you should be able to

1 Explain the importance of collaborative, two-way communication in personal selling.

2 Explain the primary types of questions and how they are applied in selling.

3 Illustrate the diverse roles and uses of strategic questioning in personal selling.

4 Identify and describe the five steps of the ADAPT questioning sequence.

5 Discuss the four sequential steps for effective active listening.

6 Discuss the superiority of pictures over words for explaining concepts and enhancing comprehension.

7 Describe the different forms of nonverbal communication.

103

as the comprehensive resource. "The best compliment I could ever get at the end of my process of helping someone is 'thank you. We would have never done this without you.' It really helps cement the relationship for the long term."

Source: Personal interview with John Klich, financial representative, July 27, 2004.

John Klich's experience with the potency of collaborative, relational sales communication illustrated in this module's opening vignette is not uncommon. In reality, it is quickly becoming the norm for effective selling. On the one hand, selling is basically communication. The skill and effectiveness of a salesperson's interpersonal communication are fundamental determinants of selling performance. However, at the same time, communication continues to be one of the least understood and studied skills for successful selling.

This module addresses the need to better understand and master the art of collaborative, two-way communication by first examining the basic nature of **relational sales communication**. Building on this understanding, the text breaks relational sales communication down into its component and subcomponent parts to facilitate the study and application of relational communication. The verbal dimension of communication is examined first with an emphasis on three communication subcomponents: (1) developing effective questioning methods for use in uncovering buyers' needs and expectations, (2) using active listening skills to facilitate the interchange of ideas and information, and (3) maximizing the responsive dissemination of information to buyers to explain and bring alive the benefits of proposed solutions. Finally, the nonverbal dimension of communication is examined with an emphasis on its application and meaningful interpretation in selling.

SALES COMMUNICATION AS A COLLABORATIVE PROCESS

Neither people nor organizations buy products. Rather, they seek out the satisfaction and benefits that are provided by certain product features. Although traditional selling has been described as "talking *at* the customer," relational selling has been referred to as "talking *with* the customer." Relational sales communication is a two-way and naturally collaborative interaction that allows buyers and sellers alike to develop a better understanding of the need situation and work together to generate the best response for solving the customer's needs. Although trust-based, relational selling has become the preeminent model for contemporary personal selling, the situation described in "An Ethical Dilemma" should serve as a reminder that some salespeople and sales organizations continue to practice more traditional and manipulative forms of selling.

Relational sales communication is the sharing of meaning between buying and selling parties that results from the interactive process of exchanging information and ideas. It is important to note that the purpose of sales communication is not agreement but rather the maximization of common understanding among participants. With this emphasis on establishing understanding, communication is fundamental throughout each stage of the personal selling process. Effective communication skills are needed to identify buying needs and to demonstrate to buyers how a salesperson's proposed solution can satisfy those needs better than competitors. The critical capabilities for effective selling include questioning, listening, giving information, nonverbal communication, and written communication skills. Although each of these skills is pervasive in everyday life, they are literally the heart and soul of the interpersonal exchange that characterizes relational selling.

Ryan Jameson, a junior marketing major, has just completed a summer-long internship in the St. Louis-based commercial accounts office of a national cell phone company. In his required paper summarizing his internship experience, Ryan noted that the first week of his internship was spent in a training class with seven additional students from several other universities. Most of the training was on the technology of cellular communication and the different products and services the company offers for sale. There was some discussion of selling skills and techniques, but most of the training was focused on product knowledge. At the beginning of the second week, each student was given a list of prospective leads that they were to use for making phone calls to potential business and commercial customers along with a three-ring binder of selling tips to incorporate and use as needed. The first page of the selling tips contained a motivational message followed by what was titled "The 5 Keys to Successful Selling." These keys to success were as follows:

Key #1: Everybody needs a cell phone! Make your daily calls, demonstrate the product, and ask for the order.

Key #2: Prospective buyers do not know what they need! Follow the standard selling message showing each of our products and ask for the order each time until the buyer makes a choice.

Key #3: Always be closing! If you don't ask, nobody will buy!

Key #4: Success in selling is simply a numbers game! Contact enough prospects and you will make your quota. Want to sell more? Make more contacts!

Key #5: Product knowledge is the key! Have a good opening, explain the products, handle objections, and close the sale by leading the buyer where you want them to go.

How does this company's selling philosophy compare with the trust-based, consultative selling approach explained in your text and discussed in class? How will these keys to selling success work in today's marketplace? Why?

VERBAL COMMUNICATION: QUESTIONING

There are two ways to dominate or control a selling conversation. A salesperson can talk all the time, or the salesperson can maintain a more subtle level of control by asking well thought out questions that guide the discussion. As highlighted in "Professional Selling in the 21st Century: Importance of Preparation and Well Thought Out Questions," successful salespeople must be masters at thinking through what they need to know and planning the questions they need to ask. They should know exactly what information they need and which type of question is best suited for eliciting that information from a prospective buyer.

Purposeful, carefully crafted questions can encourage thoughtful responses from buyers and provide richly detailed information about the buyers' current situation, needs, and expectations. This additional detail and understanding is often as meaningful for the buyer as it is for the salesperson. That is, proper questioning can facilitate both the buyer's and seller's understanding of a problem and its possible solutions.[1] For example, questions can encourage meaningful feedback regarding the buyer's attitude and the logical progression through the purchase decision process. Questioning also shows interest in the buyer and his or her needs and actively involves the buyer in the selling process. Questions can also be used to tactically redirect, regain, or hold the buyer's attention should it begin to wander during the conversation. In a similar fashion, questions can provide a convenient and subtle transition to a different topic of discussion and provide a logical guide promoting sequential thought and decision making.

PROFESSIONAL SELLING IN THE 21ST CENTURY

Importance of Preparation and Well Thought Out Questions

Alex Cruz, corporate account manager for CDW Corporation talks about the critical importance of carefully thinking through and purposefully crafting questions to successfully gain the specific information needed to advance the selling process.

Consistent with the time-tested CDW selling model, virtually all of our communication with customers is by phone and Internet. Keeping a client's attention on the phone is not always the easiest thing to accomplish. However, the phone allows me to reach people all across the country. The majority of my clients have many responsibilities and typically have full schedules that are often interrupted by internal mishaps, which causes them to fall behind in their day-to-day responsibilities. For this reason, it is very important that when I decide to make a sales call I am *able to quickly and consistently demonstrate the utmost value to the client in our conversation. If I misstep and am unable to present that value quickly I may not only lose a sale or an opportunity, but most importantly, it may also sour the credibility that I have worked hard to establish in the relationship. This is why it is important that I make sure to do my best to prepare for all of my sales calls by reviewing the account history and the relevant information that I have previously discussed with the contact before making the call. Planning and preparing appropriately enables me to ask the right questions, stay focused, and get the information I need regarding my client's situation. Only then can I add value and demonstrate to my clients that I am there to work with them to provide a solution that is built around their needs. Preparation and consideration of the questions I need to ask allows me to demonstrate expertise, build customer value, and distinguish myself from my competition.*

Questions are typed by the results they are designed to accomplish. Does the salesperson wish to receive a free flow of thoughts and ideas or a simple yes/no confirmation? Is the salesperson seeking a general description of the overall situation or specific details regarding emergent needs or problematic experiences with current suppliers? To be effective, salespeople must understand which type of question will best accomplish their desired outcome. In this manner, questions can be typed into two basic categories: (1) amount of information and level of specificity desired and (2) strategic purpose or intent.

Types of Questions Classified by Amount and Specificity of Information Desired

Open-end Questions

Open-end questions, also called nondirective questions, are designed to let the customer respond freely. That is, the customer is not limited to one- or two-word answers but is encouraged to disclose personal and/or business information. Open-end questions encourage buyers' thought processes and deliver richer and more expansive information than closed-end questions. Consequently, these questions are typically used to probe for descriptive information that allows the salesperson to better understand the specific needs and expectations of the customer. The secret to successfully using open-end questions lies in the first word used to form the question. Words often used to begin open-end questions include *what, how, where, when, tell, describe,* and *why*.[2] "What happens when . . . ," "How do you feel . . . ," and "Describe the . . ." are examples of open-end questions.

Closed-end Questions

Closed-end questions are designed to limit the customers' response to one or two words. This type of question is typically used to confirm or clarify information gleaned from previous responses to open-end questions. Although the most common form is the yes/no question, closed-end questions come in many forms—provided the response is limited to one or two words. For instance, "Do you . . . ," "Are you . . . ," "How many . . . ," and "How often . . ." are common closed-end questions.

Dichotomous/Multiple-Choice Questions

Dichotomous questions and multiple-choice questions are directive forms of questioning. This type of question asks a customer to choose from two or more options and is used in selling to discover customer preferences and move the purchase decision process forward. An example of this form of question would be, "Which do you prefer, the _____ or the _____?"

Types of Questions Classified by Strategic Purpose

[handwritten: Role Playtime]

[handwritten: (PETR)]

Probing Questions

Probing questions are designed to penetrate below generalized or superficial information to elicit more articulate and precise details for use in needs discovery and solution identification. Rather than interrogating a buyer, probing questions are best used in a conversational style: (1) requesting clarification ("Can you share with me an example of that?" "How long has this been a problem?"), (2) encouraging elaboration ("How are you dealing with that situation now?" "What is your experience with _____?"), and (3) verifying information and responses ("That is interesting, could you tell me more?" "So, if I understand correctly, _____. Is that right?").

[handwritten: – general fact finding]

Evaluative Questions

Evaluative questions use open- and closed-end question formats to gain confirmation and to uncover attitudes, opinions, and preferences held by the prospect. These questions are designed to go beyond generalized fact finding and uncover prospects' perceptions and feelings regarding existing and desired circumstances as well as potential solutions. Exemplary evaluative questions include "How do you feel about _____?" "Do you see the merits of _____?" and "What do you think _____?"

[handwritten: – uncovering perceptions, opinion, feelings]

Tactical Questions

Tactical questions are used to shift or redirect the topic of discussion when the discussion gets off course or when a line of questioning proves to be of little interest or value. For example, the salesperson might be exploring the chances of plant expansion only to find that the prospect cannot provide that type of proprietary information at this early stage of the buyer–seller relationship. To avoid either embarrassing the prospect or him- or herself by proceeding on a forbidden or nonproductive line of questioning, the seller uses a strategic question designed to change topics. An example of such a tactical question might be expressed as "Earlier you mentioned that _____. Could you tell me more about how that might affect _____?"

[handwritten: Probing Evaluative Tactical Reactive]

Reactive Questions

Reactive questions are questions that refer to or directly result from information previously provided by the other party. Reactive questions are used to elicit additional information, explore for further detail, and keep the flow of information going. Illustrative reactive questions are "You mentioned that _____. Can you give me an example of what you mean?" and "That is interesting. Can you tell me how it happened?"

These different groupings of question types are not mutually exclusive. As depicted in the guidelines for combining question types in Exhibit 4.1, effective questions integrate elements from different question types. For example, "How do you feel about the current trend of sales in the industry?" is open end (classified by format) and evaluative (classified by purpose) in nature.

Regardless of the types of questions combined, Robert Jolles, senior sales training consultant for Xerox Corporation, cautions against the natural tendency to use closed-end questions rather than open-end questions. His experience and research indicate

EXHIBIT 4.1   Guidelines for Combining Types of Questions for Maximal Effectiveness

		Strategic Objective or Purpose of Questioning			
		Explore and Dig for Details	**Gain Confirmation and Discover Attitudes/Opinions**	**Change Topics or Direct Attention**	**Follow Up Previously Elicited Statements**
Amount and Specificity of Information Desired	**Discussion and Interpretation**	*Open-end* Questions Designed to Be *Probing* in Nature	*Open-end* Questions Designed to Be *Evaluative* in Nature	*Open-end* Questions Designed to Be *Tactical* in Nature	*Open-end* Questions Designed to Be *Reactive* in Nature
	Confirmation and Agreement	*Closed-end* Questions Designed to Be *Probing* in Nature	*Closed-end* Questions Designed to Be *Evaluative* in Nature	*Closed-end* Questions Designed to Be *Tactical* in Nature	*Closed-end* Questions Designed to Be *Reactive* in Nature
	Choice from Alternatives	*Dichotomous* or *Multiple-choice* Questions Designed to Be *Probing* in Nature	*Dichotomous* or *Multiple-choice* Questions Designed to Be *Evaluative* in Nature	*Dichotomous* or *Multiple-choice* Questions Designed to Be *Tactical* in Nature	*Dichotomous* or *Multiple-choice* Questions Designed to Be *Reactive* in Nature

that for every open-end question the average salesperson asks, there will be 10 closed-end questions.[3] This overuse of closed-end questions is dangerous in selling. The discovery and exploration of customer needs are fundamental to relational selling, and discovery and exploration are best done with open-end questions. As previously discussed, closed-end questions certainly have their place in selling, but they are best used for clarification and confirmation, not discovery and exploration. An additional issue in overusing closed-end questions is that when they are used in a sequence, the resulting communication takes on the demeanor of interrogation rather than conversation.

Strategic Application of Questioning in Personal Selling

Effective questioning skills are indispensable in selling and are used to address critical issues throughout all stages of the selling process. In practice, salespeople combine the different types of questions discussed earlier to accomplish multiple and closely related sales objectives:

- *Generate Buyer Involvement.* Rather than the salesperson dominating the conversation and interaction, purposeful and planned questions are used to encourage prospective buyers to actively participate in a two-way collaborative discussion.

- *Provoke Thinking.* Innovative and effective solutions require cognitive efforts and contributions from each participant. Strategic questions stimulate buyers and salespeople to thoroughly and pragmatically think about and consider all aspects of a given situation.

- *Gather Information.* Good questions result from advance planning and should be directed toward gathering the information required to fill in the gap between "What do we need to know?" and "What do we already know?"

- *Clarification and Emphasis.* Rather than assuming that the salesperson understands what a buyer has said, questions can be used to further clarify meaning and to further emphasize the important points within a buyer–seller exchange.

- *Show Interest.* In response to statements from buyers, salespeople ask related questions and paraphrase what the buyer has said to demonstrate their interest in and understanding of what the buyer is saying.

- *Gain Confirmation.* The use of simple and direct questions allow salespeople to check back with the prospective buyer to confirm the buyer's understanding or agreement and gain his or her commitment to move forward.

- *Advance the Sale.* Effective questions are applied in a fashion that guides and moves the selling process forward in a logical progression from initiation through needs development and on through needs resolution and follow-up.

With the aim of simultaneously targeting and achieving each of these objectives, several systems have been developed to guide salespeople in properly developing and using effective questions. Two of the more prominent questioning systems are SPIN and ADAPT. Both of these systems use a logical sequencing—a sort of funneling effect—that begins with broad-based, nonthreatening, general questions. Questioning progressively proceeds through more narrowly focused questions designed to clarify the buyer's needs and to logically propel the selling process toward the presentation and demonstration of solution features, advantages, and benefits.

SPIN Questioning System

The **SPIN** system sequences four types of questions designed to uncover a buyer's current situation and inherent problems, enhance the buyer's understanding of the consequences and implications of those problems, and lead to the proposed solution.[4] SPIN is actually an acronym for the four types of questions making up the multiple question sequence: situation questions, problem questions, implication questions, and need-payoff questions.

[handwritten margin note: Situation Problem Implication Need payoff]

- *Situation Questions.* This type of question solicits data and facts in the form of general background information and descriptions of the buyer's existing situation. **Situation questions** are used early in the sales call and provide salespeople with leads to fully develop the buyer's needs and expectations. Situation questions might include "Who are your current suppliers?" "Do you typically purchase or lease?" and "Who is involved in purchasing decisions?" Situation questions are essential, but they should be used in moderation as too many general fact-finding questions can bore the buyer. Further, their interrogating nature can result in irritated buyers.

- *Problem Questions.* **Problem questions** follow the more general situation questions to further probe for specific difficulties, developing problems and areas of dissatisfaction that might be positively addressed by the salesperson's proposed sales offering. Some examples of problem questions include "How critical is this component for your production?" "What kinds of problems have you encountered with your current suppliers?" and "What types of reliability problems do you experience with your current system?" Problem questions actively involve the buyer and can assist him or her in better understanding his or her own problems and needs. Nevertheless, inexperienced and unsuccessful salespeople generally do not ask enough problem questions.

- *Implication Questions.* **Implication questions** follow and relate to the information flowing from problem questions. Their purpose is to assist the buyer in thinking about the potential consequences of the problem and understand the urgency of resolving the problem in a way that motivates him or her to seek a solution. Typical implication questions might include "How does this affect profitability?" "What impact does the slow response of your current supplier have on the productivity of your operation?" "How would a faster piece of equipment improve productivity and

[handwritten margin note: ★ Role playing]

profits?" and "What happens when the supplier is late with a shipment?" Although implication questions are closely linked to success in selling, even experienced salespeople rarely use them effectively.

- *Need-Payoff Questions.* Based on the implications of a problem, salespeople use **need-payoff questions** to propose a solution and develop commitment from the buyer. These questions refocus the buyer's attention to solutions rather than problems and get the buyer to think about the positive benefits derived from solving the problems. Examples of need-payoff questions are "Would more frequent deliveries allow you to increase productivity?" "If we could provide you with increased reliability, would you be interested?" "If we could improve the quality of your purchased components, how would that help you?" and "Would you be interested in increasing productivity by 15 percent?" Top salespeople effectively incorporate a higher number of need-payoff questions into sales calls than do less successful salespeople.

ADAPT Questioning System

As illustrated by Figure 4.1, the ADAPT questioning system uses a logic-based funneling sequence of questions, beginning with broad and generalized inquiries designed to

FIGURE 4.1   Funneling Sequence of ADAPT Technique for Needs Discovery

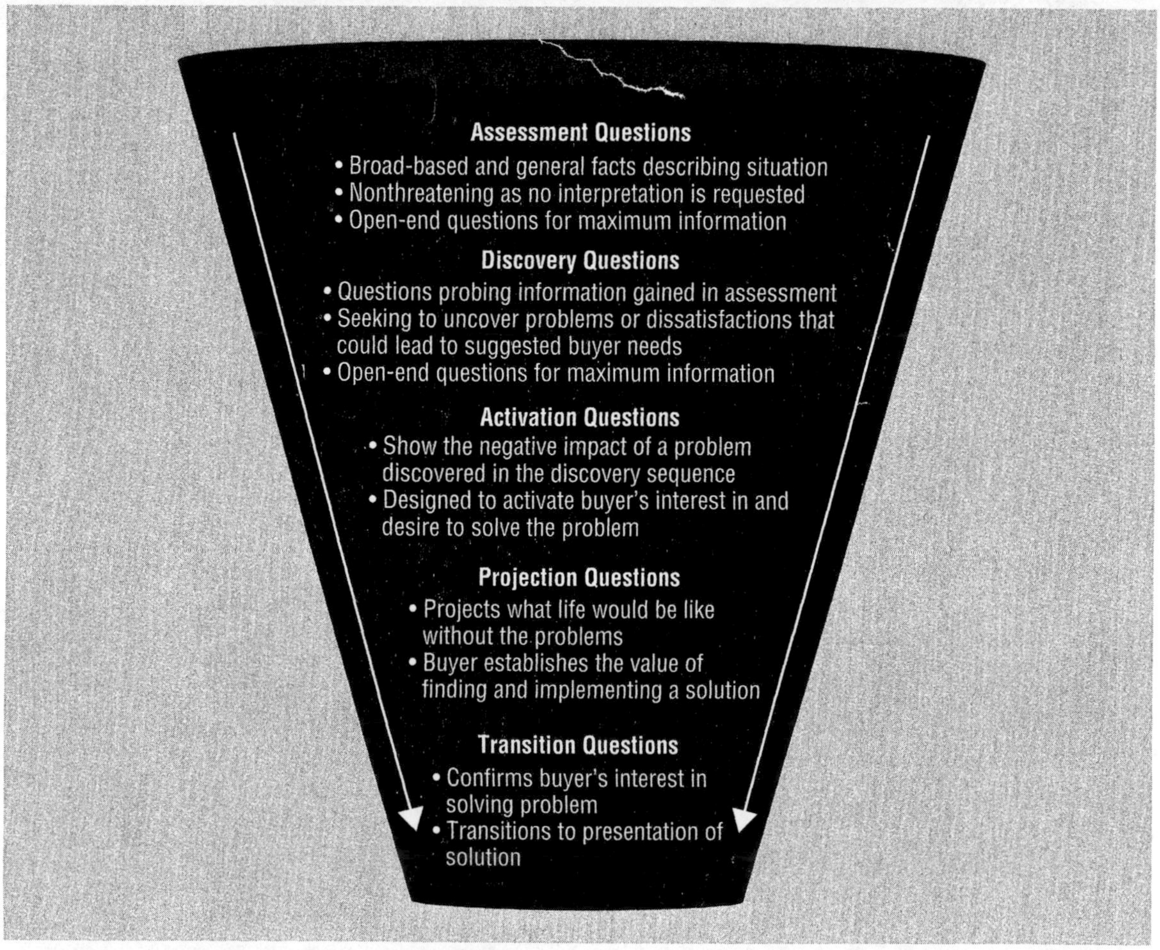

Assessment Questions
- Broad-based and general facts describing situation
- Nonthreatening as no interpretation is requested
- Open-end questions for maximum information

Discovery Questions
- Questions probing information gained in assessment
- Seeking to uncover problems or dissatisfactions that could lead to suggested buyer needs
- Open-end questions for maximum information

Activation Questions
- Show the negative impact of a problem discovered in the discovery sequence
- Designed to activate buyer's interest in and desire to solve the problem

Projection Questions
- Projects what life would be like without the problems
- Buyer establishes the value of finding and implementing a solution

Transition Questions
- Confirms buyer's interest in solving problem
- Transitions to presentation of solution

The ADAPT questioning technique logically sequences questions from broad and general inquiries through increasingly detailed questions for effective needs discovery.

identify and assess the buyer's situation. Based on information gained in this first phase, further questions are generated to probe and discover more details regarding the needs and expectations of the buyer. In turn, the resulting information is incorporated in further collaborative discussion in a way that activates the buyer's motivation to implement a solution and further establishes the buyer's perceived value of a possible solution. The last phase of ADAPT questioning transitions to the buyer's commitment to learn about the proposed solution and grants the salesperson permission to move forward into the presentation and demonstration of the sales offering. ADAPT is an acronym for the five stages of strategic questioning and represents what the salesperson should be doing at each stage: assessment questions, discovery questions, activation questions, projection questions, and transition questions.[5]

- *Assessment Questions.* This initial phase of questioning is designed to be nonthreatening and to spark conversation that elicits factual information about the customer's current situation that can provide a basis for further exploration and probing. As illustrated in Exhibit 4.2, **assessment questions** do not seek conclusions—rather, at a macro or 40,000-foot level of focus, these questions should address the buyer's company and operation, goals and objectives, market trends and customers, current suppliers, and even the buyer as an individual. The information sought should augment or confirm precall research. Examples would include "What is the current level of your production?" "How long has the current equipment been in place?" "How many suppliers are currently being used?" "What are the growth objectives of the company?" and "What individuals have input into purchase decisions?"

- *Discovery Questions.* As portrayed in Exhibit 4.3, these questions follow up on the responses gained from the preceding assessment questions. At a more micro and ground-level focus, **discovery questions** should drill down and probe for further details needed to fully develop, clarify, and understand the nature of the buyer's problems. Facts as well as the buyer's interpretations, perceptions, feelings, and opinions are sought in regard to the buyer's needs, wants, dissatisfactions, and expectations relevant to product, delivery requirements, budget and financing issues, and desired service levels. The goal is to discover needs and dissatisfactions that the salesperson's sales offering can resolve. Examples of discovery questions might include "How often do these equipment failures occur?" "How well are your current suppliers performing?" "What disadvantages do you see in the current process?" "How satisfied are you with the quality of components you are currently purchasing?" and "How difficult are these for your operators to use?"

- *Activation Questions.* The implied or suggested needs gained from discovery questions are not usually sufficient to gain the sale. Often, a buyer will believe that a particular

---

These questions are designed to elicit factual information about the customer's current situation. These questions do not seek conclusions; rather they seek information that describes the customer and his or her business environment. The information sought should augment or confirm precall research.

Examples:

1. Question—"What types of operating arrangements do you have with your suppliers?"
   Answer—We use a JIT system with our main suppliers . . .
2. Question—"Who is involved in the purchase decision-making process?"
   Answer—I make the decisions regarding supplies . . .

Assessment questions are generally open end; however, closed-end questions are used when seeking confirmation or basic descriptive information. For example, "So, you currently work with 10 different suppliers?" or "How many years have you been in business?" Assessment questions are necessary for drawing out information early in the sales cycle.

EXHIBIT 4.3   Discovery Questions

Discovery questions are used to uncover problems or dissatisfactions the customer is experiencing that the salesperson's product or company may be able to solve. Basically, these questions are used to "distill" or "boil down" the information gained from the preceding assessment questions and from precall research into suggested needs.

Examples:

1. Question—"I understand you prefer a Just-in-Time (JIT) relationship with your suppliers—how have they been performing?"
    Answer—Pretty well . . . an occasional late delivery . . . but pretty well.
2. Question—"So, your current suppliers are occasionally late with deliveries?"
    Answer—Yes . . . sometimes.

The *suggested* needs gained from discovery questions are used as a foundation for the rest of the sales call. Yet, a *suggested* need is usually not sufficient to close the sale. Often, a customer will believe that a particular problem does not cause any significant negative consequences. If this is the case, finding a solution to the problem will be a very low priority. The professional salesperson must then help the customer to reevaluate the impact of the *suggested* need by asking activation questions.

problem does not cause any significant negative consequences, hence the motivation to solve the problem will carry a low priority. Successful salespeople help the customer realistically evaluate the full impact of the implied need through the use of **activation questions**. As detailed in Exhibit 4.4, the objective is to "activate" the customer's interest in solving discovered problems by helping him or her gain insight into the true ramifications of the problem and to realize that what may initially seem to be of little consequence is, in fact, of significant consequence. Examples include "What effects do these equipment breakdowns have on your business operations?" "To what extent are these increases in overtime expenses affecting profitability?" "How will the supplier's inability to deliver on time affect your planned expansion?" and "When components fail in the field, how does that influence customer satisfaction and repurchase?"

- *Projection Questions.* As a natural extension of the activation questions, **projection questions** encourage and facilitate the buyer in "projecting" what it would be like without the problems that have been previously "discovered" and "activated." The use of good projection questions accomplishes several positive outcomes. First, the focus is switched from problems and their associated consequences to the upside—the benefits to be derived from solving the problems. What were initially perceived as costs

EXHIBIT 4.4   Activation Questions

Activation questions are used to show the impact of a problem, uncovered through discovery questions, on the customer's entire operation. The objective is to "activate" the customer's interest in solving the problem by helping him or her to gain insight into the true ramifications of the problem and realize that what may seem to be of little consequence is, in fact, of significant consequence.

Examples:

1. Question—"What effect does your supplier's late delivery have on your operation?"
    Answer—It slows production . . . Operating costs go up . . .
2. Question—"If production drops off, how are your operating costs affected, and how does that affect your customers?"
    Answer—Customer orders delayed . . . Potential to lose customers . . .

Activation questions show the negative impact of a problem so that finding a solution to that problem is desirable. Now, the salesperson can help the customer to discover the positive impact of solving the problems by using projection questions.

Projection questions help the customer to "project" what life would be like without the problems or dissatisfactions uncovered through activation questions. This helps the customer to see value in finding solutions to the problems developed earlier in the sales call.

Examples:

1. Question—"If a supplier was never late with a delivery, what effects would that have on your JIT operating structure?"
    Answer—It would run smoother and at lower cost . . .
2. Question—"If a supplier helped you meet the expectations of your customers, what impact would that have on your business?"
    Answer—Increased customer satisfaction would mean more business . . .

These questions are used to let the customer tell the salesperson the benefits of solving the problem. By doing so, the customer is reinforcing in his or her mind the importance of solving the problem and reducing the number of objections that might be raised.

and expenses are now logically structured as benefits to the buyer and his or her organization—the payoff for taking action and investing in a solution. Second—and equally important—the benefit payoff allows the buyer to establish the realistic value of implementing a solution. In this manner, the benefit payoff is perceived as a positive value received and serves as the foundation for demonstrating what the solution is worth—what the buyer would be willing to pay. As illustrated in Exhibit 4.5, projection questions encourage the buyer to think about how and why he or she should go about resolving a problem. In essence, projection questions assist the buyer in selling himself or herself by establishing the worth of the proposed solution. The customer, rather than the salesperson, establishes the benefits of solving the problem. This reinforces the importance of solving the problem and reduces the number of objections that might be raised. Examples of projection questions include "If a supplier was never late with a delivery, what effects would that have on your overall operation?" "What would be the impact on profitability if you did not have problems with limited plant capacity and the resulting overtime expenses?" "How would a system that your operators found easier to use affect your business operations?" and "If component failures were minimized, what impact would the resulting improvement in customer satisfaction have on financial performance?"

*   *Transition Questions.* **Transition questions** are used to smooth the transition from needs discovery into the presentation and demonstration of the proposed solution's features, advantages, and benefits. As exemplified in Exhibit 4.6, transition questions are

Transition questions are simple closed-end questions that confirm the customer's desire to solve the problem(s) uncovered through the previous questions.

Examples:

1. Question—"So, having a supplier who is never late with deliveries is important to you?"
    Answer—Yes, it is.
2. Question—"If I can show you how our company ensures on-time delivery, would you be interested in pursuing a formal business arrangement with our company?"
    Answer—Yes, if I'm convinced your company can guarantee on-time delivery . . .

The primary function of these questions is to make the transition from need confirmation into the sales presentation. In addition, these questions can lead to a customer commitment, provided the salesperson adequately presents how his or her company can solve the customer's problems.

typically closed end and evaluative in format. These questions confirm the buyer's desire to seek a solution and give their consent to the salesperson to move forward with the selling process. Examples include "So, having suppliers that are consistently on time is important to you—if I could show you how our company assures you of on-time delivery, would you be interested?" "It seems that increasing capacity is a key to reducing overtime and increasing profitability—would you be interested in a way to increase capacity by 20 percent through a simple addition to your production process?" and "Would you be interested in a system that is easier for your operators to use?"

VERBAL COMMUNICATION: LISTENING

Listening is the other half of effective questioning. After all, asking the customer for information is of little value if the salesperson does not listen. As illustrated by "Professional Selling in the 21st Century: Effective Listening is the Foundation for Making a Sale" effective listening is rated among the most critical skills for successful selling. Yet, most of us share the common problem of being a lot better at sending messages than receiving them, and effective listening is often considered to be the number one weakness of salespeople.[6]

Poor listening skills have been identified as one of the primary causes of salesperson failure.[7] In order to get the information needed to best serve, identify and respond to needs, and nurture a collaborative buyer–seller relationship, salespeople must be able to listen and understand what was said *and* what was meant. Nevertheless, situations similar to the one depicted in "An Ethical Dilemma" are all too common. As illustrated by Figure 4.2, effective listening can be broken down into six primary facets:

1. *Pay attention*—Listen to understand, not to reply. Resist the urge to interrupt and receive the full message the buyer is communicating.
2. *Monitor nonverbals*—Make effective eye contact and check to see if the buyer's body language and speech patterns match what is being said.

PROFESSIONAL SELLING IN THE 21ST CENTURY

Effective Listening is the Foundation for Making a Sale

As a sales representative for Dallas-based Holt Equipment, Jennifer Blessin works with all types of construction companies and helps them solve myriad equipment needs with Caterpillar's line of compact construction equipment. Jennifer underscores the importance of active listening in today's trust-based selling environment.

Salespeople know the importance of researching information about the prospect before making the sales call. But don't count on it telling you exactly what the prospect needs. The ultimate source for information about the prospect's needs is the prospect, and how well a salesperson listens will determine whether they make the sale or not. Effectively listening to buyers is at the heart of trust-based, consultative selling: finding out what

buyers are trying to accomplish, discovering what their needs and concerns are, and providing them with a unique, value-added solution. The only way to achieve this is to listen, and listen well.

As long as buyers are providing useful information, the salesperson should give them undivided attention and focus on what they are saying. Rather than interrupting to give his or her own thoughts on the subject, the salesperson must encourage buyers to finish their thoughts by providing them with positive feedback—nodding the head in agreement and paraphrasing what they have just said. This encourages them to continue. As much as a salesperson might want to jump in and respond to a buyer's comments, he or she must resist the temptation. The words that might be cut off and missed could be the key to making a sale.

AN ETHICAL DILEMMA

Naturally outgoing and enthusiastic, Tim Stratton is a person whom friends refer to as a natural-born salesperson. In his role as a regional sales representative for R&S Publishing, a major publisher of business catalogs, directories, and brochures, Tim combines these natural traits with his 11 years of experience and undergraduate degree in graphic arts to bring innovative ideas and solutions to his clients. However, Tim's sales productivity has peaked out over the previous two years and there has been a noticeable decline in repeat business and a number of his accounts have been lost to the competition. Hoping to assist Tim in getting over this continuing slump, Tim's sales manager has spent two days with him out in the field calling on prospects and customers. During these ride-a-longs, the sales manager has noticed that Tim has a tendency to interrupt when his buyer is discussing problems and desired achievements. Rather than allowing the buyer to fully describe the nature of problems and needs, Tim interjects his opinions and seems to be telling the buyer what to do. Tim continues to close sales, but his batting average is low and several customers have begun using other companies for their catalog programs.

What is going on here that might explain Tim's declining sales performance? What changes would you suggest to Tim? Why?

3. *Paraphrase and repeat*—Confirm your correct understanding of what the buyer is saying by paraphrasing and repeating what you have heard.
4. *Make no assumptions*—Ask questions to clarify the meaning of what the buyer is communicating.
5. *Encourage the buyer to talk*—Encourage the flow of information by giving positive feedback and help the buyer stay on track by asking purposeful, related questions.
6. *Visualize*—Maximize your attention and comprehension by thinking about and visualizing what the buyer is saying.

The practiced listening skills of high performance salespeople enable them to pick up, sort out, and interpret a higher number of buyers' verbal and nonverbal messages than lower-performing salespeople. In addition to gaining information and understanding critical to the relational selling process, a salesperson's good listening behaviors provide the added benefits of positively influencing the formation and continuation of buyer–seller relationships. The effective use and demonstration of good listening skills by a salesperson are positively associated with the customer's trust in the salesperson and the anticipation of having future interactions with the salesperson.[8] Clearly, effective listening is a critical component in trust-based, relational selling, and success requires continuous practice and improvement of our listening skills.

Using Different Types of Listening

Communications research identifies two primary categories of listening: *social* and *serious*.[9] **Social listening** is an informal mode of listening that can be associated with day-to-day conversation and entertainment. Social listening is characterized by low levels of cognitive activity and concentration and is typically used in conversation with a friend or a store clerk or listening to music, a concert, a TV program, or even a play. The received messages are taken at face value and do not require a high degree of concentration or thinking to sort through, interpret, and understand. However, **serious listening** is associated with events or topics in which it is important to sort through, interpret, understand, and respond to received messages. The serious form

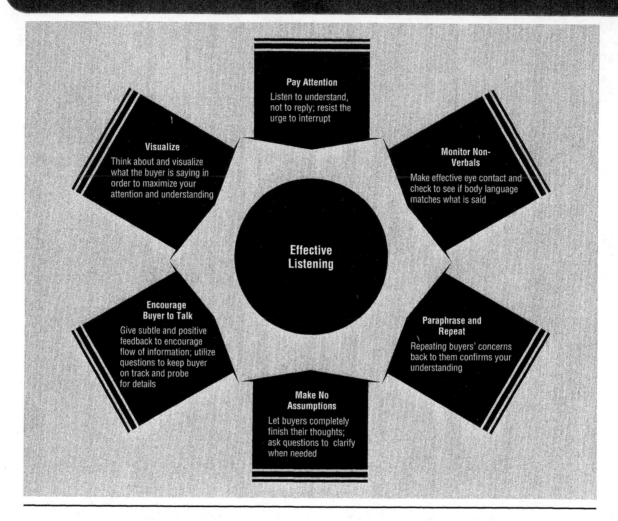

The six facets of effective listening enable salespeople to better pick up, sort out, and interpret buyers' verbal and nonverbal messages.

of listening is often referred to as *active listening*, as it requires high levels of concentration and cognition about the messages being received. *Concentration* is required to break through the distractions and other interference to facilitate receiving and remembering specific messages. *Cognition* is used to sort through and select the meaningful relevant messages and interpret them for meaning, information, and response.

Active Listening

Active listening in a selling context is defined as "the cognitive process of actively sensing, interpreting, evaluating, and responding to the verbal and nonverbal messages of present or potential customers."[10] This definition is very useful to those wishing to master active listening skills. First, it underscores the importance of receiving and interpreting both verbal and nonverbal cues and messages to better determine the full and correct meaning of the message. Second, it incorporates a well-accepted model of listening. As illustrated in Figure 4.3,[11] the **SIER** model depicts active listening as a hierarchical, four-step sequence of sensing, interpreting, evaluating, and

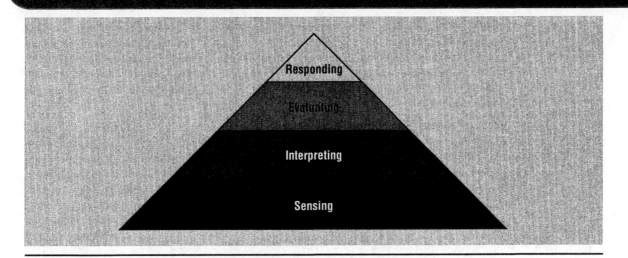

SIER Hierarchy of Active Listening   FIGURE 4.3

Responding

Evaluating

Interpreting

Sensing

Active listening is a cognitive process of actively sensing, interpreting, evaluating, and responding to verbal and nonverbal messages from buyers and prospects.

responding.[12] Effective active listening requires each of these four hierarchical process activities to be carried out successfully and in proper succession.

- *Sensing.* Listening is much more than simply hearing. Nevertheless, the first activities in active listening are **sensing** (i.e., hear and see) and receiving (i.e., pay attention to) the verbal and nonverbal components of the message being sent. Sensing does not occur without practice and should not be taken for granted. In fact, research indicates that most of us listen at only 25 percent of our capacity. Think about yourself. How often have you had to ask someone to repeat what he or she said or perhaps assumed you knew what the sender was going to say before they could say it? Increased concentration and attention can improve sensing effectiveness. Taking notes, making eye contact with the sender, and not interrupting can improve sensing skills. Let the sender finish and provide the full content of the message. This not only improves the concentration of the receiver but also encourages the sender to provide more information and detail.

- *Interpreting.* After the message is received, it must be correctly interpreted. **Interpreting** addresses the question of "What meaning does the sender intend?" Both content and context are important. That is, in addition to the semantic meaning of the words and symbols, we must consider the experiences, knowledge, and attitudes of the sender to fully understand what was meant. Hold back the temptation to evaluate the message until the sender is through. Note the nonverbal and verbal cues along with possible consistencies and inconsistencies between them. Incorporate knowledge of the sender's background and previous relevant statements and positions into the message interpretation.

- *Evaluating.* Active listening requires the receiver to decide whether he or she agrees with the sender's message. The results from the interpretation stage are evaluated to sort fact from opinion and emotion. Too often, receivers complete this activity prior to receiving the full message, and on hearing something with which they disagree, the sender is effectively tuned out. As a result, communication is stifled. **Evaluating** can be improved through improved concentration and thoughtful consideration of the full message. Summarizing the key points as if they were going to be reported to others can further enhance evaluation skills. Searching for areas of interest rather than prejudging the message can also facilitate the evaluation process.

- *Responding.* **Responding** is both an expectation and requirement for active listening to be effective. Collaborative, two-way communication requires that the listener respond to the sender. Responses provide feedback to the other party, emphasize understanding, encourage further elaboration, and can serve as a beginning point for the receiver to transition into the role of sender for the next message set. Responses can take many forms. Nonverbal cues such as nodding and smiling can indicate that the receiver's message was received. Responses in the form of restating and paraphrasing the sender's message can provide strong signals of interest and understanding. Asking questions can elicit additional details and clarification.

The SIER model provides a useful framework for evaluating communication accuracy and pinpointing the sources of problems. Similarly, it can be effectively used for planning activities and behaviors designed to improve communication effectiveness. As depicted by the SIER model, active listening is a hierarchical and sequential process. One must sense the message before it can be interpreted. In turn, the message must be interpreted before it can be evaluated. Finally, it must be effectively evaluated prior to generating a proper response. When diagnosing a listening breakdown, one should look for the lowest level in the hierarchy where the breakdown could have originated and take proper action to remedy the problem. Exhibit 4.7[13] describes 10 specific keys to effective listening that can be used in conjunction with the SIER model to pinpoint and improve listening problems.

EXHIBIT 4.7 Ten Keys to Effective Listening

The Key Practice	The Weak Listener	The Strong Listener
1. Find areas of interest	Tunes out dry subjects	Actively looks for opportunities of common interest
2. Judge content, not delivery	Tunes out if the delivery is poor	Skips over delivery errors and focuses on content
3. Hold your fire until full consideration	Evaluates and enters argument prior to completion of message	Does not judge or evaluate until message is complete
4. Listen for ideas	Listens for facts	Listens for central themes
5. Be flexible	Takes intensive and detailed notes	Takes fewer notes and limits theme to central theme and key ideas presented
6. Work at listening	Shows no energy output Attention is faked	Works hard at attending the message and exhibits active body state
7. Resist distractions	Distracted easily	Resists distractions and knows how to concentrate
8. Exercise your mind	Resists difficult expository material in favor of light recreational materials	Uses complex and heavy material as exercise for the mind
9. Keep an open mind	Reacts to emotional words	Interprets color words but does not get hung up on them
10. Capitalize on fact that thought is faster than speech	Tends to daydream with slow speakers	Challenges, anticipates, mentally summarizes, weighs evidence, and listens between the lines

VERBAL COMMUNICATION: GIVING INFORMATION

Verbal information refers to statements of fact, opinion, and attitude that are encoded in the form of words, pictures, and numbers in such a way that they convey meaning to a receiver. However, many words and symbols mean different things to different people. Different industries, different cultures, and different types of training or work experience can result in the same word or phrase having multiple interpretations. For instance, to a design or production engineer, the word *quality* might mean "manufactured within design tolerance." However, to a customer it might be translated as "meeting or exceeding expectations." To maximize clarity and minimize misunderstandings, understand and use the vocabulary and terminology that corresponds with the perspective of the customer.

Understanding the Superiority of Pictures Over Words

Studies in cognitive psychology have found that pictures tend to be more memorable than their verbal counterparts.[14] The fact that pictures enhance understanding and are more easily recalled than abstract words and symbols has several implications for effective selling.

- The verbal message should be constructed in a manner that generates a mental picture in the receiver's mind. For example, the phrase "Tropicana juices are bursting with flavor" is more visual than the more abstract version "Tropicana juices have more flavor." This can also be accomplished by providing a short and illustrative analogy or illustrative story to emphasize a key point and bring it alive in the buyer's mind.

- Rather than abstract words that convey only a broad general understanding, use words and phrases that convey concrete and detailed meaning. Concrete expressions provide the receiver with greater information and are less likely to be misunderstood than their abstract counterparts. For example, "This web transfer system will increase weekly production by 2,100 units" provides more detail than "This web transfer system will increase production by 10 percent." Similarly, "This conveyor is faster than your existing system" does not deliver the same impact as "This conveyor system will move your product from production to shipping at 50 feet per second as compared with your current system's 20 feet per second."

- Integrate relevant visual sales aids into verbal communication. Sales support materials that explain and reinforce the verbal message will aid the receiver's understanding and enhance recall of the message. As an additional benefit, sales aids such as samples, brochures, graphs, and comparative charts can be left with the buyer to continue selling until the salesperson's next call on the buyer.

Impact of Grammar and Logical Sequencing

Grammar and logical sequencing are also important in the process of giving information to others. The use of proper grammar is a given in business and social communication. In its absence, the receiver of the message tends to exhibit three closely related behaviors. First, the meaning and credibility of the message are significantly downgraded. Second, the receiver begins to focus on the sender rather than the message, which materially reduces the probability of effective communication. Last, the receiver dismisses the sender and the sender's organization as being unqualified to perform the role of an effective supplier and partner. The importance of proper grammar should not be overlooked.

Similarly, whether one is engaged in simply explaining details or making a formal proposal, logical sequencing of the material is critical. The facts and details must be organized and connected in a logical order. This is essential to clarity and assists the receiver in following the facts. A discussion or presentation that jumps around risks being inefficient and ineffective. At best, the receiver will have to ask a high number of clarification questions. At worst, the receiver will dismiss the salesperson as incompetent and close off the sales negotiation. Advance planning and preparation can improve organization. Outline what needs to be covered and organize it into a logical flow. The outline becomes the agenda to be covered and can serve as an aid for staying on track.

NONVERBAL COMMUNICATION

Nonverbal behaviors have been recognized as an important dimension of communication since medieval times. As early as 1605, Francis Bacon focused on the messages conveyed by *manual language*. Verbal communication deals with the semantic meaning of the message itself while the nonverbal dimension consists of the more abstract message conveyed by how the message is delivered. **Nonverbal communication** is the conscious and unconscious reactions, movements, and utterances that people use in addition to the words and symbols associated with language. This dimension of communication includes eyes and facial expressions; placement and movements of hands, arms, head, and legs as well as body orientation; the amount of space maintained between individuals; and variations in voice characteristics. Collectively, the various forms of nonverbal communication carry subtle as well as explicit meanings and feelings along with the language message and are frequently more informative than the verbal content of a message.[15]

Research indicates that highly successful salespeople are capable of picking out and comprehending a higher number of behavioral cues from buyers than less successful salespeople are able to sense and interpret. In addition, evidence shows that 50 percent or more of the meaning conveyed within the communication process stems from nonverbal behavior.[16] As the nonverbal components of a message carry as much or more meaning than the language portions, it is critical for salespeople to effectively sense, accurately interpret, and fully evaluate the nonverbal elements of a message in addition to the verbal components. In addition to sensing verbal messages, learn to sense between the words for the thoughts and feelings not being conveyed verbally.

Facial Expressions

Possibly reflecting its central point of focus in interpersonal communication, the various elements of the face play a key role in giving off nonverbal messages. Frowning, pursed lips, and squinted eyes are common in moments of uncertainty, disagreement, and even outright skepticism. Suspicion and anger are typically accompanied by tightness along the jaw line. Smiles are indicative of agreement and interest while biting of one's lip can signal uncertainty. Raised eyebrows can signify surprise and are often found in moments of consideration and evaluation.

Eye Movements

In North America and western Europe, avoidance of eye contact results in a negative message and is often associated with deceit and dishonesty. However, increased eye contact by the sender infers honesty and self-confidence. Increased eye contact by the receiver of the message signals increasing levels of interest and concentration. However, when eye contact becomes a stare and continues unbroken by glances away or blinking, it is typically interpreted as a threat or inference of power. A blank stare or eye contact directed away from the conversation can show disinterest and boredom. Repeated glances made toward one's watch or possibly an exit door often indicate that the conversation is about to end.

Placement and Movements of Hands, Arms, Head, and Legs

Smooth and gradual movements denote calm and confidence, whereas jerky and hurried movements are associated with nervousness and stress. Uncrossed arms and legs signal openness, confidence, and cooperation. However, crossed arms and legs psychologically close out the other party and express disagreement and defensiveness. Increased movement of the head and limbs hints at increasing tension, as does the tight clasping of hands or fists. The placement of a hand on the chin or a tilted head suggests increased levels of evaluation, whereas nodding of the head expresses agreement. Growing impatience is associated with drumming of the fingers or patting of a foot. The fingering of one's hair and rubbing the back of the neck signifies increasing nervousness and apprehension.

Body Posture and Orientation

Fidgeting and shifting from side to side is generally considered to be a negative message associated with nervousness and apprehension. Leaning forward or sitting forward on the edge of a chair is a general sign of increasing interest and a positive disposition in regard to what is being discussed. Similarly, leaning away can indicate disinterest, boredom, or even distrust. Leaning back with both hands placed behind one's head signifies a perceived sense of smugness and superiority. A rigid erect posture can convey inflexibility or even defensiveness whereas sloppy posture suggests disinterest in the topic. Similar to sitting backward in a chair, sitting on the edge of the table or the arm of a chair is an expression of power and superiority.

Proxemics

Proxemics refers to the personal distance that individuals prefer to keep between themselves and other individuals and is an important element of nonverbal communication. The distance that one places between oneself and others implies a meaningful message and affects the outcome of the selling process. If a salesperson pushes too close to a prospect who requires more distance, the prospect may perceive the salesperson to be manipulative, intimidating, and possibly threatening. However, salespeople who put too much distance between themselves and the customer risk being perceived as rigidly formal, aloof, or even apprehensive.

Proxemics differs across cultures and regions of the world. For example, in North Africa and Latin America business is conducted at a much closer distance than in North America. As depicted in Figure 4.4, North Americans generally recognize four distinct proxemic zones. The *intimate zone* is reserved for intimate relationships with immediate family and loved ones. The *personal zone* is for personal relationships with close friends and associates. The *social zone* is for business client relationships and is the zone

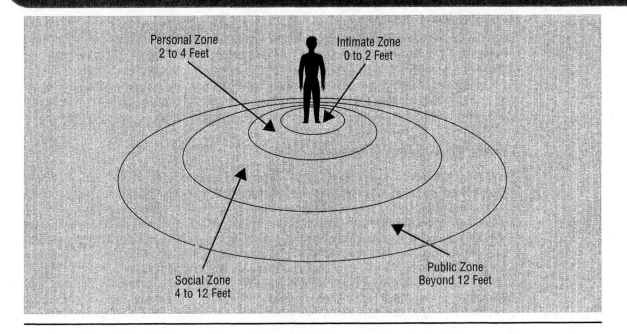

Personal Space and Interpersonal Communication   Figure 4.4

Individuals utilize four preferred spatial zones for interaction in different social and business situations.

in which most business is conducted. The *public zone* is for the general public and group settings such as classrooms and presentations.

It is critical that salespeople understand proxemics and monitor the progression of their buyer–seller relationships so as to properly position themselves with different customers. Typically, salespeople begin working with a prospect at the far end of the *social zone*. As the salesperson–buyer relationship develops, the salesperson is in a position to move closer without violating the customer's space and causing him or her to become defensive.

Variations in Voice Characteristics

Nonverbal voice characteristics such as speaking rates, pause duration, pitch or frequency, and intensity have been linked to communication effectiveness and selling performance. These voice characteristics convey direct as well as subtle and implied meanings and feelings that can complement or accent the corresponding verbal message.[17]

Speaking Rates and Pause Duration

Within normal speaking rates, faster speakers are generally evaluated more favorably than slower speakers. Contrary to the often-cited fast-talking salesperson being perceived as high pressure, faster rates of speech and shorter pause duration are actually associated with higher levels of intelligence, credibility, and knowledge.[18] Slower speakers are perceived as being less competent as well as less benevolent. However, speech rates that are jerky and beyond normal rates of speech can present problems in sensing and interpreting the complete message. Varying the rate of speech has also been found to be conducive to maintaining interest.

Pitch or Frequency

Voice pitch carries a great deal of information to the receiver. Varying pitch and frequency during the course of a message is used to encourage attentiveness of the listener and to accent certain forms of statements. A rising pitch during the message is associated with questions and can often be perceived as reflecting uncertainty. Just the opposite, a falling pitch is associated with declarative statements and completion of the message. Overall, high-pitched voices are judged as less truthful, less emphatic, less potent, and more nervous. Lower-pitched voices have been found to be more persuasive and truthful and have a positive impact on selling performance.

Intensity and Loudness

Dominance, superiority, intensity, and aggression are commonly associated with loud voices, whereas soft voices characterize submission and uncertainty. However, it is the variability of intensity that has been found to be most effective in communication. Varying levels of loudness allow the sender to adapt to different situations and environments. Variation also increases the receiver's attention and can provide additional information inputs by accenting key points of a message.

Using Nonverbal Clusters

Nonverbal clusters are groups of related expressions, gestures, and movements. Similar to a one-word expression, a single isolated gesture or movement should not be taken as a reliable indication of the true intent or meaning of a message. Sensing and interpreting groups or clusters of nonverbal cues provide a more reliable indicator of the message and intent. When the individual behaviors and gestures begin to fit together, they form a common and unified message that should be considered by the salesperson. Common nonverbal clusters applicable to selling communication are described in Exhibit 4.8.[19]

Just as nonverbal messages can be interpreted by salespeople to better interpret and understand communication with prospects and buyers, those same prospects and buyers can also sense and interpret the nonverbal messages being sent by the salesperson. Consequently, it is important that salespersons monitor the nonverbal cues they are sending to ensure consistency with and reinforcement of the intended message.

| | Common Nonverbal Clusters | | EXHIBIT 4.8 | |

Cluster Name	Cluster Meaning	Body Posture and Orientation	Movement of Hands, Arms, and Legs	Eyes and Facial Expressions
Openness	Openness, flexibility, and sincerity	• Moving closer • Leaning forward	• Open hands • Removing coat • Unbutton collar • Uncrossed arms and legs	• Slight smile • Good eye contact
Defensiveness	Defensiveness, skepticism, and apprehension	• Rigid body	• Crossed arms and legs • Clenched fists	• Minimal eye contact • Glancing sideways • Pursed lips
Evaluation	Evaluation and consideration of message	• Leaning forward	• Hand on cheek • Stroking chin • Chin in palm of hand	• Tilted head • Dropping glasses to tip of nose
Deception	Dishonesty and secretiveness	• Patterns of rocking	• Fidgeting with objects • Increased leg movements	• Increased eye movement • Frequent gazes elsewhere • Forced smile
Readiness	Dedication or commitment	• Sitting forward	• Hands on hips • Legs uncrossed • Feet flat on floor	• Increased eye contact
Boredom	Lack of interest and impatience	• Head in palm of hands • Slouching	• Drumming fingers • Swinging a foot • Brushing and picking at items • Tapping feet	• Poor eye contact • Glancing at watch • Blank stares

SUMMARY

1. **Explain the importance of collaborative, two-way communication in personal selling.** The two-way exchange process inherent in collaborative communication facilitates accurate and mutual understanding of the objectives, problems, needs, and capabilities of each of the parties. As a result of this heightened level of understanding, solutions and responses can be generated that provide mutual benefits to all participants. Without mutual sharing, this would not be possible, and one party or the other would benefit at the expense of the other. Although this might be good for the "winning" party, the disadvantaged party would be less inclined to continue doing business and would seek out other business partners.

2. **Explain the primary types of questions and how they are applied in selling.**
   Questions can be typed into two basic categories according to (1) the amount of information and level of specificity desired and (2) the strategic purpose of the question.
   * **Typed by the Amount of Information and Level of Specificity Desired.**
     This category includes open-end questions, closed-end questions, and dichotomous questions. *Open-end questions* are designed to let the customer respond freely and deliver richer and more expansive information than more directed forms of questioning. They are typically used to probe for descriptive information that allows the salesperson to better understand the specific needs and expectations of the customer. *Closed-end questions* are designed to limit the customer's response to one or two words. This type of question is typically used to confirm or clarify information gleaned from previous responses to open-end questions. *Dichotomous questions* are directive forms of questioning in which the buyer is requested to make a choice between two or more alternatives. These questions are used to discover buyer preferences and move the selling process forward.

   * **Types of Questions Classified by Strategic Purpose.** This category of questions includes questions designed for (1) probing, (2) evaluative, (3) tactical, and (4) reactive purposes. *Probing questions* are designed to penetrate beneath surface information to provide more useful details. *Evaluative questions* use an open-end format to uncover how the buyer feels about things (e.g., attitudes, opinions, and preferences held by the prospect). *Tactical questions* are used to shift the topic of discussion when a line of questioning proves to be of little interest or value. *Reactive questions* respond to previous information provided by the other party and ask for additional details about the previous information. Salespeople *use reactive questions to elicit additional details regarding facts, attitudes, or feelings the customer has mentioned.*

3. **Illustrate the diverse roles and uses of strategic questioning in personal selling.**
   The most obvious use of questioning is to elicit detailed information about the buyer's current situation, needs, and expectations. Properly applied, questioning facilitates both the buyer's and seller's understanding of a problem and proposed solutions. Questioning can also test the buyer's interest in a problem or solution and increase their cognitive involvement and participation in the selling process. Questions can also be used to subtly and strategically redirect, regain, or hold the buyer's attention should it begin to wander during the conversation. Similarly, questions can provide a convenient and subtle transition to a different topic of discussion and provide a logical guide promoting sequential thought and decision making while advancing the selling process in moving forward.

4. **Identify and describe the five steps of the ADAPT questioning sequence.**
   Corresponding to the ADAPT acronym, the five steps making up this sequence of effective questioning are assessment questions, discovery questions, activation questions, projection questions, and transition questions.
   * *Assessment Questions.* These are broad and general questions designed to be nonthreatening and to spark conversation. Rather than asking for feelings or conclusions, assessment questions elicit factual information about the customer's current situation that can provide a basis for further exploration and probing. These questions should address the buyer's company and operation, goals and objectives, market trends and customers, current suppliers, and even the buyer as an individual.

   * *Discovery Questions.* Following up responses from assessment questions, discovery questions drill down and probe for further details needed to further clarify and understand the buyer's problems. In addition to facts, the buyer's interpretations, perceptions, feelings, and opinions are sought in regard to their needs, wants, dissatisfactions, and expectations relevant to product, delivery requirements, budget and financing issues, and desired service levels. The goal is to discover needs and dissatisfactions that the salesperson's sales offering can resolve.

- *Activation Questions.* The implied or suggested needs that might be gained from discovery questions are not usually sufficient to gain the sale. Often a buyer will believe that a particular problem does not cause any significant negative consequences, hence the motivation to solve the problem will carry a low priority. Activation questions help the customer realistically evaluate the full impact of the implied need. The objective is to "activate" the customer's interest in solving discovered problems by helping him or her to gain insight into the true ramifications of the problem and realize that what may initially seem to be of little consequence may, in fact, carry significant consequence to the buyer's organization.

- *Projection Questions.* A natural extension of the activation questions, projection questions encourage and facilitate the buyer in "projecting" what it would be like if the problems or needs did not exist. Projection questions switch the focus from problems to the benefits to be derived from solving the problems—the payoff for taking action and investing in a solution. Focusing on the benefit payoff allows the buyer to establish his or her perceived value of implementing a solution. In this manner, the benefit payoff is perceived as what the solution is worth—what the buyer would be willing to pay. Projection questions assist the buyer in selling himself or herself by establishing the worth of the solution. More important, the customer, rather than the salesperson, establishes the value of solving the problem.

- *Transition Questions.* Transition questions smooth the transition from needs discovery and activation into the presentation and demonstration of the proposed solution's features, advantages, and benefits. Typically, closed end and evaluative in format, these questions confirm the buyer's desire to seek a solution and give his or her consent to the salesperson to move forward with the selling process.

5. **Discuss the four sequential steps for effective active listening.** Active listening consists of the sequential communication behaviors of (1) sensing, (2) interpreting, (3) evaluating, and (4) responding.
   - *Sensing.* The first activity in active listening is to sense and receive the verbal and nonverbal components of the message. Sensing is much more than just hearing the message and requires practice and concentration. Poor or weak sensing can create significant problems in the latter stages of interpreting and evaluating.

   - *Interpreting.* After sensing and receiving the message, it must be correctly interpreted in terms of what the sender actually meant. In addition to the meaning of the words and symbols, the experiences, knowledge, and attitudes of the sender should be considered to fully understand what was meant.

   - *Evaluating.* Effective communication requires the receiver to decide whether or not he or she agrees with the sender's message. This requires evaluating the results from the interpretation stage to sort fact from opinion and emotion.

   - *Responding.* Collaborative communication requires listeners to provide feedback to the other party. Responses can take the form of restating and paraphrasing the sender's message, answering questions, or asking questions to gain additional details and clarification.

6. **Discuss the superiority of pictures over words for explaining concepts and enhancing comprehension.** Evidence is provided by studies in cognitive psychology supporting pictures as being more memorable than words. Using descriptive words to "draw" mental pictures in the buyer's mind can enhance understanding and are more easily recalled than abstract words and symbols. This carries several implications for successful selling:
   - Understanding and recall can be aided by providing a short and illustrative analogy or illustrative story to emphasize a key point and bring it alive in the buyer's mind.

   - Rather than abstract words that convey only a broad general understanding, utilize words and phrases that convey concrete and detailed meaning. Concrete expressions provide the receiver with greater information and are less likely to be misunderstood than their abstract counterparts.

• Integrate relevant visual sales aids into verbal communication. Sales support materials that explain and reinforce the verbal message will aid the buyer's understanding and enhance recall of the message.

7. **Describe the different forms of nonverbal communication.** Nonverbal behaviors are made up from the various movements and utterances that people use in addition to the words and symbols associated with language. These can be conscious or unconscious and include eye movement and facial expressions; placement and movements of hands, arms, head, and legs as well as body orientation; the amount of space maintained between individuals; and variations in voice characteristics. Sensing and interpreting groups or clusters of nonverbal cues can provide a reliable indicator of the underlying message and intent. When the individual behaviors and gestures begin to fit together, they form a common and unified message that should be considered by the salesperson. Evidence shows that 50 percent or more of the meaning conveyed in the process of interpersonal communication is carried by nonverbal behaviors. Consequently, it is critical that salespeople learn to effectively sense, accurately interpret, and fully evaluate the nonverbal elements of a message.

UNDERSTANDING PROFESSIONAL SELLING TERMS

relational sales communication	discovery questions
open-end questions	activation questions
closed-end questions	projection questions
dichotomous questions	transition questions
probing questions	social listening
evaluative questions	serious listening
tactical questions	active listening
reactive questions	SIER
SPIN	sensing
situation questions	interpreting
problem questions	evaluating
implication questions	responding
need-payoff questions	nonverbal communication
ADAPT	proxemics
assessment questions	nonverbal clusters

DEVELOPING PROFESSIONAL SELLING KNOWLEDGE

1. Explain why talking *with* buyers rather than talking *at* buyers is critical to success in selling.

2. Discuss how salespeople use effective questioning to maintain subtle control over the buyer–seller communication dialogue.

3. Distinguish between open-end and closed-end questions and describe how each of these question formats might best be used in the personal selling process.

4. Explain the difference in the uses of probing, evaluative, tactical, and reactive questions in personal selling.

5. Discuss how effective questioning skills help accomplish the seven closely related sales objectives identified in this module.

6. Identify and explain each of the individual steps involved in the SPIN sequence of questioning. Develop two example questions for each step.

7. Identify and explain each of the individual steps involved in the ADAPT sequence of questioning. Develop two example questions for each step.

8. Discuss how the four sequential elements of sensing, interpreting, evaluating, and responding (SIER) combine to create what is referred to as active listening.

9. Explain what is meant by nonverbal clusters and why they are important to salespeople.

10. What is meant by proxemics? Why is it important for salespeople to understand the concept of proxemics?

BUILDING PROFESSIONAL SELLING SKILLS

1. Listening skill development is an ongoing process. Good listening is a key to success in any business environment. Discovering your attitude about listening and assessing your listening behaviors are important for self-development and improvement. Complete the following exercise and score your listening habits. If the statement describes your listening habits, check "Yes," if not, check "No." After completing the assessment, score your listening habits according to the scale following the checklist.[20]

	YES	NO
a. I am interested in many subjects and do not knowingly tune out dry-sounding information.	❏	❏
b. I listen carefully for a speaker's main ideas and supporting points.	❏	❏
c. I take notes during meetings to record key points.	❏	❏
d. I am not easily distracted.	❏	❏
e. I keep my emotions under control.	❏	❏
f. I concentrate carefully and do not fake attention.	❏	❏
g. I wait for the speaker to finish before finally evaluating the message.	❏	❏
h. I respond appropriately with a smile, a nod, or a word of acknowledgment as a speaker is talking.	❏	❏
i. I am aware of mannerisms that may distract a speaker and keep mine under control.	❏	❏
j. I understand my biases and control them when I am listening.	❏	❏
k. I refrain from constantly interrupting.	❏	❏
l. I value eye contact and maintain it most of the time.	❏	❏
m. I often restate or paraphrase what the speaker said to make sure I have the correct meaning.	❏	❏
n. I listen for the speaker's emotional meaning as well as subject matter content.	❏	❏
o. I ask questions for clarification.	❏	❏
p. I do not finish other people's sentences unless asked to do so.	❏	❏
q. When listening on the phone, one hand is kept free to take notes.	❏	❏
r. I attempt to set aside my ego and focus on the speaker rather than myself.	❏	❏
s. I am careful to judge the message rather than the speaker.	❏	❏
t. I am a patient listener most of the time.	❏	❏

The following scale will help you interpret your present listening skill level based on your current attitudes and habits.

1–5 "NO" answers	You are an excellent listener. Keep it up!
6–10 "NO" answers	You are a good listener but can improve.
11–15 "NO" answers	Through practice you can become a much more effective listener in your business and personal relationships.
16–20 "NO" answers	Listen up!!

How do your listening skills compare to those of your class peers? What steps might you take to strengthen your listening skills?

2. Developing ADAPT question sequences takes thought and practice. Using the ADAPT questioning process discussed in this module as a guide, develop a scripted series of salesperson questions and possible buyer responses that might be typical in the following selling situation. For your convenience, a sample ADAPT questioning script template is included following the description of the selling scenario.

THE SELLING SCENARIO

This scenario involves a salesperson representing the Direct Sales Department of American Seating Company (ASC) and Rodney Moore, a buyer representing the Seattle Music Arts Association (SMAA). Although there are some 12 major manufacturers of auditorium seating, ASC's market share of 21 percent makes the company a leader in this industry. ASC's selling efforts are organized on a basis of market types: one department sells direct to end-users and a second department sells to distributors who in turn sell to retailers of business furniture. Direct sales to end-users are restricted to minimum orders of $200,000.

As an integral part of a major remodeling project, SMAA wants to replace the seats in the Seattle Metropolitan Auditorium. ASC estimates a potential sale of between $350,000 and $500,000. This range represents differences in both quantity and types of seating desired. According to the Request for Proposals, funding for this project is being provided through a bond issue. From this very basic level of knowledge of the buyer's situation, the salesperson is working through the ADAPT questioning sequence with the buyer to better identify and confirm the actual needs and expectations regarding seating.

Use the following ADAPT script template to develop a series of salesperson questions and anticipated buyer responses that might apply to this selling situation.

Assessment Questions:

Seller: _____
Buyer: _____

Seller: _____
Buyer: _____

Seller: _____
Buyer: _____

Seller: _____
Buyer: _____

Discovery Questions:

Seller: _____
Buyer: _____

Seller: _____
Buyer: _____

Seller: _____
Buyer: _____

Seller: _____
Buyer: _____

Activation Questions:

Seller: _____
Buyer: _____

Seller: _____
Buyer: _____

Seller: _____
Buyer: _____

Seller: _____
Buyer: _____

Projection Questions:

Seller: _____
Buyer: _____

Seller: _____
Buyer: _____

Seller: _____
Buyer: _____

Seller: _____
Buyer: _____

Transition Questions:

Seller: _____
Buyer: _____

Seller: _____
Buyer: _____

Situation: Read the selling scenario in item 2.

Characters: Yourself, salesperson for American Seating Company (ASC); Rodney Moore, director of purchasing for the Seattle Music Arts Association (SMAA)

Scene: *Location*—Rodney Moore's office at the Seattle Music Arts Association (SMAA). *Action*—As an integral part of the remodel of the Seattle Metropolitan Auditorium, SMAA will be replacing all the seating. As a salesperson for ASC, you are making an initial sales call to Rodney Moore for the purpose of identifying and detailing the specific needs and expectations SMAA has for seating in the new auditorium.

ROLE PLAY

Role play this needs discovery sales call and demonstrate how you might utilize SPIN or ADAPT questioning sequences to identify the needs for seating.

Upon completion of the role play, address the following questions:

2a. What additional information does the salesperson need in order to fully understand the seating needs of SMAA? Develop assessment and discovery questions designed to elicit the needed information.

2b. What additional activation and projection questions might be effective for motivating the buyer to take action and advance the sale forward?

3. Used in combination, open- and closed-end questions help salespeople uncover and confirm customer needs, dissatisfactions, and opportunities. Observe a salesperson calling on a new prospect and notice the different types of questions used and the information that is received in exchange.
   • What open-end questions did the salesperson use?
   • What types of information were gathered by using these open-end questions?
   • What closed-end questions did the salesperson use?
   • What types of information were gathered by using these closed-end questions?

ROLE PLAY

4. **Situation:**   MidComm specializes in providing cell phones and wireless services for small businesses with 10 to 100 employees having needs that call for mobile, wireless communication. As an account development specialist for MidComm, you are making an initial sales call to Dan Goebel, the director of your university's maintenance division to assess their current use and needs for wireless mobile communication services. According to the initial information you gained from a short phone conversation with Dan, they are currently using Sprint cellular service for a number of their maintenance supervisors. Having staff members wirelessly linked and able to communicate from anywhere on campus has proven beneficial in terms of efficiency and productivity. In fact the university is considering rolling cell phones out to all building maintenance workers. They have been pleased with the positive aspects of wireless communication, but during your phone conversation Dan made a couple of comments that there might be some problems with the present vendor and concerns about potential employee misuse of the phone services.

Characters: Yourself, salesperson for MidComm; Dan Goebel, director of facilities maintenance for your university

Scene: *Location*—Dan Goebel's office at the university. *Action*—Role play this needs discovery sales call and demonstrate how you might utilize SPIN or ADAPT questioning sequences to identify the needs and concerns of the prospect.

Upon completion of the role play, address the following questions:

4a. What additional information does the salesperson need in order to fully understand the communication needs and concerns? Develop assessment and discovery questions designed to elicit the needed information.

4b. What additional activation and projection questions might be effective for motivating the prospect to take action and advance the sale forward?

5. Strong and effective interpersonal communication skills play a critical role in trust-based, consultative selling. The Northwest Regional Educational Laboratory (NWREL) has developed two different assessment systems for use in evaluating the effectiveness of interpersonal communication: (1) the E.A.R. Assessment System and (2) SCANS Interpersonal Communication Competencies. Using these instruments, individuals can work to further enhance their communication with other individuals and groups. Both of these instruments are explained and compared on the NWREL Web site.

Go to the Web site **http://www.nwrel.org/assessment/.** Click on "Oral Communication" in the upper left portion of the Web page. Click on "EAR related to SCANS Comparison Chart."

Read and study the comparison chart found on this last Web page. The EAR Assessment System can be found on the vertical axis (left margin) and the SCANS Interpersonal Communication Competencies can be found on the horizontal axis (at the top of the chart). The cells making up the body of the chart describe the activities and competencies that have been found to be positively associated with effective interpersonal communication.

Upon completion of the Web activity, address the following questions:

5a. Compare the activities and competencies described in this effective interpersonal communication chart with the activities and behaviors you have learned as comprising trust-based, consultative personal selling. How are they similar? How are they different? Why?

5b. Identify five competencies detailed in the various cells making up the chart that you feel are most applicable to trust-based, consultative selling. As part of your response, explain why you selected each of these five items.

MAKING PROFESSIONAL SELLING DECISIONS

Case 4.1: Pre-Select, Inc.

Background

You are a salesperson for Pre-Select, Inc. (PSI), the Chicago-based industry leader in preinterview assessment and testing for the insurance industry. Focusing primarily on sales-related recruiting and selection, PSI's Interactive Employee Assessment System (IEAS) has been successful in lowering overall payroll costs by reducing sales agent turnover rates. Because of its highly recognized rate of success, PSI's customers include 13 of the top 20 insurance companies in the United States.

Although the system is continuously revised and updated, the basic program has been operating for six years. Using a personal computer in the field—usually at the branch office or general agency location—the IEAS consists of three computer-based components:

1. Preinterview attitude and aptitude testing
2. Interactive simulations of critical work situations for use as part of the interview process
3. Periodic posthiring assessment for input into future training needs

Current Situation

Ron Lovell, national agency director for Secure Future Insurance Company (SFIC), is interested in improving his company's recruiting and selection process for sales agents. SFIC is a national company with 150 agents across the United States. Although not ranked among the top 20 insurers, SFIC is a large and successful firm listed in the *Fortune 1000*. You have met with Ron on four previous occasions exploring problems, opportunities, and needs. During these meetings, you discovered that SFIC's turnover rate among its sales agents approaches 42 percent. Compared with industry averages, that is not all that bad, but it does require hiring 375 new salespeople every year. SFIC's own estimate of hiring, training, and licensing costs is $7,500 per new salesperson hired, for a total annual cost exceeding $2.8 million. Well-documented field experience indicates that, using PSI's computer-based system, turnover would drop to an average turnover rate ranging from 15 to 20 percent, which offers considerable savings to SFIC.

You have been working up the figures for implementing the system at SFIC's headquarters and in each of the company's 150 general agency offices. One-time hardware costs total $610,000. Although minimal training is required, installation and training would be priced out at $75,000 plus another $5,500 for chargeable travel expenses. Software licensing fees would total $135,000 per year. Sales tax on the hardware and software would be computed at 6.5 percent. Finally, software maintenance fees run 15 percent of the annual licensing cost. According to the technical support department, this installation could be completed, with the full system operating and all staff training completed, in just four months from the date of the order.

The Learning Assignment

Review your text materials discussing "Verbal Communication: Giving Information." This section details three fundamentals for maximizing information exchange: (1) generating mental pictures in your buyer's mind, (2) using phrases that convey concrete and detailed meaning, and (3) integrating effective visual aids to enhance your buyer's understanding. Demonstrate your understanding of these three concepts by responding to the following discussion items:

Questions

1. Think through and create a seller–buyer script that explains the advantageous capabilities and beneficial outcomes of your assessment system.
2. Develop a set of visual aids that could be used to illustrate the capabilities and beneficial outcomes identified.

ROLE PLAY

Situation: Read Case 4.1.

Characters: Yourself, salesperson for Pre-Select, Inc.; Ron Lovell, national agency director for Secure Future Insurance Co.

Scene: *Location*—Ron Lovell's office at Secure Future Insurance Co. *Action*—This is your fifth sales call to Secure Future. On the previous sales calls, you have worked with Lovell to discover and detail a great deal of information about the prospect's problems and needs to do a better job in selecting and hiring sales agents. Lovell has requested this meeting so that you might illustrate how your Interactive Employee Assessment System (IEAS) program can help them address and resolve these problems.

Role play this meeting with Ron Lovell and demonstrate how you might explain the capabilities of and beneficial outcomes offered by IEAS as they are described in Case 4.1.

Upon completion of the role play, address the following questions:

1. What might the salesperson do to generate vivid mental pictures of the advantages offered by the IEAS program?
2. What other ways might the salesperson maximize the detailed meaning and understanding through the use of concrete expressions?
3. What other visual sales aids could be used to further support and illustrate the capabilities and benefits of this system?

Case 4.2: STAGA Financial Services

Background

Bart Waits, account manager for Data Intelligence, LLC, arrived just a few minutes early for his 9:00 A.M. meeting with Kerri Williams, director of purchasing for STAGA Financial Services. This was his first in-person call at STAGA, and he had flown in explicitly for this meeting to present his proposal for a data-mining software package that would be used by the client's IT department. On arrival, Bart did the obligatory check-in with the receptionist in the main lobby. After contacting the purchasing office, the receptionist informed him that they would be right down to escort him to Williams' office. About 12 minutes later, Williams' executive assistant entered the lobby and advised Bart that she would escort him to the office where they would be meeting. The executive assistant was friendly and open and provided Bart with a fresh cup of coffee just before taking him into Williams' office.

Current Situation

On entering the large and well-furnished office, Bart noticed that the layout was a bit different than he had expected. Kerri was sitting behind a large walnut executive desk that was located at an angle in one corner and faced toward the opposite wall of windows. No guest chairs were located adjacent to the desk. Rather, the chairs were set some 10–12 feet from the desk, adjacent to a small table, and facing the desk. In another area of the room, there was a worktable with several chairs pulled up to it.

Kerri was on the phone as he entered and signaled for him to go ahead and be seated. It was obvious that the conversation was drawing to a close, and she made eye contact and smiled at him once or twice to acknowledge his presence. When the phone call was over, she popped up from the desk and walked over to meet him. While shaking hands, each of them introduced themselves, and she mentioned that he should address her as Kerri. She apologized for being on the phone and inquired about his flight. After some small talk, Bart transitioned into his presentation by first outlining the needs as specified in STAGA's original Request for

Proposals (RFP). As Bart provided many additional details beyond those in the RFP, Kerri smiled and looked him in the eye as she shifted her chair closer to the table and commented that it was apparent that he had done his homework on the company.

Several times during his presentation, she placed her hand on her cheek and shifted forward to ask numerous questions. Although sparingly, she also took notes at several points of his presentation. Bart's appointment was for one and one-half hours, and he figured that he would need every minute of it. However, about 50 minutes into the meeting he noticed that Kerri would glance at her watch occasionally. After making a major point and demonstrating several significant benefits to STAGA, he noticed that Kerri uncrossed her legs and leaned forward with her glasses on the tip of her nose as she began asking him a series of questions about his software package.

Questions

1. Identify the different nonverbal cues that the buyer was providing to Bart.
2. If you were in Bart's place, how would you have interpreted and responded to these different nonverbal cues?

ROLE PLAY

Situation:	Read Case 4.2.
Characters:	Bart Waits, account manager for Data Intelligence, LLC; Kerri Williams, director of purchasing for STAGA Financial Services
Scene:	*Location*—Kerri Williams' office at STAGA Financial Services. *Action*—Bart has arrived for his first meeting with Williams. As he is escorted to Williams' office to begin his sales call, he begins to pick up a variety of verbal and nonverbal cues that might prove very useful as he advances through the agenda of this initial sales call.

Role play this meeting between Bart and Kerri as described in Case 4.2.

Upon completion of the role play, address the following questions:

1. Based on the patterns of verbal and nonverbal clusters, what interpretations might the salesperson make as to the meaning of these various communication signals?
2. How should Bart respond to these nonverbal cues in order to further advance his sales call objectives?

Initiating Customer Relationships

The two modules in Part Two concentrate on initiating relationship with customers. Module 5 discusses prospecting, the process of locating and screening potential customers. Strategic prospecting and various prospecting methods are presented as means of overcoming unique challenges in this early stage of the sales process. The preapproach is also discussed in Module 5. In the preapproach, salespeople gather and study information to be used in subsequent sales calls.

In Module 6, we offer insights into how to plan sales presentations and approach the customer. A comprehensive sales presentation checklist provides a framework for sales presentation planning. The checklist reminds salespeople to define the buying situation, buyer needs and motives, the competitive situation, presentation objectives, and additional information needed to plan a successful presentation. Module 6 also gives valuable advice on how to approach the customer, which involves securing an appointment and getting the sales presentation off to a good start.

PROSPECTING AND PREAPPROACH

USING QUESTIONS TO QUALIFY POTENTIAL CUSTOMERS

The wireless phone industry is highly competitive, and salespeople in this industry must continually add new customers to be successful. Mike Ciccheto, a major account executive with Nextel Communications in Indianapolis, sells wireless services to companies with 250 to 1,000 employees. He has learned the importance of asking the right questions to determine if prospective customers are good prospects, and if so, for which of his services.

Ciccheto's prospects fall into one of two categories: those who embrace technology and those who are reluctant to use it. The first group is typically looking for solutions to problems, while the second group is resistant to learning how Nextel's technology works. To categorize prospects into one of these two groups, Ciccheto asks an initial question: "How much do you use the Internet in your business now?" He asks that prospects answer on a scale of 1 to 10, with 1 representing "not at all," and 10 meaning "all digitized." If a prospect answers 1 through 4, Ciccheto classifies them as a prospect for cell phone service with walkie-talkie capability, which can enhance communications both in and out of the office. If the response falls between 7 and 10, Ciccheto knows that the account is more likely interested in how Nextel's wireless solutions can work with credit card scanners.

For Mike Ciccheto, a simple questioning method is a powerful prospecting tool. Not only is it an efficient sales tool, but it also focuses on customer needs and helps build lasting relationships.

Source: "Bridge the Difference," by Steve Atlas, from *Selling Power*, (April 2004), 34–38.

As illustrated in the opening vignette, successful salespeople such as Nextel's Mike Ciccheto realize the importance of effective prospecting and gathering pre-call information. Unless salespeople cultivate future business, they typically will not be able to sustain the sales volume growth rates required in most sales jobs. There are many different methods of prospecting and salespeople should use those methods that work for him or her. In this module we will examine strategic prospecting and take a closer look at prospecting reluctance. First, the critical role of prospecting is examined. This is followed with a discussion of prospecting methods and techniques that have been documented and proven successful in identifying prospective customers. Finally, the importance of the precall collection, analysis, and utilization of information relevant to the upcoming sales call and prospect—the preapproach—is discussed.

THE CHALLENGES OF PROSPECTING

The glamour in sales is bringing in the big order. It is much more exciting for a salesperson to make an immediate sale than to spend countless hours prospecting for new customers. Unfortunately, many salespeople are focused on the immediate sale instead of doing the tedious task of gathering information about their prospects.

Objectives

After completing this module, you should be able to

1 Explain strategic prospecting.

2 Discuss why prospecting can be a challenging task for a salesperson.

3 Explain where salespeople find prospects.

4 Understand the importance of gathering and studying precall information.

Salespeople will often say that they find it difficult to allocate enough time to prospecting. In most cases, the more accurate statement would be that salespeople find it easier to spend time with existing customers, as they are more comfortable calling on familiar faces than dealing with strangers. Truthfully, the biggest reason most salespeople find prospecting challenging is their fear of rejection. Today's buyers are busy, and many are reluctant to see salespeople with whom they are not currently doing business. Experienced salespeople know that preplanning their sales calls greatly increases their chances of getting a commitment from the buyer. However, cold calls rarely result in a sale. This can be discouraging. Conventional wisdom indicates that less than 5 percent of unplanned cold calls result in a sale, whereas roughly 25–30 percent of preplanned calls produce a sale. Here are some of the reasons buyers will not take the time to see a salesperson:

1. They may have never heard of the salesperson's firm.
2. They may have just bought the salesperson's product category, and there is presently no need.
3. Buyers may have their own deadlines on other issues, and they are not in a receptive mood to see any salespeople.
4. Buyers are constantly getting calls from salespeople and do not have time to see them all.
5. Gatekeepers in any organization screen their bosses' calls and sometimes are curt and even rude.

A novice salesperson who is not used to rejection can find this experience unsettling. Training programs and experienced sales reps must help new hires learn the prospecting process. Time and experience help salespeople learn what techniques work in their product category and territory.

Strategic Prospecting

The first step in the selling process is **prospecting.** Strategic prospecting is actually a series of sequential activities designed to identify, qualify, and prioritize organizations and individuals that have the need for and potential to purchase the salesperson's market offering of products and services. Through this procedure of prospecting, a salesperson determines whether a potential buyer candidate possesses the characteristics to become a profitable account.

As illustrated in Figure 5.1, prospecting begins with the identification of **leads.** Often referred to as a "suspect," a lead is simply a potential candidate that may or may not prove to be a valid prospect. The value of the suspected buyer candidate is determined through a procedure called **qualifying a lead.** In this second phase of the prospecting process, the salesperson searches out, collects, and analyzes information to determine the likelihood of

FIGURE 5.1   Salespeople Must Develop Leads into Qualified Prospects

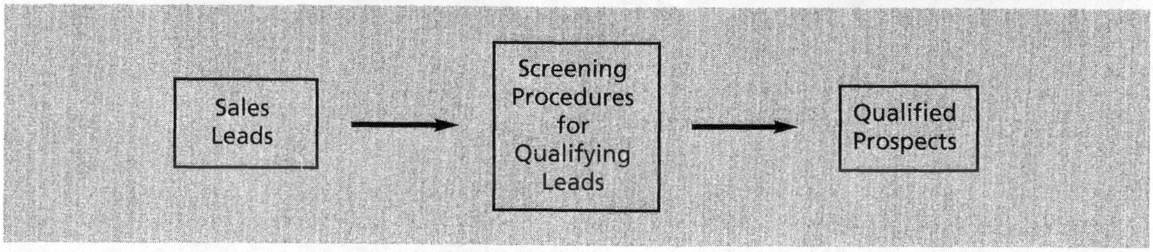

The objective of strategic prospecting lies not only in accumulating sales leads, but also turning a lead into a qualified prospect.

the lead being a good candidate for making a purchase. That is, does the lead have a potential need for your product and the capability for making the purchase decision? As will be discussed in detail later in this module, only those leads passing these initial screening questions are true **prospects**—qualified strong candidates for making a purchase. For example, Wal-Mart and Neiman Marcus are major retail outlets for ready-to-wear clothing and would certainly be found on most manufacturers' lists of leads. However, the low-price needs and requirements of Wal-Mart would not meet the screening criteria for selling organizations such as Tommy Hilfiger and Liz Claiborne, two companies that seek a limited number of upscale retail distribution outlets. Consequently, Wal-Mart would not advance through the lead qualifying process. On the other hand, the needs of Neiman Marcus are aligned with Tommy Hilfiger and Liz Claiborne, and Neiman Marcus would advance as a qualified prospect with high priority.

Prospecting is extremely important to most salespeople. Salespeople who do not regularly prospect are operating under the assumption that the current customer base will be sufficient to generate the desired level of future revenue. This is a shaky assumption in that market conditions may change, causing existing customers to buy less. Another possibility is that customers may go out of business or be bought by another firm, with the buying decisions now being made outside the salesperson's territory. The salesperson may simply lose customers due to competitive activity or dissatisfaction with the product, the salesperson, or the selling firm. Because there is typically a considerable time lag between the commencement of prospecting and the conversion of prospects to customer status, salespeople should spend some time prospecting on a regular basis. Otherwise, lost sales volume cannot be regained quickly enough to satisfy the large majority of sales organizations—those that are growth oriented.

In the midst of the current knowledge and technology explosion, information about prospective customers is readily available. For example, cumbersome printed directories have been replaced by computer disks and online services. These computerized directories can be easily searched for specific keyword criteria, and prospects can be categorized by size, location, and many other variables. The *Harris Directory* data, for instance, can be searched for headquarter locations or whether companies export or not. Some computerized directories can be linked with mapping software so that it is possible to identify the number of prospects in different geographic locations. This is only one example of how salespeople learn about prospects. "Professional Selling in the 21st Century: Getting Appointments over the Phone," describes the importance of using the telephone to prospect and the difficulty in securing appointments. Taking time to prospect

PROFESSIONAL SELLING IN THE 21ST CENTURY

Getting Appointments over the Phone

John Klich, college unit director and agent for Northwestern Mutual Financial Network in Skokie, Illinois, understands the importance of prospecting to gain new business. Here are a few of his thoughts on how he uses the telephone in his prospecting process:

I need to make two appointments per day to be successful and meet my personal selling targets. Many times it takes 25–40 phone calls to make those two good appointments. I understand that the phone is my lifeline. If I don't get a commitment in a matter of seconds, I have lost the prospect. This means that my primary points have to be direct, *compelling, and brief—very brief. I have to be well organized. I don't use a script, but I do have my key points outlined on paper and in front of me when I make my prospecting calls.*

My philosophy is to keep my opening short and sweet. I briefly introduce myself. I mention referrals right away when I can, and I resist the temptation to make a full-blown sales presentation over the phone. I try to sell the appointment. It may sound obvious, but always be polite. One last thought, if someone already has a good relationship with an agent, I thank him or her for their time and let them know that I'm available if anything changes.

FIGURE 5.2   Prospecting Plans Are the Foundation for Effective Prospecting

The *Strategic Prospecting Plan* sets goals, allocates specific times to be used for prospecting, and continuously evaluates results in order to maximize the effectiveness of prospecting time and effort.

---

and having a plan are critical to prospecting success. With all the different prospecting methods available (you will learn about these in this module), it is important that salespeople have a prospecting plan or system.

A **strategic prospecting plan** should fit the individual needs of the salesperson. As illustrated in Figure 5.2, the focal point of a prospecting plan should be the goal stating the number of qualified prospects to be generated. Formalized goals serve as guides to what is to be accomplished and help to keep a salesperson on track. The plan should also allocate an adequate and specific daily or weekly time period for prospecting. Having specific time periods set aside exclusively for prospecting helps to prevent other activities from creeping in and displacing prospecting activities. A good **tracking system** should also be a part of the prospecting plan. A tracking system can be as low-tech as a set of 3- by 5-inch note cards or employ one of the many computerized and online contact management or customer relationship management software applications. An example of a simple, but effective, paper and pencil tracking form can be found in Exhibit 5.1. The tracking system should record comprehensive information about the prospect, trace the prospecting methods used, and chronologically archive outcomes from any contacts with the prospect. A fourth element of the prospecting plan is a system for analyzing and evaluating the results of prospecting activities. Continuous evaluation should be employed to assure the salesperson is meeting prospecting goals and using the most effective prospecting methods. The fifth and final element of a prospecting plan should be a program to review and stay up to date on product knowledge and competitor information to emphasize and underscore that the salesperson's products and services offer the best solutions to customer needs and problems. Self-confidence is critical to success in selling and a base of comprehensive knowledge and understanding is the key to believing in one's self.

As with all phases of the sales process, salespeople must exercise judgment and set priorities in prospecting. There is a limited amount of time for prospecting, and a better understanding of the concepts and practices illustrated in this module can help a salesperson be more productive. An added bonus is that the sales process is more enjoyable for salespeople calling on bona fide prospects who can benefit from the salesperson's offering.

Personal Prospecting Log   **EXHIBIT 5.1**

Personal Prospecting Log

Name   _Tom Jenkins_

Team   _Indianapolis Commercial_   Date   _4/16_

1st Contact	Organization	Contact Person	Source of Lead	Phone	Date of Appointment	Outcome of Call	Follow-up Activity
6/02/05	Cummins Engine	Tyler Huston	Personal contact	765-444-1234	4/11 8:30 AM	Need info on printer	Send in mail
9/01/04	Cosco	Fred Banks	Referral Tom Oats John Deere	219-888-4111	will call with dates/times	Liked our numbers decision next week	Send info on satisfied customers
9/02/04	Ball-Foster	MaryLou Hinkle	Called in on 800#	765-365-4242	4/13 Lunch	Great lunch need proposal	Will work up proposal set date and present
4/19/05	Ontario Systems	Darrell Beaty	Referral	765-223-4117	4/19 4 PM		
4/17/05	Cincinnati Reds	Sharon Bristow	Referral Stacey Jones Indianapolis, Indiana	513-452-REDS	4/17 8 AM		
2/02/05	BANK ONE	Alice Arnold	Direct mail sent back 6/02	317-663-2214	4/16 Lunch	Didn't seem impressed need more work	Need more contact with Alice PACER GAME?
2/03/05	Davis & Davis	Frank Chapman	800 call in	317-211-8811	Bob Evans 4/15 Breakfast 7 AM	Will include their DP department at next call	Schedule DP
3/03/05	ABB	Jerome Parker	Personal contact	317-927-4321	4/14 2 PM	Liked our proposal	Call Monday for answer
3/03/05	Thomson Consumer Electronics	Doug Lyon	Phone	317-212-4111	4/15 3 PM	Had bad experience with us several year ago	This one will take time

Locating Prospects

Many different sources and methods for effective prospecting have been developed for use in different selling situations. The more popular prospecting methods are highlighted in Exhibit 5.2 and will be described shortly. A good selling organization and successful salespeople will have a number of ongoing prospecting methods in place at any given time. The salesperson must continually evaluate prospecting methods to determine which methods are bringing in the best results. New methods must also be evaluated and tested for their effectiveness.

EXHIBIT 5.2   Popular Prospecting Sources and Methods

External Sources	Internal Sources	Personal Contact Sources
• Referral • Introductions • Centers of Influence • Organization • Noncompeting Salespeople • Visible Accounts	• Company Records • Lists and Directories • Advertising Inquiries • Telephone Inquiries • Commercial Lead Lists • Internet & World Wide Web	• Observation • Cold Canvassing • Trade Shows • Bird Dogs (Spotters) • Sales Seminars

---

External Sources

Referrals

A **referral** is a name of a company or person given to the salesperson as a lead by a customer or even a prospect who did not buy at this time. Many training programs teach their salesforce to ask each prospect for the name(s) of other potential prospects. This can be a risky, ineffective tactic if done prematurely. A salesperson who practices relationship selling should wait until a customer has been able to judge a salesperson and his or her ability to meet and exceed the customer's expectations prior to asking for a referral. Logic should tell a salesperson that if a prospect is not willing to buy at this time, the prospect probably will be reluctant to pass on the names of business associates. A good referral program can be started after the salesperson has cultivated strong relationships by keeping promises and providing outstanding service.

Introductions

The **introduction** is a variation of the referral technique. In addition to requesting the names of prospects, the salesperson asks the prospect or customer to prepare a note or letter of introduction that can be sent to the potential customer. The best letter is actually a testimonial prepared by a satisfied customer. This technique can also be done on the phone or in person. The buyer must hold the person doing the referring in high esteem for the technique to be effective.

Centers of Influence

A well-known and influential person that can help the salesperson prospect and gain leads is known as a **center of influence.** A good relationship-building salesperson will first gain this person as a satisfied client and then ask him or her to help locate new prospects. Accountants, bankers, lawyers, business owners, teachers, politicians, and government officials can be good center-of-influence individuals. Salespeople can join civic organizations and social organizations such as country clubs and fraternal organizations to meet key community people.

Organizations

Some salespeople will seek memberships in various civic groups that give them the opportunity to meet individuals who can become prospects for their product or service. These groups generally meet on a regular basis, and this gives the salesperson time to build relationships. A salesperson must set contact goals for each meeting to make this approach beneficial. Salespeople must let the group know what they do and that they are interested in helping others. If a salesperson joins only to get something from the group (e.g., names, leads), other members will soon see that agenda as self-serving, and this technique will not be beneficial.

Noncompeting Salespeople

Salespeople for noncompeting products can be a good source for getting prospects' names. Reciprocity is the key for agreeing to be another set of eyes for a **noncompeting**

salesperson. This approach was demonstrated when a Hershey Chocolate, U.S.A., salesperson went out of his way to tell a Hormel sales representative about a new food mart going into their territory. The Hormel representative was the first of his competitors to meet with the new food mart management team and was given valuable shelf space that his competitors could not get. A few months later, the Hormel sales representative returned the favor when he found that an independent grocer was changing hands. The Hershey salesperson was able to get into the new owner's store early and added valuable shelf space for his products. The operating principle of "you scratch my back, and I scratch yours" works when information flows in both directions.[1]

It is important for salespeople to strike up conversations with other sales representatives while waiting to see buyers. Noncompeting salespeople can be found everywhere and can help in getting valuable information about prospects.

Visible Accounts

In addition to making community contacts or working with key center-of-influence types, salespeople can also cultivate visible and influential accounts that will influence other buyers. In smaller communities, buyers may be impressed if a salesperson is selling to one of the community's larger companies (e.g., GM, Ford, Westinghouse). Doing business with this customer may give the salesperson credibility with other prospects, and these customers could become key accounts, especially if the larger company is well respected for choosing good suppliers. Testimonials from a key account may influence other companies in the salesperson's territories.

Internal Sources

Company Records

Any company that is looking for more business should examine their company records and make a list of former customers that stopped ordering during the past 5 or 10 years. There may be a number of reasons (not all bad) why customers stop ordering. Perhaps a new buyer took over the account and is buying from his or her previous supplier. Whatever the reason, a call asking about their status may determine that the buyer is ready to resume purchasing from the salesperson and company again. Although it sounds difficult, the salesperson should ask why the company lost the business and not be afraid to ask what it will take to win it back. A good relationship-building salesperson realizes that it is going to take a number of calls to regain the buyer's confidence.

Lists and Directories

Published lists and directories, also often available in electronic form, offer an inexpensive, convenient means of identifying leads. Telephone books today contain a business section that lists all the community's businesses. This list is usually broken down further by business type. Manufacturers, medical facilities, pharmacies, and grocery stores, to name a few, can be easily identified by using the business pages of the phone book. Many **lists and directories** exist, such as chamber of commerce directories, trade association lists, *Moody's Industrial Directory, Standard & Poor's Register of Corporations, Directors, and Executives,* to name a few.

Directories are a gold mine of information if they are used correctly. A salesperson must remember that the day these lists are published they start to become obsolete. Sending a letter to a buyer who is no longer with the company makes the salesperson look bad. Companies change their names, merge with others, and even change their addresses. Salespeople must verify information before using it. Exhibit 5.3 refers to many of the directories that salespeople have at their disposal.

Advertising Inquiries

One manufacturer's rep in the natural gas industry speaks highly of his company's advertising plan. They only advertise in trade magazines that they believe their buyers read. The salesperson's territory is Idaho, Utah, Montana, and Wyoming. Their advertising message is simply, "If we can help you with any of your natural gas needs (e.g., flow

EXHIBIT 5.3   **List of Secondary Lead Sources**

1. *Harris Directory,* Harris InfoSource, Indiana, Illinois, Kentucky, Michigan, Ohio, Pennsylvania, Virginia, West Virginia; features company profiles, key contacts with titles, street and mailing addresses, extended zip codes, phone, fax and toll-free numbers, headquarters location and phone, employment figures, import/export, product description, annual sales, facility size, and more. Find information at www.harrisinfo.com.

2. *Sales & Marketing Management* magazine discusses strategies and tactics of marketing and evaluates the market for various products and services. Of more interest to salespeople in the field is its *Annual Survey of Buying Power,* which helps salespeople determine how many individuals in a particular territory can afford their particular product or service. It also provides information about the most promising sales targets and tips on applying statistical data to your particular marketing plans. See www.salesandmarketing.com.

3. *Moody's Industrial Directory* is an annual publication with a wide range of statistical information about particular firms that might be prospects for a specific product or service. Names of executives, description of the company business, and a brief financial statement for more than 10,000 publicly held firms are on the Web at www.moodys.com.

4. *Standard & Poor's Register of Corporations, Directors, and Executives* is an excellent source of personal information about individuals in companies. Such information can be used for qualifying prospects and for learning enough about them to plan an effective approach and presentation. This annual publication lists names, titles, and addresses for 50,000 firms. See www.standardandpoors.com.

5. *Thomas Register of American Manufacturers,* published annually, provides information about who makes what and where almost anything may be purchased. Information is also provided about the corporate structure of the manufacturer and about its executives. If a company sells supplies, raw materials, or components used by a certain type of manufacturer, a salesperson can find an exhaustive list of all companies that might need that product. If a company markets a service, a salesperson can find companies in his or her area whose business fits the description of the ideal client. An index allows recovery of information by geographic location, by product or service, by company name, and by product trade name. Find more information at www.thomasregister.com.

6. *Polk City Directory* supplies detailed information on individuals living in specific communities. Polk publishes more than 1,100 directories covering 6,500 communities throughout the United States and Canada. The local chamber of commerce should have access to this directory. See www.citydirectory.com.

7. *Trade Shows & Professional Exhibits* lists more than 3,500 trade shows including their location, when they are held, and attendance expected.

8. *The International Corporate 1000* provides information and profiles of the 1,000 largest companies in the world: 350 are from the United States and Canada; the remaining 650 are from Europe, South America, the Pacific Basin, and the Middle East.

9. *Database America* has 14 million businesses and 104 million households in their databases. They provide prospect lists (perfect for sales lead generation and telemarketing), tape and PC diskettes (enables printing of sales leads and labels), and mailing labels (useful for direct mail campaigns). Visit Web site: http://www.databaseamerica.com.

10. *Million Dollar Directory* (Dun & Bradstreet) lists names, addresses, and business lines of firms worth more than $1 million. See www.dnbibl.com/mddi.

11. *Encyclopedia of Associations* (Thomson Gale) lists 22,200 national associations, more than 22,300 international organizations, and more than 115,000 regional, state, and local organizations.

12. *Directory of Corporate Affiliations* The Web site www.corporateaffiliations.com provides information on 170,000 parent companies, affiliates, subsidiaries, and divisions worldwide.

13. *World Scope: Industrial Company Profiles* (Wright Investor's Service) provides extensive coverage of 5,000 companies from 25 countries, within 27 major industry groupings. See www.wisi.com.

14. *National Trade and Professional Associations* (Columbia Books) lists more than 7,500 trade and professional associations, along with pertinent information about each. See www.columbiabooks.com.

meters, odorizers), please give us a call." These leads are then turned over to the salesperson who calls on that territory. Territories of this size cannot be covered extensively by one salesperson. The advertising program qualifies the prospect (with the help of the telephone) before the salesperson is sent out on the call.[2]

Telephone Inquiries

Many organizations today use both inbound (prospect calls the company) and outbound (salesperson contacts the prospect) telemarketing. **Inbound telemarketing** involves a telephone number (usually a toll-free number) that prospects or customers can call for information. Companies distribute toll-free numbers by direct mail pieces (brochures), advertising campaigns, and their **outbound telemarketing** program. United Insurance Agency in Muncie, Indiana, uses both inbound and outbound telemarketing to serve their market niche of hotels across America.[3] They use outbound telemarketing to generate and then qualify leads for their salesforce. Qualified leads are turned over to experienced salespeople. Usually, interns do all the outbound telemarketing. Inbound telemarketing is used to resolve problems, answer questions of prospects, as well as take orders from existing customers.

Commercial Lead Lists

A large variety of commercial list providers offer lead lists designed to focus on virtually any type of business and/or individual. Available on paper or in convenient computer formats such as Excel and Word, **commercial lead lists** range from simple listings of names, addresses, and phone numbers to more detailed listings with a full profile of the different entities included in the list. Salespeople should keep in mind that even while list services guarantee a range of accuracy, commercial lists typically contain a number of errors. Also, response rates with commercial lists are usually lower than for more customized lists compiled by the individual salesperson. Typically, only a few prospects will be generated for every 100 names on the lead list.

Internet and World Wide Web

Many firms today have turned to **Web** sites to attract potential customers. A Web site is a collection of information about the company that usually includes company history, products, prices, and how to order or reach a salesperson if there is an interest in the products. Companies today are creatively using text, pictures, sound, and video to attract prospects. Advertising and promotion campaigns focus on Web site addresses and encourage prospects to browse their site.

The disadvantage of using a Web site occurs if companies do not update them periodically. One farm implement dealer learned this the hard way when posting used farm equipment on its Web site. Seventy-five percent of the equipment was sold the first month the Web site was available. Before the site was updated later that year, sales reps had to tell prospective buyers that the equipment had been sold. In fact, almost everything on the site was sold. Some companies find they have to update their sites weekly and even daily.

Personal Contact Sources

Observation

Careful **observation** in a salesperson's territory can reveal the names of potential customers. Pharmaceutical salespeople are constantly looking for new offices being built by hospitals, new pharmacies being built in neighborhoods, and even grocery stores adding their own pharmacies. These are new places to call on that competitors may not have noticed.

Salespeople who work for the natural gas industry usually keep a pair of boots in their car. They are looking for heavy moving equipment. Whenever they see ground being moved, they tromp across the field and ask the operators if they know what is going to be built on the land. Sometimes, they hear a strip mall is going in, other times a middle

PROFESSIONAL SELLING IN THE 21ST CENTURY

What Is Your Prospecting Advantage?

Greg Burchett, district sales manager from Moore Wallace, spends quite a bit of time with each of his sales reps going over Moore Wallace's prospecting advantage.

I know every Moore Wallace product or service has some advantage over the others on the market. By defining our advantages and then fitting them to the market, we make prospecting a more rewarding activity. I have my salespeople list their present customers and how they use Moore Wallace's products, what they like about it, and what benefits it has *brought to them. Next, we have them make a list of prospects they think could use our products. Next, we have them cross-match the lists to show which benefits would fit each prospect. Those who cross-match in many ways will be priority prospects. Those who do not cross-match at all are very low-priority prospects. By assigning a numerical value to each prospect, we automatically eliminate wasted prospecting time and develop a prospecting advantage image of our ideal prospect. When it's time to prospect again, we already know exactly what prospects will be the best for Moore Wallace to call.*

school. The rep then drives to the school system and asks for the plans and whether the heating and cooling decisions have been made yet.[4] Observation can play a big role in beating competitors to the punch when looking for new prospects. As described in "Professional Selling in the 21st Century: What Is Your Prospecting Advantage?," observation plays a big role in how a salesperson's present customers are using his or her product. This information can be used in prioritizing which prospects are the best candidates to purchase those products.

Cold Canvassing

Making unannounced calls on prospects is called **cold canvassing,** or cold calling. This is probably the least successful form of prospecting. Buyers may be annoyed by the salesperson for not having an appointment. Other buyers may have full schedules and no time to see the salesperson. Still others may not be in, and the cold call resulted in a wasted trip. Many salespeople only use cold canvassing as a last resort when other techniques are not producing good leads or if their day is not full of scheduled appointments.

It takes a lot of time and persistence to knock on every door in a prospecting area to uncover potential buyers. Salespeople who do cold calls should set goals as to what they hope to accomplish during a cold call. At a minimum, they should introduce themselves to the receptionist or secretary and start to build rapport with them. At a later date when they phone, the receptionist will now have a face with the name. Ask the receptionist or secretary for information about the company and the buyer. A second goal may be to get an appointment for a later date. It is easier to turn down an appointment request over the phone than it is in person. Finally, one may get in to see the buyer and actually get to make a sales call. In any case, this time should be used wisely to set the stage for further prospecting.

Trade Shows

Attending conventions and **trade shows** presents salespeople with excellent opportunities to collect leads. Generally, the company purchases booth space and sets up a stand that clearly identifies the company and its offerings. Salespeople are available at the booth to demonstrate their products or answer questions. Potential customers walk by and are asked to fill out information cards indicating an interest in the company or one of its products. The completed information card provides leads for the salesperson. Trade shows can stimulate interest in products and provide leads. For example, bank loan officers attend home improvement trade shows and can offer the homeowner immediate credit to begin a project. Those who sign immediately may be offered a reduction in interest rate.

Bird Dogs (Spotters)

Bird dogs (sometimes referred to as **spotters**) are individuals who provide leads to a salesperson for a fee. A variety of agreements have been found to exist. Sometimes the salesperson pays the fee for each lead provided. However, the more common arrangement is for the fee to be paid only if the lead actually makes a purchase. One example of a bird dog program is the agreement that business equipment salespeople have with equipment repair personnel. When the repairperson encounters a machine that is nearing or past the end of its useful life, the contact information is provided to the salesperson by the repairperson. If the salesperson is successful in selling a new piece of equipment, the repairperson receives a fee for providing the lead.

Sales Seminars

Firms can use **seminars** to generate leads and provide information to prospective customers. For example, a financial planner will set up a seminar at a local hotel, inviting prospects by direct mail, word of mouth, or advertising on local television and radio, to give a presentation on retirement planning. The financial consultant discusses a technique or investing opportunities that will prepare the audience for retirement. Those present will be asked to fill out a card expressing their interest for follow-up discussions. The financial consultant hopes this free seminar will reward him or her with a few qualified prospects.

"An Ethical Dilemma" illustrates the difficulty in getting sales reps to locate potential new business.

Qualifying Prospects

Prospects must meet criteria such as being financially capable of making the purchase, able to truly benefit from what is being sold, accessible to the salesperson, and in a position to make or support a purchase decision. In addition to these common criteria, it is likely that salespeople or their companies will impose additional criteria for qualifying prospects (e.g., salesperson can only sell to financial institutions or companies with gross sales of $10 million or more). The personal attributes of the buyer will

AN ETHICAL DILEMMA

Tom Linker has sold office furniture for the past 10 years. The second year he was with the company he won a district contest and placed eighth in the national contest during his third year. The past seven years have been very disappointing. Tom has had some success at getting his current clients to upgrade and make repeat purchases. His downfall has been his inability to locate new business. Tom's boss, Larry Davis, started a new prospecting program in which each salesperson had to contact five new leads per month and discuss them at their monthly sales meetings. After several months, Tom still seems to be having problems generating new business from the leads that he has been turning in to his boss. After six months of no new business, Larry decided to investigate to find out what Tom's problem might be. Larry had to make only three phone calls to determine that Tom has been turning in names that he has never called on! What should Larry do?

also come into play. Honeywell has had a history of allowing their salespeople to turn prospects over to another salesperson if the personalities of the salesperson and buyer did not mesh.[5]

Initiating customer relationships includes the search for and identification of qualified prospects. At a minimum, qualified prospects are those who:

1. Can benefit from the sales offering.
2. Have the financial wherewithal to make the purchase, whether cash, credit, or barter capacity.
3. Play an important role in the purchase decision process.
4. Are eligible to buy based on a fit within the selling strategy (i.e., they fit the profile of the desired customer).
5. Are reasonably accessible and willing to consider the sales offering.
6. Can be added to the customer base at an acceptable level of profitability to allow a mutually beneficial relationship between buyer and seller. This is hard to judge at this stage in the sales cycle, but a preliminary assessment must be made.

In addition to those listed, there may be additional criteria required by the seller based on a particular situation. Additional criteria might include: Does the buyer have a sense of urgency? Are the buyers working under a time constraint such as their copier is broken and work is piling up? Is the buyer open minded to the offering? Have the buyers been known to try new technologies or must they see it working somewhere else before they will try it? Does the buyer give feedback or must the salesperson continually probe to get any feedback at all? Some buyers will tell the salesperson everything they know; others will be tight lipped. Is the buyer trusting in nature, or will it take a lot of effort to win this buyer's trust?

A firm may have a need for a new fax machine, but if the buyer is not open minded to the technology, he or she might not be a good prospect at this time. Other buyers have needs but are unwilling to listen for a variety of reasons (e.g., busy on other projects, recently burned by a salesperson and the buyer is taking it out on all salespeople). A good prospect readily gives feedback. A silent buyer makes it difficult to determine the extent of interest by the buyer. Possibly, the best prospect is the one who has a sense of urgency and wants to act now. Regular calls by the salesperson are needed to stay close to each buyer so that when a need arises, the salesperson will be positioned to get the order.

THE PREAPPROACH: GATHERING AND STUDYING PRECALL INFORMATION

Once potential customers are identified, the salesperson must begin the process of collecting information. During this stage, the salesperson gathers information about the prospect that will be used to formulate the sales presentation. Buyer's needs, buyer's motives, and details of the buyer's situation should be determined. Some organizations spend a great amount of time determining the salesperson's and buyer's communication style. Effectively sensing and interpreting customers' communications styles allow salespeople to adapt their own interaction behaviors in a way that facilitates buyer–seller communication and enhances relationship formation.

The more the salesperson knows about his or her buyer, the better chance he or she has to sell. Over time, the salesperson should be able to accumulate knowledge about the prospect. The information that the salesperson needs varies with the kind of product that he or she is selling. As a rule, a salesperson should definitely know a few basic things about his or her customers (e.g., the prospect's name, correct spelling, and correct pronunciation).

A salesperson can learn a great deal about a customer over time by collecting bits and pieces of information, sorting them out, and developing a personalized presentation for the customer.

Obtaining Precall Information on the Buyer

A salesperson must do some preliminary homework once a company has been identified as a potential client. The first stage of information gathering is to concentrate on the individual prospect. Several questions need to be answered that will identify how the buyer will behave toward the salesperson. Exhibit 5.4 details some of the questions that a salesperson needs to ask.

It is not unusual for gatekeepers to prohibit the salesperson access to the buyer over the phone if the salesperson mispronounces the buyer's name. Mail is thrown away without being opened if the name is misspelled or the title is incorrect.

Precall information should be used to develop rapport with the prospect and to eventually tailor the presentation to fit the buyer's needs. A salesperson can establish a relationship with a prospect by discussing such mutual points of interest as an alumni association with the same college or support for the same athletic team. As illustrated in "An Ethical Dilemma," information gathering must be done thoughtfully. It can take many sales calls and months to gather all the useful information needed by a salesperson.

Gathering Information on the Prospect's Organization

Gathering information about the prospect's company helps salespeople better understand the environment in which they will be working. Exhibit 5.5 details some of the questions that provide useful information about the prospect's organization. Is

---

Information to Gather on a Prospect and Who to Contact   EXHIBIT 5.4

Information Needed	How to Collect Information
The prospect's name.	Correct spelling and pronunciation can be gathered by asking the receptionist or secretary to verify information.
The prospect's correct title.	This can be determined by asking the gatekeepers to verify.
Is this prospect willing to take risks? Are they confident with decision making?	The salesperson may have to ask the prospect about willingness to take risks.
Is the prospect involved in the community? Does the prospect belong to any clubs or professional organizations?	The salesperson may be able to observe club or organizational honors displayed in the office.
Does the prospect have hobbies or interests he or she is proud of? (coin collector, sports enthusiast)	Observation of the office might give away this information.
What is the prospect's personality type? Easygoing? All business?	Observation and experience with the buyer will give the answer to the salesperson.
Where was the prospect educated? Where did this prospect grow up?	Look for diploma on the wall. The salesperson may have to ask for this information.

Teresa Wolf had just completed her sales training with Foster Supply (a distributor of component parts for small engines), and she really took to heart the importance of precall information gathering. Her company kept a customer profile and planning sheet that gathered information such as

Name _____
Address _____
Type of Business _____
Name of Buyer _____
Buyer's Hobbies _____
Decision Maker _____
Key Influences in the Company _____
Buyer Profile _____
Buyer Personality Type _____
Name of Owner _____
Age of Company _____
Primary Products Produced, etc. _____

She had only been in her territory two weeks when her sales manager, Ted Hart, started receiving complaints from Teresa's prospects and customers. The callers complained that she had been aggressively collecting information on their company and buyers by interviewing everyone in their respective companies that would agree to see her. One caller, Jane VanWay (the lead buyer for Wisconsin Power Corporation and a key account for Foster Supply) even termed one of her sales calls an "interrogation." Upon reviewing her profile sheets, Ted was amazed at how complete they were. Nevertheless, there was still the problem in how Teresa was going about getting the information. If you were Teresa, how might you go about researching and collecting the needed company and individual buyer information in a fashion that would not be perceived as so intrusive and aggressive?

the prospect presently buying from a single supplier? How long has the prospect been buying from this supplier? If the answer is 20 years and he or she is extremely satisfied with the current salesperson, products, and services, then the prospect should be thanked for his or her time, and the salesperson should move on to other accounts.

Sources of Information

A good salesperson uses all available information sources to gather valuable information. Lists and directories will have names, addresses, phone numbers, and other key information. The Web can be a valuable tool as companies provide more than enough vital

EXHIBIT 5.5   Gathering Information about the Organization

Information Needed	How to Collect Information
What type of business are we dealing with: manufacturer, wholesaler, retailer, government, educational, medical, financial institution?	This can be gathered from a directory.
To what market does the company sell? Who are the organization's primary competitors? What does the company make and sell?	Annual reports may be helpful in answering these questions.
Who does the prospect presently buy from? Do they buy from a single vendor? Multiple vendors? How long have they purchased from their suppliers? What problems does the company face? In what volume does the company buy? What is the organization's financial position?	The salesperson may have to ask for this information.

information for a salesperson. Walker Group in Indianapolis has one person dedicated to daily seeking critical Web information about their clients and competitors.[6] Salespeople have access to a large quantity of current information and should use it to gain a competitive edge over their competitors.

Secretaries and receptionists can be a friendly source of information. They can certainly be used to verify name, title, pronunciation, and correct spelling. Also, noncompeting salespeople can help a salesperson fill in information on accounts.

Finally, a salesperson should be gathering information about each of its companies and buyers. Some companies provide the salesforce with contact management software like ACT or Goldmine. Salespeople may develop their own system for gathering pertinent information. Exhibit 5.6 illustrates the types of information that can be gathered in a customer profile.

Determining Other Buyers' Influences

As products become more complex, we often see an increase in the number of buying influencers and decision makers involved in the purchase. The salesperson should attempt to determine the various buying influencers. For example, if a salesperson concentrates on the purchasing agent in an organization and ignores other key players (e.g., department head, data processing) in the decision-making process, the salesperson takes the risk that he or she is potentially selling to the wrong person.

The salesperson must use observation and questioning to determine the role of each member of the buying team and the amount of influence each exerts; each member's needs should be determined before or during the presentation. Department heads may

---

Customer Profile EXHIBIT 5.6

1. Name of Business _____
2. Address _____
3. Phone _____
4. Name of Buyer(s) _____ Title _____
   Personality, Hobbies, Interests _____
   _____ Title _____
   _____ Title _____
   _____ Title _____
5. Source of prospect (i.e., referral, cold call) _____
6. Other Key People
   Receptionists _____
   Personality, Hobbies, Interests _____
   Secretaries _____
   Personality, Hobbies, Interests _____
   Department Heads _____
   Personality, Hobbies, Interests _____
   Other Influencers—Who? _____
   Personality, Hobbies, Interests _____
7. What products does the company produce? _____
8. History and current standing in the industry _____
9. How many employees? _____
10. Extent of operations—local, regional, national, international _____
11. Is buying done by individuals or committee? _____
12. Does the company buy from single or multiple sources? _____

be interested in how the product will benefit their department, whereas the CFO may only care about the price. During group presentations, all the members of the buying party must feel involved. The salesperson must be sure to direct questions and comments to all potential decision makers in the group.

If a salesperson has only one contact (e.g., purchasing agent) in an organization, he or she runs the risk that the key contact could die, get fired, change jobs, get transferred, or retire. By having contact with many influencers in an organization, the salesperson will always have a number of people who have had previous experiences to pass on to the new purchasing agent or team member. In the first instance, the salesperson must start the entire relationship process again; in the second, the salesperson will have help keeping the relationship in place.

SUMMARY

1. **Explain strategic prospecting.** Strategic prospecting involves the identification of qualified potential customers, usually called prospects. When we say a prospect is qualified, it means that the prospect meets or exceeds screening criteria that have been established by the salesperson or the sales organization. Prospects must meet criteria such as being financially capable of making the purchase, able to truly benefit from what is being sold, accessible to the salesperson, and in a position to make or support a purchase decision.

2. **Discuss why prospecting can be a challenging task for a salesperson.** Prospective buyers may be difficult to contact because they have never heard of a salesperson's firm and do not want to take the time with a potential new supplier. Buyers are constantly getting calls from salespeople and do not have time to see them all. Gatekeepers have been trained to screen their bosses' calls and often are not pleasant to the salesperson.

3. **Explain where salespeople find prospects.** A good sales organization and salesperson will have a number of ongoing prospecting methods in place at any given time. Asking present customers for leads (referral), working with noncompeting salespeople, buying directories or lists, advertising for interested companies to call or mail in their interest, telemarketing, the Web, direct mail, and observation are a few of the techniques that salespeople can use to generate leads.

4. **Understand the importance of gathering and studying precall information.** Salespeople must gather information about the prospect that will be used to help formulate the sales presentation. Buyer's needs, buyer's motives, and details about the buyer's situation should be determined. The more a salesperson knows about the buyer, the better chance he or she will have to meet the buyer's needs and eventually earn the commitment.

UNDERSTANDING PROFESSIONAL SELLING TERMS

prospecting	referral
leads	introduction
qualifying a lead	center of influence
prospects	noncompeting salesperson
strategic prospecting plan	lists and directories
tracking system	inbound telemarketing

outbound telemarketing   cold canvassing
commercial lead lists   trade shows
Web   bird dogs (spotters)
observation   seminars

DEVELOPING PROFESSIONAL SELLING KNOWLEDGE

1. Why should a salesperson be concerned with prospecting—isn't it enough to concentrate on your present customers and grow your new business from them?

2. What should be the objectives of strategic prospecting?

3. Why is prospecting difficult for some salespeople?

4. Why should a salesperson wait until they have a track record with a buyer before they ask for a referral?

5. Why is there the potential for cold canvassing to be an ineffective prospecting method?

6. At a minimum, what criteria should be used to qualify prospects?

7. Why is it important to collect precall information on the buyer and the company?

8. What sources of information can a salesperson use to gather information on their prospects?

9. Why is it important to determine other buying influences?

10. What are some typical objectives a salesperson might hope to accomplish when calling on a prospect?

BUILDING PROFESSIONAL SELLING SKILLS

1. You have recently graduated from college and are selling a new line with X-tra Clear Copiers. You have been assigned to a new territory in a city of 100,000 near your campus. You do not have any clients who currently own X-tra Clear Copiers. Your boss asks you to develop a prospect list in 10 days. How might you go about generating this list of prospects?

Provide a list of sources that you might use to generate leads.

1. _____
2. _____
3. _____
4. _____
5. _____
6. _____
7. _____
8. _____
9. _____
10. _____

Provide a list of establishments that would be prospects for X-tra Clear Copiers. Can you identify a person to call on? What information should you try to collect?

1. Company _____
   Whom to call on _____
   Info to collect _____

2. Company _____
   Whom to call on _____
   Info to collect _____

3. Company _____
   Whom to call on _____
   Info to collect _____

4. Company _____
   Whom to call on _____
   Info to collect _____

5. Company _____
   Whom to call on _____
   Info to collect _____

6. Company _____
   Whom to call on _____
   Info to collect _____

7. Company _____
   Whom to call on _____
   Info to collect _____

8. Company _____
   Whom to call on _____
   Info to collect _____

9. Company _____
   Whom to call on _____
   Info to collect _____

10. Company _____
    Whom to call on _____
    Info to collect _____

ROLE PLAY

2. **Situation:**   Read the Ethical Dilemma on page 148.

   Characters: Teresa Wolf, salesperson for Foster Supply; Jane VanWay, lead buyer for Wisconsin Power Corporation

   Scene: *Location*—Jane VanWay's office at Wisconsin Power Corporation. *Action*—Teresa has been doing a commendable job in getting complete company and buyer profile information to complete the account profile sheets that her company requires her to complete and keep updated. However, Teresa's sales manager has received a number of complaints about her aggressiveness in getting the information. Jane VanWay, lead buyer for Wisconsin Power Corporation and long-time key account for Foster Supply, has even complained that Teresa seems to interrogate everyone who is willing to see her.

Role play a sales call interaction with Jane VanWay and demonstrate how information about the buyer and the buyer's company might be collected without it being an interrogation.

Upon completion of the role play, answer the following questions:

2a. What other methods might Teresa use to gain the information she needs?

2b. How might Teresa handle the fact that many of her prospects and buyers have developed a negative impression of her information-gathering techniques?

ROLE PLAY

3. **Situation:**   Read "Professional Selling in the 21st Century" on page 138.

   Characters: John Klich, salesperson for Northwestern Mutual Financial Network; Tracy Hanna, high school math teacher

   Scene: *Location*—John Klich's office at Northwestern Mutual Financial Network. *Action*—John is making his daily phone calls to qualify prospects and set up appointments to present a variety of financial services and products as solutions for individual life insurance and retirement needs. He has obtained Tracy's name and phone number from a lead list of community teachers.

Role play the phone conversation between John and Tracy as John gathers the information needed to screen Tracy as a qualified prospect and gain an appointment for an initial sales call to explore Tracy's needs for financial services and products and begin developing the relationship as a satisfied client.

Upon completion of the role play, answer the following questions:

3a. What other ways might John introduce himself, generate Tracy's positive involvement, and gain the appointment?

3b. Why is it important for John to avoid making a full-blown sales presentation to Tracy over the phone?

4. As an account manager for Chemical Coating Corporation (CCC) you have national responsibility for selling Syntex, a new paint additive that significantly extends the shelf life and improves the application of all forms of latex-based paints. This is a breakthrough product just coming onto the market and you are in the process of identifying, qualifying, and prioritizing latex paint manufacturers across the United States that offer high potential for buying the new additive.

Prior information gathered from CCC's customer account records indicates that the best prospects would be larger manufacturers of latex paint. The larger manufacturers tend to be characterized by having an asset base of $10 million or higher and 25 or more employees.

Having become a regular user of the Internet and World Wide Web in digging out business-related information on prospects and accounts, you are aware that the *Thomas Register* site has the capability to search specific product categories by name, identify manufacturers, and provide a summary profile of each company identified.

Access the *Thomas Register* site at the URL **http://thomasregister.com** and generate a listing of firms manufacturing the product described as latex paint. Print the listing in a format suitable to hand in to your instructor. You may have to complete a free registration process to use the site.

- On the *thomasregister* home page, select "search for product or service," enter the product name "latex paint" into the "Containing The Words" text box, and select "Find It."
- The results page entitled "Product Headings Found" will indicate the number of latex paint manufacturers listed in the Thomas Register Data Base.
- Click on the hotlink heading "paints: latex" to pull up a more detailed page listing the companies by name and location.
- Click on each company's hot linked company name to obtain the summary description page for the individual company.
- Click on the "Company Profile" hotlink to access a more detailed profile of the company including asset size, number of employees, and full description of what the organization does.

Discussion Questions

4a. How many total leads did you find?

4b. Use CCC's description of the characteristics that denote major manufacturers to provide an initial qualification screen. How many of the leads pass this initial screening test?

4c. Prioritize the remaining accounts according to CCC's screening criteria and list the companies in the order of priority for contact.

4d. What problems do you see with using a commercial database such as the *Thomas Register* as a lead generating tool? Explain.

5. A large number of computer-based and online tools are available to facilitate tracking prospects and customerss. Some of these tools are known simply as contact management applications while others have evolved into full customer relationship

management tools. ACT! is one of the consistent leaders in this category of products and is used by a large number of companies of all sizes.

 Access the ACT! Web site at the URL **http://act.com.** Click on the link to see the ACT! demo. This tour will walk you through the features of the newest release and allow you to experience firsthand how versatile these contact management tools have become.

Discussion Questions

5a. As a salesperson, how might you use ACT! to increase your selling effectiveness?

5b. What five features of ACT! would be most beneficial to you? Why?

MAKING PROFESSIONAL SELLING DECISIONS

Case 5.1: How to Prospect for New Customers

Background

Pete Tsuleff has been interested in the food and beverage industry since he was a little boy. His father owned a restaurant/tavern. Pete spent his evenings, weekends, and summers working in the restaurant. At age 21, he began to work as a bartender. He had firsthand experience ordering food, hiring, firing, and running the entire operation by the time he was 25. At age 30, he bought his father out.

During the next 10 years, he opened another restaurant/bar and two package liquor stores. Peter's first love was experimenting with new recipes. He had a chili that won competitions in his hometown. He made a spaghetti sauce that was world class. His garlic bread and garlic cheese bread were legendary. Pete decided to get out of the tavern and liquor business, and he opened a line of spaghetti shops. Sales over the first five years were outstanding, and he opened a new store every six months.

Pete continued to experiment with recipes and developed a line of barbecue sauces. He believes that he is the first to dual franchise spaghetti and barbecue in the same building.

Current Situation

Pete is convinced that a good market exists (e.g., groceries, restaurants, gas stations) for his garlic bread and spaghetti and barbecue sauces. He has seen his sales grow by 18 percent per year over the past five years, and the trend is expected to continue for at least the next three years.

One of his first problems is to obtain a list of prospects.

Questions

1. What prospecting methods should Pete use?
2. How can Pete qualify the leads he receives? What qualifying factors will be most important?
3. How can Pete organize his prospecting activities?
4. How should he keep records of his prospects?
5. What precall information is needed by Pete? How will he collect this information?

ROLE PLAY

Situation: Read Case 5.1.

Characters: Pete Tsuleff, owner and salesperson for Specialty Foods & Sauces; Sue Almont, specialty products buyer for Cub Food Stores.

Scene: *Location*—Pete Tsuleff's office at Specialty Foods & Sauces. *Action*—In the course of Pete's prospecting activities, Sue Almont and Cub Foods have scored a high priority as a qualified prospect for his new line of garlic breads and sauces. Cub Foods is a major supermarket chain with significant market penetration in Iowa, Missouri, Illinois, and Indiana.

Role play the phone conversation between Pete and Sue as Pete introduces himself and his company to Sue, gathers needed information about the prospect, and asks for an appointment for an initial sales call.

Upon completion of the role play, answer the following questions:

1. In what other ways might Pete introduce himself and his company?
2. How might Pete elicit sufficient interest from Sue to gain an appointment for a sales call?
3. Why is it important for Pete to avoid making a full-blown sales presentation to Sue over the phone?

Case 5.2: Prospecting and Gaining Precall Information

Background

Preston Adams has just completed the sales training program for the Office Equipment Division of Xerox. Preston has been assigned a territory in Illinois that includes the metro areas of Bloomington, Decatur, and Peoria. The company once commanded a significant market share in these markets. However, due to a problem with a previous salesperson in these markets three years ago, Xerox has not been directly working this particular region of central Illinois. Although there are a large number of Xerox machines still in use across this territory, it has been a while since a salesperson has called on any accounts. As with any geographic area, there have likely been a lot of changes with existing companies moving or even going out of business and new companies opening up.

Current Situation

Preston's sales manager, Eric Waits is coming in two weeks to spend three days in the field with Preston calling on prospective accounts. Preston is working to develop a list of leads that he can qualify and then contact in order to set up the sales calls he will be making with his manager.

Questions

1. What prospecting methods and sources might Preston use to develop his list of leads?
2. How might Preston go about qualifying the leads he develops? What qualifying factors will be most important?
3. What precall information would be needed by Preston?
4. How might Preston go about obtaining that information?

Situation:	Read Case 5.2.
Characters:	Preston Adams, salesperson for Xerox Business Machines Division; Jerri Spencer, office manager with purchasing responsibilities for Peoria-based McKelvey and Walters, Attorneys-at-Law.
Scene:	*Location*—Preston Adam's office at Xerox Business Machines Division. *Action*—In the course of Preston's prospecting activities, Jerri Spencer and the McKelvey and Walters law firm have come up as a strong

ROLE PLAY

prospect for Xerox's new line of professional copiers. McKelvey and Walters operate a large office in Peoria that occupies most of two floors in the Planter's Bank Building and a branch office in Bloomington. They were previously a customer of Xerox, but the information that Preston has obtained indicates that they are using an unspecified variety of different brands of copiers.

Role play the phone conversation between Preston and Jerri as Preston introduces himself and his company to Jerri, gathers needed information to better qualify the prospect, and asks for an appointment for an initial sales call.

Upon completion of the role play, answer the following questions:

1. In what other ways might Preston introduce himself and his company?
2. How might he handle the likely questions as to why it has been so long since they have heard from a Xerox salesperson?
3. What information does Preston need in order to qualify McKelvey and Walters as a good prospect?

PLANNING THE PRESENTATION
AND APPROACHING
THE CUSTOMER

SUCCESSFUL SALES PRESENTATIONS REQUIRE PLANNING, CUSTOMER FOCUS

According to Linda Navarro, CEO of Sonnet Supply, a California specialty cutting tools distributor, a good sales presentation comes from 80 percent preparation and 20 percent actual presentation. Chip Wernig, president of a Denver, Colorado, industrial distributor, says a good presentation results from three things, "preparation, preparation, and preparation." John Graham, president of a marketing services and sales consulting firm, is brutally honest when he says: "Only stupid people wing it. Those salespeople think they are experienced, and that experience will give them the ability to get through the appointment without all the preparation. But those who don't prepare, don't make sales."

Experts agree that planning is the key to making productive sales calls. In today's busy business environment, buyers simply do not have time to waste on poorly planned sales presentations that do not focus on their unique needs and opportunities. By focusing on the buyer's situation, salespeople must be able to show how they add value for their customers. In many cases, adding value boils down to improving the customer's financial situation, either by generating additional revenue or by saving money.

A key to successful sales presentation planning is to set a specific action objective for the customer as a result of the presentation. In some cases, this will be to make a purchase, while other presentations are focused on an intermediate step that could move the customer closer to making a purchasing decision. For example, the salesperson might seek approval for a product usage test, which could lead to a sale as a result of a presentation at a later date.

Sales presentation planning is a fairly simple process, but it is not completed without careful thought. To optimize the process, think like a customer, present information the way a customer wants to receive it, and use a customer-action objective to measure presentation success.

Source: Kimberly Griffiths, "Making a Good Sales Presentation is All About the Preparation Put in Beforehand, and Making the Pitch Customer Centric," *Industrial Distribution*, (July 2004): 44–46.

SALES PRESENTATION PLANNING

Sales presentation planning has become more important in recent years, as evidenced by increased coverage on the topic in sales training programs. The requirements of professional selling today make **sales presentation planning** imperative, and it is often extensive, because it is increasingly viewed as a critical link in the sales process.

As with other planning processes, the salesperson must begin with a specifically stated objective, or perhaps multiple objectives, for each sales presentation.

It is recommended that the major objective for all sales presentations be stated in terms of the specific customer action being sought as a result of the presentation. In many cases, this will be for the customer to make a purchase. In other cases, the customer action sought is to agree to a next step that brings the buyer and seller closer to a purchase decision. For example, in the first call on a prospect,

Objectives

After completing this module, you should be able to

1 Discuss the different types of sales presentations and what goes into their planning.

2 Determine when it is best to use the three types of sales presentations.

3 Discuss the importance of using a sales presentation checklist.

4 Discuss the importance of planning the initial sales call.

5 Discuss how the sales mix model enhances the planning effort.

6 Explain how to approach and initiate contact with each prospect.

157

salespeople might introduce the capabilities of their company and seek customer approval to meet with others who share decision-making authority in a subsequent follow-up meeting. If this request is successful, the salesperson, then sets one or more appropriate customer-action objectives for the follow-up meeting.

Typical objectives might be stated as order quantities or dollar values, or even in communications terms, such as reaching an agreement in principle with the prospect. Once a clearly stated objective has been formulated, the salesperson can focus on how the benefits of his or her offering can best serve the needs of the prospect.

Taken to the ultimate, sales presentation planning might actually result in a script to guide sales encounters. Not to be confused with a scripted sales message to be delivered over the telephone, this script would be a guide to expected sales activities given a particular buying situation. Research has been conducted that suggests that scripts could help salespeople learn how to adapt to the customer and the selling situation, while developing their own personal style and sales tactics.[1]

After a great deal of planning and preparation, a salesperson will get an appointment with the prospect for a face-to-face meeting. The approach represents the first time the salesperson and the prospect come into contact with one another. The approach has a couple of important objectives. First, the salesperson wants to make a good first impression. Second, the salesperson must generate interest in the product in order for the buyer to agree to a presentation. The following discussion provides a summary of the three basic types of presentations: memorized or canned presentations, organized presentations, and written sales proposals. First, types of sales presentations will be presented. Next, the importance of using a checklist as an effective sales tool will be discussed. A brief overview follows of the sales mix model. Finally, various techniques to approach the customer are covered.

SALES PRESENTATION FORMAT

To plan the sales presentation, salespeople must decide on a basic presentation format, such as a canned sales presentation, an organized presentation, and the written sales proposal. Exhibit 6.1 summarizes the types of presentations used by sales professionals. A salesperson might use one or more of these formats with a particular customer. Each format has unique advantages and disadvantages. To be successful, these presentations must be credible and clear. In addition, the salesperson must deliver the presentation in the right environment at an appropriate time to maximize the probability of a successful outcome.

For any of the three presentation types, salespeople must plan to be as specific as possible in developing their sales message. For example, it is better to tell a prospect "This electric motor will produce 4800 RPM and requires only one hour of maintenance per week" than to say "This motor will really put out the work with only minimum maintenance."

Canned Sales Presentations

Canned sales presentations include scripted sales calls, memorized presentations, and automated presentations. Automated presentations rely heavily on computer images, movies, tapes, or slides to present the information to the prospect.

Most canned sales presentations have been tested for effectiveness with real customers before dissemination to the salesforce. Canned presentations are usually complete and logically structured. Objections and questions can be anticipated in advance, and appropriate responses can be formulated as part of the presentation. The highly structured and inflexible canned sales presentation does not vary from customer to customer. When properly formulated, it is logical and complete and minimizes sales resistance by anticipating the prospect's objections. It can be used by relatively inexperienced salespeople and perhaps is a confidence builder for some salespeople.

Canned sales presentations make an implicit assumption that customer needs and buying motives are homogeneous. Therefore, canned presentations fail to capitalize on a key advantage of personal selling—the ability to adapt to different types of customers and various selling situations. Most consumer-based telemarketing sales calls are canned and follow this formula. The canned presentation can be effective but is not appropriate for many

Types of Sales Presentations   **EXHIBIT 6.1**

Canned Presentations
- Include
  - scripted sales calls
  - memorized presentations
  - automated presentations
- Should be tested for effectiveness
- Must assume buyer needs are the same

Organized Presentations
- Address individual customer and different selling situations
- Allow flexibility to adapt to buyer feedback
- Most frequently used format for sales professionals

Written Sales Proposals
- The proposal is a complete self-contained sales presentation
- Customer may receive proposal and a follow-up call to explain and clarify the proposal
- Thorough assessment should take place before a customized proposal is written

situations—simply because customer opportunity to interact is minimized. During a memorized presentation, the salesperson talks 80 to 90 percent of the time, only occasionally allowing the prospect to express his or her feelings, concerns, or opinions. Figure 6.1 illustrates this process. Unfortunately, the salesperson does not attempt to determine the prospect's needs during the sales interview but gives the same memorized sales talk to all

Prepared Approach to a Sales Presentation   **FIGURE 6.1**

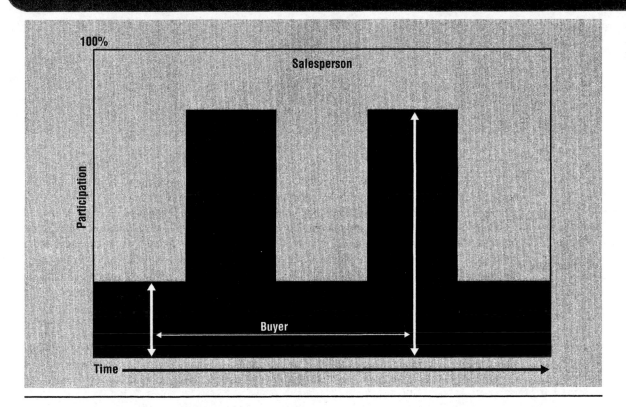

During a memorized presentation, the salesperson talks 80 to 90 percent of the time, only occasionally allowing the prospect to express his or her feelings, concerns, or opinions.

prospects. The salesperson can only assume the buyer's need and must hope that a lively presentation of product benefits will cause the prospect to buy. The major limitation of the canned sales presentation is that it fails to capitalize on the strength of personal selling—the ability to tailor the message to the prospect. Further, it does not handle interruptions well, may be awkward to use with a broad product line, and may alienate buyers who want to participate in the interaction.

Despite its limitations, the canned sales presentation can be effective in some situations. If the product line is narrow and the salesforce is relatively inexperienced, the canned presentation may be suitable. Also, many salespeople find it effective to use in a sales presentation to introduce their company, to demonstrate the product, or for some other limited purpose.

ORGANIZED SALES PRESENTATIONS

Sales presentations that are tailored to each prospect are far more popular with salespeople than are canned sales presentations. In the **organized sales presentation**, the salesperson organizes the key points into a planned sequence that allows for adaptive behavior by the salesperson as the presentation progresses. Feedback from the prospect is encouraged, and therefore this format is less likely to offend a participation-prone buyer. "An Ethical Dilemma" demonstrates the problem for a salesperson who is not willing to ask questions and gain feedback.

AN ETHICAL DILEMMA

Tom Lawrence was not one who liked to do a lot of precall planning or ask questions of his prospects. Tom had a good idea about which of his product's features were hot buttons for most prospects. During each of his sales calls, he hammered home those features that he thought were important to most of his prospects. His sales manager made calls with him for a few days and made the observation that he should do more questioning and listening and only sell those features and benefits that were relevant to each prospect. Tom stated: "I feel that is a waste of time. Most of my buyers are busy. They don't have time to answer questions all day. I'm the expert, I should know what they need." What are the dangers in the way Tom thinks? What can his sales manager do to help Tom change?

To best address individual customers and different selling situations, salespeople should consider an organized presentation, which allows the implementation of appropriate sales strategies and tactics. Such an approach allows much-needed flexibility to adapt to buyer feedback and changing circumstances during the presentation. Organized presentations may also include some canned portions. For example, a salesperson for Caterpillar may show a videotape to illustrate the earth-moving capabilities of a bulldozer as one segment of an organized presentation. Due to its flexibility during the sales call and its ability to address various sales situations, the organized presentation is the most frequently used format for professional sales presentations.

One reality of this presentation format is that it requires a knowledgeable salesperson who can react to questions and objections from the prospect. Steve Kehoe, president of Kehoe Financial Services, confirms this in "Professional Selling in the 21st Century: Being Prepared for My Sales Calls." Further, this format may extend the time horizon before a purchase decision is reached, and it is vulnerable to diversionary delay tactics by the prospect. Presumably, those who make these arguments think that a canned presentation forces a purchase decision in a more expedient fashion.

Being Prepared for My Sales Calls

Steve Kehoe, president of Kehoe Financial Services in Cincinnati, Ohio, knows the importance of planning and organizing each of his sales calls.

My clients are very knowledgeable, they want answers to questions and I must be prepared to answer them. It may sound simple but my clients want to know what I am selling and why do they need it. If they have high schoolers, it's my job to explain the college savings plan and how it works. I represent many different companies so my clients want to know what company I am recommending and why. It is not unusual to be asked if I have other satisfied clients using the product. I have to be prepared to talk about my satisfied clients and how I helped them. Yes, price always comes up and my clients want to know if my prices are truly competitive. We're not always the lowest, but we better be close. Many of my clients are not confident in their decision making. I must be prepared to explain why they need to act now and not wait. I cannot go into my sales calls having not thought about these questions. As a professional salesperson, I must plan for them before the fact and be ready to answer them.

The trust-based relational selling presentation often referred to as the need-satisfaction/consultative model, is a popular form of an organized presentation. It is different from the canned presentation as it is designed as a flexible interactive dialog with the customer. The first stage of the process, the need development stage, is devoted to a discussion of the buyer's needs. As seen in Figure 6.2, during this phase the buyer should be talking 60 to 70 percent of the time. The salesperson accomplishes this by using the

The Trust-Based Selling Process:
A Need-Satisfaction Consultative Model   **FIGURE 6.2**

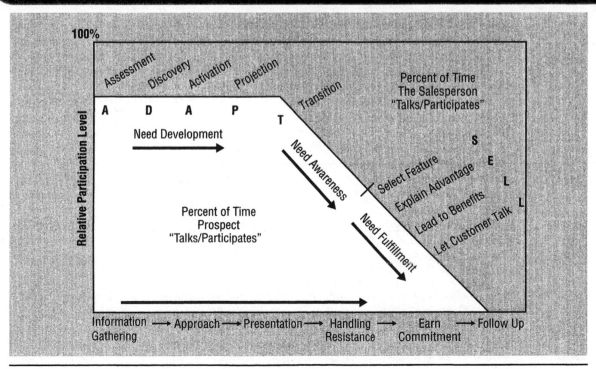

first four questioning techniques of the ADAPT process. The second stage of the process (need awareness) is to verify what the buyer thinks his or her needs are and to make the buyer aware of potential needs that may exist. For instance, fast-food restaurants were generally slow to recognize the need to offer more low-fat and low-carbohydrate menu items until their sales volume suffered. Others, such as Subway, gained a competitive advantage by working with their suppliers to formulate a significant number of menu alternatives for the health-conscious consumer. The need-awareness stage is a good time to restate the prospect's needs and to clarify exactly what the prospect's needs are. During the last stage of the presentations, (the need-fulfillment stage), the salesperson must show how his or her product and its benefits will meet the needs of the buyer. As seen in Figure 6.2, the salesperson during the need-fulfillment stage will do more of the talking by indicating what specific product will meet the buyer's needs. The salesperson, by being a good listener early in the process, will now have a better chance to gain the buyer's interest and trust by talking about specific benefits the buyer has confirmed as being important.

Overall, however, most agree that the organized presentation is ideal for most sales situations. Its flexibility allows a full exploration of customer needs and appropriate adaptive behavior by the salesperson.

Written Sales Proposals

The third basic type of sales presentation is the **written sales proposal**. The proposal is a complete self-contained sales presentation, but it is often accompanied by other verbal sales presentations before or after the proposal is delivered. With widespread usage of word processing, computer graphics, and desktop publishing, the written sales proposal is being used in a growing number of situations. These technologies have minimized the traditional disadvantage of the written proposal—the time it takes to prepare it.

In some cases, the customer may receive a proposal and then request that the salesperson make a sales call to further explain the proposal and provide answers to questions. Alternatively, preliminary sales presentations may lead to a sales proposal. In any event, the sales proposal should be prepared after the salesperson has made a thorough assessment of the buyer's situation as it relates to the seller's offering.

The sales proposal has long been associated with important, high-dollar-volume sales transactions. It is frequently used in competitive bidding situations and in situations involving the selection of a new supplier by the prospect. One advantage of the proposal is that the written word is usually viewed as being more credible than the spoken word. Written proposals are subject to careful scrutiny with few time constraints, and specialists in the buying firm often analyze various sections of the proposal.

Sales proposal content is similar to other sales presentations, focusing on customer needs and related benefits offered by the seller. In addition, technical information, pricing data, and perhaps a timetable are included. Most proposals provide a triggering mechanism such as a proposed contract to confirm the sale, and some specify follow-up action to be taken if the proposal is satisfactory.

With multimedia sales presentations becoming more routine, it is natural to think that written sales proposals would be declining in importance. Actually, the opposite is true. With the widespread use of multimedia, the standards for all sales communication continue to rise. Buyers expect clear informative sales messages, and they are less tolerant of sloppy communication. Because everyone knows that word processing programs have subroutines to check spelling and grammar, for example, mistakes are less acceptable than ever.

Because written communication provides a permanent record of claims and intentions, salespeople should be careful not to over promise, while still maintaining a positive and supportive tone. No buyer wants to read a proposal full of legal disclaimers and warnings, yet such information may be a necessary ingredient in certain written communication. As with all communication, salespeople should try to give buyers the information they need to make informed decisions.

Writing Effective Proposals

Whether the proposal is in response to a buyer's request for proposals (RFP) or generated to complement and strengthen a sales presentation, it is essential that the proposal be correctly written and convey the required information in an attractive manner. Tom Sant, an author and consultant who works with many Fortune 100 companies, gives these reasons why proposals may fail:[2]

1. Customer does not know the seller.
2. Proposal does not follow the specified format.
3. Executive summary does not address customer needs.
4. Proposal uses the seller's (not the customer's) company jargon.
5. Writing is flat and technical and without passion.
6. Generic material contains another customer's name.
7. Proposal is not convincing.
8. Proposal contains glaring grammatical errors.
9. Proposal does not address key decision criteria.
10. Proposal does not build a persuasive value proposition.

Clearly, developing a quality proposal takes time and effort. However, the process of writing an effective proposal can be simplified by breaking the proposal down into its primary and distinct parts. The five parts common to most proposals are an executive summary, a needs and benefits analysis, a company description, the pricing and sales agreement, and the suggested action and timeline.[3]

Executive Summary

This summary precedes the full proposal and serves two critical functions. First, it should succinctly and clearly demonstrate the salesperson's understanding of the customer's needs and the relevance of the proposed solution. An effective summary will spell out the customer's problems, the nature of the proposed solution, and the resulting benefits to the customer. A second function of the summary is to build a desire to read the full proposal. This is important as many key members of the organization often read little more than the information provided in the summary. A question commonly asked by new salespeople refers to the length of the executive summary. A good rule of thumb is that an executive summary should be limited to two typewritten pages—especially if the main body of the report is fewer than 50 pages in length.

Needs and Benefits Analysis

This section is typically composed of two primary parts. First, the situation analysis should concisely explain the salesperson's understanding of the customer's situation, problems, and needs. Second, the recommended solution is presented and supported with illustrations and evidence on how the proposed solution uniquely addresses the buyer's problems and needs. The emphasis in this section should be on the benefits resulting from the solution and not on the product or service being sold. It is important that these benefits be described from the perspective of the customer. Proprietary information required in the proposal can be protected in a number of ways. The most common method is to place a notice on the cover (i.e., "Confidential" or "For Review Purposes Only"). Many technology companies ask the prospect to sign a nondisclosure agreement that is part of the overall document, and in some instances, the selling organization will even copyright the proposal.

Company Description

Information about the supplier company offering the proposal is included to demonstrate why the company is the best vendor for this solution. This section offers a succinct overview and background of the firm, but the emphasis should be on the company's capabilities. Case histories of customers for whom the company solved similar problems with similar solutions have proved to be an effective method to document and illustrate organizational capabilities and past successes.

Pricing and Sales Agreement

The previous sections are designed to build the customer-value of the proposed solution. Once this value has been established, the proposal should "ask for the order" by presenting pricing information and delivery options. This information is often presented in the form of a sales agreement for the buyer to sign off on and complete.

Suggested Action and Timetable

The purpose of this section is to make it as easy as possible for the buyer to make a positive purchase decision. In effect, this section should say " . . . if you like the proposal and want to act on it, this is what you do." There may be a contract to sign, an order form to fill out, or instructions regarding who to call to place an order or request further information. A timetable that details a schedule of key implementation events should also be included.

The specific content of a written proposal will vary from situation to situation. Nevertheless, there are certain content expectations and contextual issues that are universal. Salespeople desiring to enhance their proposal writing skills should evaluate the completeness and accuracy of each proposal they write. Exhibit 6.2[4] presents a "Proposal Writing Scorecard" that can provide an effective checklist for evaluating and improving writing skills.

EXHIBIT 6.2   The Proposal Writing Scorecard

The following scorecard evaluates five dimensions that should be contained in effective written proposals: reliability, assurance, tangibles, empathy, and responsiveness. Scoring each of the items in the five sections can assist you in detecting strengths as well as weaknesses. Score each item using this scale: 5 = *Excellent*; 4 = *Good*; 3 = *Average*; 2 = *Poor*; and 1 = *Inadequate*.

Reliability: reflects your (the seller's) ability to identify creative, dependable, and realistic solutions and strategies and match them to the buyer's needs and wants.

Does the Proposal:
_____ 1. Clearly articulate proposed solutions and strategies?
_____ 2. Provide creative and innovative solutions and strategies for the buyer?
_____ 3. Present solutions and strategies appropriate for buyer's business operation and organization?
_____ 4. Provide financial justifications that support the proposed solutions and strategies?
_____ 5. Provide references that support and reflect dependability?
_____ TOTAL FOR RELIABILITY

Assurance: builds the buyer's trust and confidence in your ability to deliver, implement, produce, and/or provide the benefits.

Does the Proposal:
_____ 1. Assure the buyer that proposing organization has qualified, experienced, and competent leadership and staff?
_____ 2. Provide adequate specifications and/or benefits that substantiate ability and capability statements?
_____ 3. Present techniques, methodologies, or processes for assuring quality performance?
_____ 4. Concisely and adequately define project or implementation roles and responsibilities?
_____ 5. Clearly identify and define all fees, prices, and expenses for completing the project?
_____ TOTAL FOR ASSURANCE

Tangibles: enhance and support the communication of your message and invite readership by its overall appearance, content, and organization.

Does the Proposal:
_____ 1. Provide a logical flow of information, ideas and sense of continuity for solving buyer's business problems?
_____ 2. Convert the intangible elements of the solutions or strategies into tangibles?

(continued)

The Proposal Writing Scorecard—_continued_ **EXHIBIT 6.2**

_____ 3. Demonstrate high standards for excellence in format, structure, grammar, spelling, and appearance?

_____ 4. Provide positive indicators to differentiate the proposing organization from their competition?

_____ 5. Contain a letter of transmittal, executive summary, needs and benefits analysis, company description, and the pricing and sales agreement?

_____ TOTAL FOR TANGIBLES

Empathy: confirms your thorough understanding of the buyer's business and their specific needs and wants.

Does the Proposal:

_____ 1. Clearly identify the buyer's specific needs and wants?

_____ 2. Demonstrate a thorough understanding of the buyer's business operation and organization?

_____ 3. Provide solutions and strategies that fit within the buyer's business goals?

_____ 4. Fulfill the buyer's original expectations?

_____ 5. Identify and discuss financial and nonfinancial benefits in terms of their impact on the buyer's unique operation and organization?

_____ TOTAL FOR EMPATHY

Responsiveness: developed in a timely manner and demonstrates a willingness to provide solutions for the buyer's needs and wants and to help measure results.

Does the Proposal:

_____ 1. Meet or beat the completion deadline?

_____ 2. Reflect a genuine willingness to understand the buyer's business operation and organization and to provide viable and flexible solutions and strategies?

_____ 3. Reflect the proposing organization's willingness to work closely with the buyer by enthusiastically asking questions, gathering information, presenting options, and reviewing draft proposals?

_____ 4. Did the proposing organization thoroughly review the final proposal with the buyer and respond to their questions or clarify any outstanding issues and concerns?

_____ 5. Are the proposed solutions or strategies within the buyer's budget and implementation timeframes?

_____ TOTAL FOR RESPONSIVENESS

The expectation for _perfect_ spelling and grammar is universal. Misspelling a customer's name or misstating the title of the recipient or the exact name of the organization risks turning off a prospect. After all, the quality of a salesperson's written documents is a surrogate for that salesperson's competence and ability as well as the capabilities and overall quality of the organization. For this reason, salespeople are well advised to follow the "Twelve Simple Rules for Writing" set out in Exhibit 6.3.[5] Although a well-written proposal is no guarantee of making the sale, a poorly written proposal will certainly reduce the probability of success.

Next, the sales presentation checklist is presented as a tool salespeople can use to make the task of customizing the sales presentation easier.

SALES PRESENTATION CHECKLIST

A **sales presentation checklist** is a useful planning tool to ensure that all the pertinent content areas are covered with each prospect. The sales presentation checklist is best suited for the organized sales presentation. Information is needed from the prospect that will be used to customize the proposal presentation. Exhibit 6.4 illustrates the types of information that salespeople should be collecting throughout the sales process. Section 1 covers specific information on the company name, key contact person, the buyer's job title, and the type of business. It is critically important to determine any others who may

---

EXHIBIT 6.3 Twelve Simple Rules for Writing

- Double check company names, titles, and individuals' names.
- The spelling of words you are not sure of should always be looked up. Do not rely on your word processor's spelling checker.
- Write the proposal and get away from it before proofreading. Give your mind some time away from the document so that it will be fresh when it is time to begin the editing process.
- Proofread and edit for improvements rather than to simply catch mistakes. How can the message be improved in clarity and crispness?
- Repeat the proofreading process and, when possible, have a third party read for meaning, clarity, grammar, and spelling. Another set of eyes can find problems that the writer often overlooks. Don't submit your first draft, as it won't be your best.
- Use hyphens to avoid confusion, but do not place a hyphen after an adverb that ends with *ly*.
- Separate things in a series with a comma, and set off nonessential clauses with a comma.
- Use *that* in restrictive clauses; use *which* in nonrestrictive clauses. (e.g., The sales quota that he announced is too low. He announced the new sales quota, which is too low.)
- Avoid starting sentences with the words *and* or *but*.
- Use *like* for direct comparisons; use *such as* for examples.
- Use a dash to set off and end a thought in a sentence that differs from the preceding concept or thought.
- Periods, commas, and question marks go within quotation marks; semi-colons go outside quotation marks.

---

influence the purchase decision. What departments are involved? What role do they play? This information should be gathered and documented in part B. It is important that the salesperson make sure all the key players are receiving the appropriate information and getting the proper attention they deserve. A mistake often made by salespeople is not identifying all the buying influences.

Salespeople must take the time to uncover the prospect's needs. This can be done by determining a problem (e.g., not enough computer memory) or opportunity (e.g., plant expansion) (section 2, part A of the checklist). At this time, salespeople's ability to gather information is much more important than their ability to give information. A salesperson must refrain from dominating the sales conversation early on with product information before needs are uncovered. As needs are identified, a salesperson should match his or her product's solutions to the needs of the buyer to determine if they can solve the problem (section 2, part B). Salespeople should determine whether they have a good solution. Sometimes, it is in the salesperson's best interest to pass on the business and recommend a competitor's solution. This is a great way to build trust with a buyer.

In Section 3 of the checklist, salespeople attempt to define the prospect's buying motives. In other words, from the prospect's perspective, what is most important in making this purchase decision? What will motivate the buyer to make a purchase? Buying motives may be rational or emotional, or a combination of both rational and emotional. **Rational buying motives** typically relate to the economics of the situation, including, cost, profitability, quality, services offered, and the total value of the seller's offering perceived by the customer. **Emotional motives** such as fear, the need for security, the need for status, or the need to be liked, are sometimes difficult for salespeople to uncover as prospects are generally less likely to share such motives with salespeople. In business-to-business selling, rational motives are typically the most important buying motives, but salespeople should not ignore emotional motives if they are known to exist.

Understanding the competitive situation is essential in sales presentation planning. Since buyers make competitive comparisons in making purchase decisions, salespeople should do the same prior to the sales presentation. Section 4 of the Sales Presentation

Sales Presentation Checklist   EXHIBIT 6.4

1. Prospect Information
A. Key person information

Company Name:_____   Type of Business: _____

Contact Person: _____   Job Title:_____

B. Other influences on the purchase decision

Name(s)	Departments	Role in Purchase Decision

2. Needs and/or Opportunity Analysis
A. Statement of prospect's problem and/or opportunity as related to sales offering

_____
_____
_____
_____
_____

B. Brief description of product or service that will meet the prospect's problem/opportunity

_____
_____
_____
_____
_____

3. Prospect's Buying Motives: From the prospect's view point, what is most important in making this purchase decision?

Rational Motives (often economic issues such as cost, quality, and service capabilities)	Emotional Motives (such as status, security, and fear)

(continued)

EXHIBIT 6.4   **Sales Presentation Checklist—*continued***

4. Competitive Situation: Include current suppliers (if applicable) and other key competiton.

Competitor	Strengths	Weakness

5. Sales Presentation Objectives: State as Customer action(s) sought by the salesperson.

Major Objectives	Minor Objectives

6. Sales Presentation Planning: Linking benefits, support information, and reinforcement methods. Specific benefits should correspond to prospect's buying motives from section 3.

A. Specific Benefits: Benefits to be stressed are arranged in priority order (sequence to be followed in presentation unless prospect feedback during the presentation indicates an alternative sequence)	B. Information needed to support claims for each benefit	C. Where appropriate, methods for reinforcing verbal content (AV, collateral material, illustrations, testimonials, etc.)
1. ⟶	1. ⟶	1.
2. ⟶	2. ⟶	2.
3. ⟶	3. ⟶	3.
4. ⟶	4. ⟶	4.
List all relevant benefits for this buying situation		

7. Approach (Introduce yourself, give thanks for the appointment, build rapport, then use all or part of the ADAPT method, depending on how much is known about the prospect)

Plans for the first few minutes of the sales presentation:
Introduction, thanks, then: _____
Assessment _____
Discovery _____
Activation _____
Project _____
Transition to Presentation _____

(continued)

Sales Presentation Checklist—*continued*   EXHIBIT 6.4

8. Questions and objections

Anticipated prospect questions and objections, and planned responses

Questions and Objections	Responses

9. Prospect commitment

A preliminary plan for how the prospect will be asked for a commitment related to the sales presentation objective

10. Follow-up action

Statement of follow-up action needed to ensure that the buyer–seller relationship moves in a positive direction

Checklist asks the salesperson to specify key competitors along with their strengths and weaknesses. By knowing their own product's strengths and weaknesses as well as those of competitive products, salespeople are better equipped to position their offering competitively. If the prospect is already buying a similar product, knowledge about the current supplier can give the salesperson important insight into which buying motives and product attributes are of likely importance to the buyer.

Section 5 asks the salesperson to determine the objective for his or her sales call. Salespeople must have an objective for each sales call. Many salespeople think there is only one objective and that is to get an order. Other sales objectives do exist. For instance, during an introductory call the objective may be simply to introduce the salesperson and his or her company and to gather information on the buyer's needs. Eventually, the major sales presentation objective will be to present the proposal for the buyer's acceptance. After the sale is made, the objective may be to follow up and determine whether the customer is satisfied with the salesperson's efforts. The salesperson can also look for openings to cover additional objectives. Gwen Tranguillo of Hershey's always looks for ways to introduce other products in her presentation if the buyer expresses interest. Gwen made a major sales presentation on a Halloween display of king-size candies and found the buyer very interested in adding more king sizes immediately. She shifted gears and gained commitment on the new king-size display and later in the presentation went back to her Halloween proposal. At the very least, the heart of any presentation should be to advance the process toward an order.

Section 6 focuses on specific benefits that are important to the prospect, the information that is needed to support claims made to stated benefits, and sales tools such as visual aids that can reinforce them. After the salesperson has gathered all the information needed (i.e., buyer has need, who are the competitors, and what are the specific sales presentation objectives), he or she must determine what specific features/benefits are of interest to the buyer (part A). Those features/benefits of high importance to the buyer and his or her buying motives should be covered first. It may only take one or two benefits to gain commitment. During this stage, the salesperson should be using information (e.g., satisfied clients, success stories) to support the claims for each benefit (part B). The salesperson must be able to support competitive claims for each benefit that he or she discusses with the customer (i.e., how does this benefit compare to your competitors?). The salesperson will not always be asked to provide support for claims he or she makes, but he or she must be prepared to offer support for competitive claims if asked to do so by the customer. Different ways to support competitive claims include testimonials from satisfied customers, third-party information as provided by research studies or trade publications, and any other type of evidence that the salesperson may develop to support his or her claims.

The salesperson should have at his or her disposal visual sales aids that can help sell a point (section 6, part C in the checklist). Salespeople must realize that although what they say is important, it is extremely critical to pay attention to how they say it and how they illustrate it with appropriate sales tools. The salesperson should be cautious with the use of humor, taking care to avoid anything that may be exploitative, tactless, or self-deprecating.

Salespeople should remember that sales tools are to be used only to make the sales message more credible, more clear, and more memorable. They should support the main points in the presentation rather than bombard the prospect with information. Too many illustrations, films, and demonstrations can confuse the prospect and be counterproductive to the sales effort. Module 7 covers sales tools and their value to the sales presentation.

Section 7 addresses the critical first few minutes of the sales call. During the first few minutes of the sales call, the salesperson must establish rapport with the prospect, focus his or her attention on the offering, and make a smooth transition into the presentation. The salesperson must be sure that he or she properly introduces himself or herself when calling on a new prospect. During the first few minutes of the sales call, it is recommended that the salesperson use questions to get the prospect involved in the call and that the salesperson listen very carefully to what the prospect has to say about his or her situation. Salespeople should be positive and friendly here and throughout the sales presentation. The salesperson should tell the customer why he or she is making the call. This helps to establish an agenda and put the customer at ease. The salesperson should be flexible and willing to adjust if the customer has other ideas about the agenda. Salespeople only have a few minutes to make a good first impression with the buyer. Planning the first few minutes can help guarantee things get started well early in the sales call.

Obviously the first few minutes of the sales call will be greatly influenced by previous interaction (if any) between the buyer and the salesperson. For example, if previous sales calls have established buyer needs and the buyer has agreed to a sales presentation, the first few minutes will be quite different than if this is the first sales call on this prospect. The ADAPT questioning process (refer to Module 4) can be used in part or whole to acquire needed information and make a transition to the sales presentation. As a guide, the salesperson should respect the buyer's time and get to the presentation as soon as circumstances allow. The salesperson should not rush to get to the presentation, and certainly should not launch into a presentation without establishing buyer needs and interest in it. In section 8, salespeople should think about and practice responses to common questions and objections that they are typically asked. Salespeople should rarely be caught off guard with questions and objections that they cannot answer. Once questions have been adequately answered, this is a good time to look for commitment opportunities. As the buyer sees that his or her preliminary concerns are not concerns at all (e.g., salesperson explains deliveries can be made daily), then the salesperson must be ready to ask for the business (section 9). Strategies and methods of handling buyer questions and objections and earning a commitment are covered in Module 8 of the text.

Finally, the salesperson must always be looking for ways to enhance the relationship and move it in a positive direction (section 10). The salesperson should always make a note of any promises that he or she has made during the sales calls and especially during the proposal presentation. The buyer may ask for information that the salesperson is not prepared to give during the presentation. By taking notes, the salesperson ensures that the appropriate follow-up activities will happen.

This sales presentation checklist is an extremely useful tool for all salespeople and especially to inexperienced salespeople. It guarantees that all the appropriate steps are covered and all the pertinent information needed is collected. Using a sales presentation checklist will make the task of customizing the sales presentation easier.

SEQUENCE OF THE SALES PRESENTATION AND PLANNING THE INITIAL SALES CALL

Once the salesperson has sufficient background information, he or she is ready to plan the initial sales call. A well-planned sales call can help reduce stress and give the salesperson needed confidence. Many sales organizations today are making the first call that a salesperson makes a "getting-to-know-you" call that introduces the seller by collecting information on the buyer's background and needs. The first call is not to sell the product but to lay the groundwork for future calls and eventual sales.

The salesperson must establish presentation objectives for each sales call. The salesperson must ask himself or herself what he or she hopes to accomplish on this sales call. Salespeople know that most sales are not closed during the first or even second contact with the customer. Getting the order is the ultimate objective, but most of the time salespeople call on buyers to accomplish other objectives such as:

1. introducing the salesperson and his or her company;
2. obtaining personal and business information;
3. providing company literature for the prospect to review;
4. conducting a needs assessment;
5. demonstrating a new product offering;
6. providing post-sale service.

After completing the sales presentation checklist, the salesperson should have the information needed to determine the basic sequences for the key points in the presentation.

The tactical planning of the sales presentation is to determine the basic sequence for the key points in the presentation. With an organized presentation, there should be some flexibility to allow adaptation to prospect questions and interests. Nonetheless, it is a good idea to have the key points arranged in a logical, sequential order.

There are few ironclad rules about how to order a sales presentation. Certainly, the appropriate sequence will be dictated by the situation, including priority to the prospect's preferences. A few general rules can be offered:

- Following an adequate introduction of the salesperson and the salesperson's company, questions, and careful listening, confirmation statements should be used to clarify and define explicit customer needs as related to the salesperson's offering.

- Benefits should be presented in order of importance according to the prospect's needs, and these benefits may be repeated during the presentation and at the conclusion of the presentation.

- If the sales presentation is a continuation of one or more previous sales calls, a quick summary should be made of what has been agreed on in the past, moving quickly into the prospect's primary area of interest.

- As a general rule, pricing issues should not be focused on until the prospect's needs have been defined and the salesperson has shown how those needs can be addressed with the product or service being sold. After prospects fully understand how the product or service meets their needs, they can make informed judgments on price/value issuses.

SALES MIX MODEL

To this point, our discussion of the sales presentation planning process should have clearly suggested a need for a specific objective for each presentation and a need to determine the basic format of the presentation. In general terms, we have spoken of blending information into a palatable sales message. This is best done within the context of the **sales mix model** shown in Figure 6.3. The model includes five variables that require planning effort: presentation pace, presentation scope, depth of inquiry, degree of two-way communication, and use of visual aids.

Presentation pace refers to the speed with which the salesperson intends to move through the presentation. The appropriate pace will be determined largely by the preference of the prospect and may be affected by such variables as complexity of the product or the number of products to be presented. Another determinant of pace would be past experiences with a particular customer, as a quicker pace may be possible with a familiar customer.

Presentation scope involves the selection of benefits and terms of sale to be included in the presentation. This narrowing-down process can be a challenge for the knowledge-laden salesperson, who may know more about the product than will be of interest to the prospect. Time and again, we see reports of jargon-spouting salespeople who have talked themselves out of a sale through indiscriminate use of their extensive product knowledge. An illustration of this problem comes from Charles O'Meara, an expert who advises

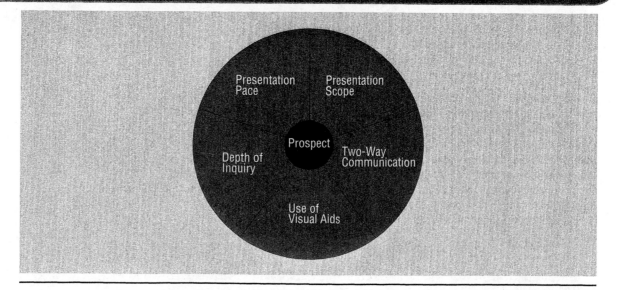

Figure 6.3 — Sales Mix Model

Five variables require planning effort after the salesperson has set objectives for the presentation and selected a basic presentation format.

customers on how to buy stereo equipment. O'Meara says that if a salesperson "tries to, say, inundate your aural sensibility with a plethora of polysyllabic terminology—watch out! Either the salesperson is trying to confuse you or he is a techie who can't relate to other human beings. The salesperson should talk technical only if the customer wants to talk technical."[6]

Depth of inquiry refers to the extent to which the salesperson goes to ascertain the prospect's needs and decision process. Some of this information may have been gained in the preapproach, and some probing is usually necessary during the presentation. The planning task is simply to identify gaps in needed information and plan the presentation accordingly.

The issue of **two-way communication** is partially addressed when the salesperson selects a basic format for the presentation. By definition, the canned presentation does not allow for significant two-way communication. The organized presentation allows for, and usually encourages, a two-way flow. The degree of interactive flow is often dictated by buyer expertise, with more allowance for two-way flow planned with expert buyers.

Visual aids to supplement the spoken word have become an important element in sales presentations, and their use must be carefully planned. Unless sales aids are used with caution, they may actually detract from, rather than enhance, the sales presentation. When properly orchestrated, visual aids ranging from flip charts to video demonstrations can be valuable tools during the sales presentation. The computer is increasingly being used as the basic tool for enhancing presentations. Multimedia packages are plentiful and inexpensive, and packages such as PowerPoint are routinely used to construct and integrate photographs, graphics, statistical data, sound effects, and video into a complete presentation.

After the sales presentation is planned, the salesperson is ready to shift to an active selling mode. Although the customer may have been contacted earlier in the sales process, the emphasis has been on information gathering and planning. Now, the actual selling begins as the salesperson seeks an interview with the prospect.

APPROACHING THE CUSTOMER

Approaching the customer involves two phases. The first phase is securing an appointment for the sales interview. The second phase covers the first few minutes of the sales call. Each step in the sales process is critical, and the approach is no exception. In today's competitive environment, a good first impression is essential to lay the groundwork for subsequent steps in the sales process. A bad first impression on the customer can be difficult or impossible to overcome.

Getting an Appointment

Most initial sales calls on new prospects require an appointment. Requesting an appointment accomplishes several desirable outcomes. First, the salesperson is letting the prospect know that the salesperson thinks the prospect's time is important. Second, there is a better chance that the salesperson will receive the undivided attention of the prospect during the sales call. Third, setting appointments is a good tool to assist the salesperson in effective time and territory management. The importance of setting appointments is clearly proclaimed in a survey of secretaries, administrative assistants, and other "gatekeepers" responsible for scheduling appointments. A majority of respondents thought that arriving unannounced to make a sales call is a violation of business etiquette.[7] Given this rather strong feeling of those who represent buyers, it is a good idea to request an appointment if there is any doubt about whether one is required.

The following "An Ethical Dilemma" demonstrates the importance of trust and why doing an end run around a gatekeeper is unacceptable.

Appointments may be requested by phone, mail (including e-mail), or personal contact. By far, setting appointments by telephone is the most popular method. Combining mail and telephone communications to seek appointments is also commonplace. Regardless of the communications vehicle used, salespeople can improve their chances of getting an appointment by following three simple directives: give the prospect a reason why an appointment should be granted; request a specific amount of time; and suggest a specific time for the appointment. These tactics recognize that prospects are busy individuals who do not spend time idly.

In giving a reason why the appointment should be granted, a well-informed salesperson can appeal to the prospect's primary buying motive as related to one of the benefits of the salesperson's offering. Being specific is recommended. For example, it is better to say that "you can realize gross margins averaging 35 percent on our product line" than "our margins are really quite attractive."

Specifying the amount of time needed to make the sales presentation alleviates some of the anxiety felt by a busy prospect at the idea of spending some of his or her already scarce time. It also helps the prospect if the salesperson suggests a time and date for the sales call. It is very difficult for busy individuals to respond to a question such as, "What would be a good time for you next week?" In effect, the prospect is being asked to scan his or her entire calendar for an opening. If a suggested time and date are not convenient, the interested prospect will typically suggest another. Once a salesperson has an appointment with the prospect and all the objectives have been established, the salesperson should send a fax or e-mail that outlines the agenda for the meeting and reminds the buyer of the appointment.

Starting the Sales Call

Having secured an appointment with a qualified, presumably interested prospect, the salesperson should plan to accomplish some important tasks during the first few minutes of the call. First in importance is to establish a harmonious atmosphere for discussion. Common rules of etiquette and courtesy apply here. Some preliminary small talk is usually part of the ritual, then the discussion should turn to business. Adaptive salespeople can learn how to interpret the prospect's signals and move into the sales message reasonably soon.

Initiating Contact

The old adage "you only get one chance to make a first impression" has never been truer than in the sales arena. Proper dress, etiquette, and courtesy will be the first things that a buyer notices about the salesperson. Kim Davenport, district manger for Shering-Plough, discusses the importance of making good first impressions in "Professional Selling in the 21st Century: Making a Good First Impression."

Making a Good First Impression

Kim Davenport, district manager for Shering-Plough, has seen his industry change since 1977, in regard to what is accepted as professional dress. Salespeople are allowed to wear beards and mustaches as long as they are groomed properly (i.e., short, neatly trimmed, not shaggy). What salespeople are allowed to wear has changed dramatically over the years. Today (particularly in the south during the summer season) men and women sales representatives routinely wear short-sleeve golf shirts that have Shering-Plough's name on the front for identification. Kim says it is almost a necessity in towns like Scottsdale, Arizona, where temperatures reach 120 degrees in the summer. First impressions are still important according to Kim and looking professional is the key. Dressing attractively and giving special attention to grooming will always pay off.

The second thing that the buyer will notice is the first few words that come out of the salesperson's mouth. Although salespeople do not want to sound as if their words and messages are memorized, they should be rehearsed and flow freely. For example,

> Mr. Smith, I want to thank you for taking the time to see me. I'm Betty Brown from Hershey Chocolate, U.S.A. The reason I am here today is to introduce myself and my company and to find out a few things about you and your store (generally done while shaking hands).

An introduction approach by itself falls short of gaining the customer's attention. The introductions are usually followed by a statement that gets the customer to react and start talking. Salespeople have used many different approaches effectively over the years. The salesperson must attempt to use an approach to gain the prospect's attention. Depending on the selling situation, several strategies can be effectively used to approach the prospect. We briefly discuss some of the more popular approaches, and they are summarized in Exhibit 6.5.

Introductory Approach

The **introductory approach** is the most frequently used technique, but by itself it is one of the weakest. It does not gain the prospect's attention. For example, the salesperson walks into the buyer's office and says: "Hello, I am Jon Jacobs from Hormel."

Possible Approach Methods	**EXHIBIT 6.5**
Introductory Approach	Professionally greet prospect with name and company.
Product Approach	Immediately show the prospect the product to see and touch.
Benefit Approach	Offer the prospect a benefit that most buyers think is appropriate.
Question Approach	Get the prospect involved in the sales call by asking an appropriate question.
Referral Approach	Mention the name of a mutual friend who referred you to the prospect.
Compliment Approach	Offer a compliment to the buyer about the buyer or the company.
Survey Approach	Ask the prospect for permission to survey the company's needs in your product category.

This approach gains minimal attention and probably generates the least interest. Therefore, an introductory approach should be used with other approaches to generate more interest. A possible approach might be: "Hello, I am Jon Jacobs from Hormel; we have introduced a new chili in our test markets that has outsold all other chili's by 35 percent. I have brought some for you to sample." This statement gathers attention, promotes interest, and provides a transition to the sales presentation.

Product Approach

Some products can be easily carried into the buyer's office to handle, try, feel, taste, or smell. Thus, the **product approach** should maximize the use of a prospect's senses. This can be an excellent way to show the buyer the benefits being offered and gain prospect involvement. Sometimes, a salesperson cannot bring the actual product to the buyer because of its size. The salesperson must use other means to simulate the actual product. Literature, sample output, or any usual tool such as computer-generated graphics, slides, or videotapes can be used.

Benefit Approach

Many successful approaches begin with a strong statement about a benefit that the product brings to the customer. Benefits might include 30 percent faster, 20 percent less expensive, better value, more efficient, or more market coverage. The **benefit approach** is especially valuable if it is addressed to the buyer's dominant buying motive. The downside to this approach centers on describing benefits that may not be important to the buyer. This approach is better left until after specific needs are determined.

Question Approach

The **question approach** is best used by describing an interesting characteristic about the product and then following it up with a question. It is hoped that a good question will trigger the prospect's thinking about a problem they need solved. The salesperson might say: "We've added three new flavors to our product line. Do you have time for me to tell you about them?"

Once the salesperson asks the question, he or she must listen carefully to the response. If the answer is yes, then the salesperson should proceed with an enthusiastic presentation of the three new flavors. If the answer is no, then the salesperson should find out when an appropriate time might be.

Referral Approach

Citing the name of a satisfied customer or friend of the prospect (after receiving their approval to use their name) can begin an effective sales call. It is important to remember that the **referral approach** can have a negative effect if the prospect and referral are not as good friends as the referral thinks. It is important not to drop names and act as if buyers are happy customers when they are not. An example of a referral approach might be: "Mr. Todd, I am here at the suggestion of your south-side store manager, Mr. Frost. He thought you might be interested in our new product line. We put it in for them last month, and Mr. Frost is very happy with the results."

Compliment Approach

Everyone enjoys a compliment. If the **compliment approach** is sincere, it may be an effective beginning to a sales call. However, insincere flattery is often obvious and offensive to prospects. Compliments must be both specific and sincere and of real interest to the prospect.

A salesperson's use of an inappropriate compliment follows: "Mr. Smith, I really like the open concept of your office building." On the surface, this compliment does not appear to be anything that a salesperson should not say. However, the compliment was not specific and agitated the buyer. The buyer hated the open concept because there was no privacy and it was impossible to shut the door when the office building was noisy.

The salesperson should have said: "Mr. Smith, the open concept of your office building really makes the rooms look bigger." The buyer could now respond that it certainly makes the rooms appear bigger, but he dislikes it because there is no privacy and the rooms are too noisy.

Survey Approach

The **survey approach** uses gathering information as an attention-getting statement. The salesperson approaches clients and offers to survey their business in a particular functional area. For instance, a computer salesperson might survey all the departments to determine whether all their data processing needs are being met. This approach is time-consuming, and the salesperson runs the risk of doing a lot of work with no guarantee of an order. Some organizations provide the survey approach as a service to promote goodwill and build the relationship with the customer.

Assessing the Situation and Discovering Needs through ADAPT

One of the most important communication skills for salespeople is questioning skills. Asking the right questions at the right time helps salespeople identify needed information about the organization's buying process. This ensures that the buyer understands what the salesperson is communicating. Developing and asking effective questions requires planning and practice. Planning a general questioning strategy can be an effective approach to actively engage a buyer during a sales interaction. The ADAPT process, as covered in Module 4, is one approach that can be used in many selling situations. The acronym ADAPT is appropriate for this questioning process because, as the name implies, it is flexible and can be made to apply to almost any situation.

SUMMARY

1. **Discuss the different types of sales presentations and what goes into their planning.** The three types of presentations most organizations use are canned presentations, organized presentations, and written sales proposals. Canned presentations include scripted sales calls, memorized presentations, and automated presentations. Most canned presentations have been tested for effectiveness with real customers before they are used by the entire salesforce. Canned presentations are usually complete and logically structured. Objectives are anticipated in advance, and appropriate responses can be formulated as part of the presentation. Organized presentations best address individual customers and different selling situations. A salesperson must be prepared to adapt to each prospect's specific needs. Only those benefits that meet that specific buyer's needs will be addressed. A written sales proposal is a complete, self-contained sales presentation. A sales proposal should be prepared after the salesperson has made a thorough assessment of the buyer's situation as it relates to the seller's offering.

2. **Determine when it is best to use the three types of sales presentations.** The canned or memorized presentation is best used when customer needs and buying motives are homogeneous. The canned presentation today is used by few companies. It is still used by telemarketers and a few companies with inexperienced salesforces (e.g., interns selling knives during the summer). The organized presentation is best used to meet the needs of individual customers that present different selling situations.

Most business-to-business sales use the organized presentation. This approach allows much needed flexibility to adapt to buyer feedback and changing circumstances during the presentation. The written sales proposal is a complete self-centered sales presentation, but it is often accompanied by other verbal sales presentations before or after the proposal is delivered. A written proposal is often used when a great deal of technical information is required. This allows the customer the opportunity to digest all the material. In some cases, the customer may receive a proposal and then request that the salesperson make a sales call to further explain the proposal and provide answers to questions.

3. **Discuss the importance of using a sales presentation checklist.** The sales presentation checklist is extremely useful to inexperienced salespeople. It guarantees that all the appropriate steps of the sales process are covered and all pertinent information is collected. Using the checklist will make the task of customizing the sales presentation easier.

4. **Discuss the importance of planning the initial sales call.** Once the salesperson has sufficient background information, he or she is ready to plan the initial sales call. A well-planned sales call can help reduce stress and give the salesperson needed confidence.

5. **Discuss how the sales mix model enhances the planning effort.** When the salesperson has to blend a great deal of information into a palatable sales message, the salesperson can use the sales mix model to get this done. The model includes five variables that require planning effort: presentation pace, presentation scope, depth of inquiry, degree of two-way communication, and use of visual aids.

6. **Explain how to approach and initiate contact with each prospect.** Salespeople only get one chance to make a first impression. Proper dress, etiquette, and courtesy will be the first things that a buyer notices about the salesperson. The first few words that come out of a salesperson's mouth may be critical to his or her success. An introduction approach should be used with other approaches to generate more interest.

UNDERSTANDING PROFESSIONAL SELLING TERMS

sales presentation planning
canned presentations
organized sales presentations
written sales proposal
sales presentation checklist
rational buying motives
emotional motives
sales mix model
presentation pace
presentation scope
depth of inquiry

two-way communication
visual aids
approaching the customer
introductory approach
product approach
benefit approach
question approach
referral approach
compliment approach
survey approach

DEVELOPING PROFESSIONAL SELLING KNOWLEDGE

1. Why is sales presentation preplanning important?
2. Do you see the need for a salesperson to ever use a canned sales presentation?
3. Most salespeople use organized presentations today. Why?
4. Explain why both verbal and written communication are a necessity for a successful salesperson.
5. Explain why written proposals are becoming a necessity for today's salesperson.

6. Why is the sales presentation checklist an important tool for today's salesperson?

7. How does the sales mix model help prepare the salesperson for an effective presentation?

8. Why is it important for a salesperson to establish objectives for each sales call?

9. Why is it important for a salesperson to have a number of different approach techniques at his or her disposal?

10. Why is the introductory approach by itself a weak opening technique?

BUILDING PROFESSIONAL SELLING SKILLS

1. The salesperson's appearance and manner must convey a favorable impression. Within the first few minutes that the prospect and the salesperson are together, the prospect makes judgments that will have a direct effect on the interaction to follow. The first few words the salesperson says set the tone of the entire presentation. There are several approaches that can be used to gain the prospect's interest and attention.

   a) Introduction—The sales rep states his or her name and the name of the company. What are the strengths and weaknesses of this opening?

   b) Referral—Start out by mentioning that so-and-so suggested the prospect would be interested in your product.
   What are the strengths and weaknesses of this opening?

   c) Question—Asking a meaningful question gets the prospect's attention, encourages a response, and initiates two-way communication.
   What are the strengths and weaknesses of this opening?

   d) Benefit—Focus the prospect's attention on a product benefit.
   What are the strengths and weaknesses of this opening?

   e) Compliment—Offer a sincere and specific compliment.
   What are the strengths and weaknesses of this opening?

   f) Develop an approach that uses a combination of the preceding methods.
   What are the strengths and weaknesses of this opening?
   Which methods did you select to combine? Why?

2. **Situation:** Read the Ethical Dilemma on page 160.

   Characters: Tom Lawrence, sales representative; sales manager; customer

   Scene 1: *Location*—Tom in his sales manager's office. *Action*—Sales manager addresses his concern that Tom doesn't do enough precall planning and talks about features not relevant to the buyer.

ROLE PLAY

   Role play Tom and his boss's conversation.

   Scene 2: *Location*—Tom in one of his customer's office. *Action*—Tom begins his sales conversation without asking any questions and determining needs. He goes right into features.

   Role play Tom and his customer's conversation.

   Upon completion of the role plays, address the following questions:

   2a. What are the potential problems for Tom?
   2b. Can you think of any reason why Tom may be afraid to precall plan and ask questions?

3. **Situation:** Read the Ethical Dilemma on page 174.

   Characters: Mary Clark, salesperson; secretary

   Scene 1: *Location*—Client's office. *Action*—Mary calls in-person on company on which she has used this technique.

ROLE PLAY

Role play the secretary asking Mary why she was selling under the guise of research when she was really calling for an appointment. The secretary and data processing manager had compared notes and knew Mary was less than truthful.

Scene 2:   *Location*—Mary's office. *Action*—Mary calls on the phone to the secretary.

Role play the secretary asking Mary a few questions about what kind of research she is doing. Who does Mary work for? For what will she use the data she is collecting?

Upon completion of the role play, address the following questions:

3a. What happens when the secretary starts asking questions?

3b. What are the potential long-term ramifications of Mary's actions? Short term?

4. Go to a search engine like Yahoo.com. Type in "sales, planning the call" or "sales, precall planning." What did you find? Browse through some of these Web sites. What do the so-called experts have to say about precall planning? Write a memo to your boss suggesting some actions your office can take to improve their precall planning based on the Web site information you found. Make sure you reference the Web sites you browsed.

MAKING PROFESSIONAL SELLING DECISIONS

Case 6.1: The New Salesperson

Lon Taylor has been working for three months for a large chemical company that sells fertilizers to farm co-ops and distributors. He has just completed his training and is ready to go into the field. He has been taught how to gather precall information and prepare for his presentation. He has targeted his biggest distributor for his first call. The appointment has been set; he is ready to go in for a fact-finding call and hopefully some preliminary talk about one of his new products that has been launched in the past two weeks. Lon is calling on Perry Martin, general manager of the distributorship. Lon was in for a big surprise. Perry greeted Lon with, "I've been waiting for you, follow me." Lon followed Perry out to the warehouse where he directed Lon's attention to three large pallets of Lon's products. The top pallet was leaking chemicals all over the pallets below and onto the floor. Perry went on to complain that he'd called the 800 number service hotline three times trying to get someone out to take care of the mess. This totally caught Lon off guard.

Questions

1. What should Lon do now?
2. Lon has a well-prepared presentation on his new product he wants to give. What should he do about this information gathering call?

Situation: Read Case 6.1

Characters: Lon Taylor, sales repre-
             sentative; Perry Martin, general
             manger; Todd Cravens, Lon's boss

Scene 1:   *Location*—Distributor's warehouse.
          Action—A rather agitated Perry
          points out the leaking chemicals.

Role play Lon's response to Perry.

Scene 2:   *Location*—Lon on the phone to his
          boss, Todd. *Action*—Lon tries to get
          to the bottom of why customer serv-
          ice has not let anyone know about his
          customer's problem.

Role play Lon's call to his boss, Todd.

Upon completion of the role play, address the following questions:

1. How should Lon handle an agitated Perry?
2. How should sales and customer service work together in the future to make sure this does not happen again?

Case 6.2: The Overhead Door Company

Mary Tyler sells for The Overhead Door Company. She has sold garage doors to contractors and individual homeowners for two years. When Mary first began selling, she used to introduce herself as the name of her company. Next, she made a brief opening remark and then moved quickly into her presentation. Although this resulted in selling many garage doors, Mary thought that there must be a better method.

Questions

1. What can you recommend to Mary to strengthen the introduction of her sales calls?
2. If Mary is successful using her present method, why should she change?

Situation: Read Case 6.2

Characters: Mary Tyler, sales represen- **ROLE PLAY**
             tative; customer

Scene 1:   *Location*—Mary is on the phone call-
          ing a new prospect. *Action*—Mary
          introduces herself.

Role play Mary's introduction and try different approach techniques.

Upon completion of the role play, address the following questions:

1. Do you think some openings are more effective than others?
2. Which ones do you find effective?
3. Which approach techniques do you find difficult to use? Why?

Developing Customer Relationships

Part Three is comprised of two modules that focus on the interpersonal interaction which results in an established relationship between buyer and seller. Module 7 discusses sales presentation delivery, while Module 8 covers addressing concerns and earning a commitment from the customer.

In Module 7, we concentrate on establishing a productive buyer–seller dialogue. To accomplish a productive dialogue, the salesperson must understand how to communicate benefits to the buyer in an effective manner. The use of sales aids such as audio visual support material is discussed. Module 7 concludes with a section on special strategies and tactics for selling to groups.

Module 8 discusses why buyers may raise objections or resist the sales proposition and how salespeople can deal with resistance in a professional, ethical manner. We present specific methods for handling objections and earning a commitment from the buyer without employing high-pressure tactics.

KRAFT PRESENTATIONS USE TECHNOLOGY THAT FOCUSES ON THE CUSTOMER

Chris Hogan, vice president of sales information for Kraft Foods, is an expert on using technology to enhance sales presentations. He was named winner of the Best Use of Technology in the National Sales and Marketing Awards competition sponsored by *Sales and Marketing Management* magazine in 2003. To build business with retailers, Kraft's 2,000 salespeople use a proprietary software tool called the 3-Step Category Insight Builder. The 3-Step Builder identifies consumer buying behavior within a product category, isolates the opportunity to build business within the category, and provides the insights to build an action-oriented business plan. The plan guides the retailer on which products to stock on specific shelves, where to position its house brand, and how to optimize promotional performance.

Kraft also uses another proprietary software tool called the Promotion Insight Builder to analyze and create promotions built around major events. For example, Mr. Hogan says, "Take the Super Bowl. We look at that and determine foods that will be eaten during the halftime show—such as dips. Kraft has many products for snacking so we develop our promotions accordingly."

Chris Hogan knows that the success of Kraft's sales technology ultimately depends on how well it delivers value to retailers and to the Kraft salesforce: "We believe that one must start with the consumer, get to know his needs, and use that technology to build a program that drives business."

Source: From Linda Strnad, "Top of Their Class," *Sales and Marketing Management,* (February 2004): 53–61.

During the **sales presentation**, the salesperson expands on the rapport, knowledge, and understanding established in the preceding portions of the sales process and during previous sales calls. It is in this phase of the selling process that the salesperson presents a solution to the buyer's needs, nurtures the buyer's perceived value of the sales offering as a unique solution for the individual buyer, and confirms the buyer's understanding of and interest in obtaining the benefits offered by the salesperson's solution.

The sales presentation has been compared to doing surgery in that it is complex and requires preparation, knowledge, and skill.[1] Prior to conducting surgery, the doctor has acquired a great deal of relevant information from a variety of sources and developed a comprehensive understanding of the patient's problems and needs. Based on this understanding of the patient's needs, the surgeon utilizes his or her training and skills in combination with an assortment of tools to conduct a surgical procedure unique to the individual patient's needs. Continuing the analogy, up to the point of the presentation in the selling process the salesperson has been developing his or her knowledge and understanding of the buyer's situation and needs. Now, in the form of an effective presentation, the salesperson presents a solution that is specific and customized to the needs of the buyer, illustrates and demonstrates the benefits of the solution, and confirms the buyer's belief in and desire to obtain the benefits.

Good salespeople are very much like good surgeons in that they are serious in what they do and leave nothing to chance. They work with the prospective buyer

Objectives

After completing this module, you should be able to

1 Describe the difference between features, potential benefits, and confirmed benefits and the role they play in benefits selling.

2 Construct complete selling points using feature and benefit statements.

3 Explain the four steps of the SELL Sequence.

4 Discuss the advantages of using response-checks in the selling presentation.

5 List and explain the different forms of presentation tools and sales aids that can increase the impact of a presentation.

6 Delineate the four steps of the SPES process for effectively utilizing sales aids in presentations.

7 Explain some of the special considerations in making sales presentations to groups.

EXHIBIT 7.1   Keys to Effective Sales Presentations

1. Sales presentations should be guided by at least one major objective that requires customer action as a result of the presentation.
2. Sales presentations should have a clear, easy to follow structure. The use of the Sales Presentation Checklist (see Module 6) provides such a structure.
3. Understand customer needs before making a complete sales presentation.
4. Focus on needs and buying motives that the customer confirms as being important.
5. Present the solution, or value proposition, in terms of benefits the customer will experience as a result of making a purchase.
6. Seek confirmation from the customer that the benefits offered are important to the customer, and that your proposition can deliver them.
7. Plan for, and encourage, customer interaction during the presentation. Strive for a productive two-way dialogue, which can be achieved through active listening and questioning.
8. Use audio visuals and other sales tools to reinforce key points, but do not let technology and sales tools overwhelm the message.
9. Guard against annoying mannerisms and statements. Be positive and specific throughout the presentation.
10. Be prepared if the presentation is successful. Make it easy for the customer to make a purchase.

---

to identify, diagnose, and clarify unsatisfied needs or problems and then show the buyer how much better the situation would be by purchasing the proposed product or service. For some keys to effective sales presentations see Exhibit 7.1.

NEEDS-GAP ANALYSIS: SELECTING APPROPRIATE CUSTOMER OFFERINGS BY ASSESSING NEEDS

The simple fact that a qualified prospect can buy does not translate that he or she will buy. Need alone is not sufficient. A prospect will buy after being convinced that by purchasing your product, he or she will be substantially better off. As discussed in Module 6, "Planning the Presentation and Approaching the Customer," the approach stage begins the information gathering stage. The salesperson works to build rapport, gets acquainted with the prospect, and initiates the process of needs identification and clarification. Using a questioning sequence such as **SPIN** or **ADAPT** (for a full discussion of SPIN and ADAPT see Module 4, "Communication Skills") the salesperson explores the buyer's situation to identify missed opportunities, dissatisfactions, needs, and problems. The salesperson must ask questions, probe for details, and listen carefully to what the prospective buyer is saying. This step may even take more than one sales call depending on the amount of probing and clarifying that must take place to understand the prospect's needs. The salesperson's primary goal is to uncover the prospect's specific needs or problems and then focus on what products or services will solve the problem or meet the specific needs.

Based on the prospective buyer's identified and confirmed needs, the salesperson reviews the possible product and service options in order to select or create a solution that satisfies the buyer's needs and problems. The salesperson describes and builds desire for the recommended solution by detailing features of the solution as they relate to specific needs of the prospective buyer and demonstrating the benefits provided by each of the relevant features. It is here, in the presentation, that solution features and benefits are linked to buyer's specific needs in a way that generates the buyer's desire to purchase and acquire the recommended solution. As illustrated in "An Ethical Dilemma," basing a presentation on anything other than a customer's true needs is a questionable tactic.

Tracey Wise has been selling computer systems for just over nine years and earned the position of senior account manager for one of the leading companies in the industry. For several months, Tracey has been working with a major insurance company that is looking for an automated information system that will solve the company's growing backlog of worker compensation claims. After reviewing the information from previous sales calls with the buyer, Tracey and her tech-support team decided that the R740 system offered the greatest benefits to this particular customer. However, a special sales promotion provided company salespeople additional commissions and double points toward the annual sales incentive trip to Hawaii for each R800 system sold. The higher priced R800 had all the same features and capabilities of the R740 along with many more. However, few of these additional capabilities would ever be of value to the insurance company. During her last sales call, Tracey explained and demonstrated the R740 and the R800 and persuaded the buyer that they would quickly "grow into the additional features" making the R800 the best deal. Based on Tracey's presentation and stated benefits, the company purchased the R800 and Tracey received the bonus commission and qualified for the Hawaii sales incentive trip.

What happened here? What are the dangers in over-selling a customer?

CREATING VALUE: LINKING SOLUTIONS TO NEEDS

It is unlikely that the customer will be interested in every detail of the salesperson's product or service offering, and certainly some aspects of the offering will be more important to a particular prospect than will others. Essentially, salespeople should strive to communicate three crucial factors: (1) how buyer needs will be met or how an opportunity can be realized as a result of a purchase; (2) how the product features translate, in a functional sense, into benefits for the buyer; and (3) why the buyer should purchase from you as opposed to a competitive salesperson. To assist salespeople in effectively communicating these three factors, most sales training programs emphasize a form of **benefit selling**, sometimes referred to as **FAB** (for features, advantages, and benefits).

BENEFIT SELLING: FEATURES, POTENTIAL BENEFITS, AND CONFIRMED BENEFITS

Any given product or service is comprised of multiple **features** that have the capability to produce different **potential benefits** and **confirmed benefits**. Features are traditionally defined as a quality or characteristic of a product or service that is designed to provide value to a buyer. Features answer the question, "What is it?" A benefit is the value provided by a feature to the buyer and addresses the always present buyer's question, "What's in it for me?" However, not all benefits will be valued at the same level by all buyers, thus the categorization of potential benefits versus confirmed benefits. A potential benefit describes a general form of value that is assumed to be of importance by the salesperson but not yet acknowledged as such by the buyer. Once the prospective buyer acknowledges the importance of a benefit to his or her buying situation, it is a confirmed benefit. Because confirmed benefits represent customer value that is provided by the proposed solution, some sales programs refer to the confirmed benefit as the **value proposition**.

Research tells us that buyers do not purchase products and features. Rather, buyers purchase the value and satisfaction provided to them in the form of relevant benefits.

Consequently, features have very little persuasive power. Salespeople can be more effective by selling benefits rather than features. However, to be most effective and gain the buyer's confirmation, stated benefits must be relevant to the prospective buyer's needs and phrased in a format that clearly translates the benefit from a generic "one-size-fits-all" description to a unique and customized benefit that has immediate meaning for the prospective buyer. While the one-size-fits-all benefit statements do not require much cognitive effort on the part of the salesperson, they typically do not pass from potential benefits to confirmed benefits. As illustrated in Exhibit 7.2, benefit statements that build on the salesperson's understanding and appreciation of the buyer's situation and are tailored to the individual buyer's needs and expectations are more likely to be confirmed by the buyer as being important.

By themselves, features and potential benefits risk the buyer thinking or asking, "So what?" Confirmed benefits are persuasive and advance the sale forward on the basis of creating added value for the buyer. This is the foundation of benefit selling. In benefit selling, the salesperson describes the benefits as they relate to specific needs of the prospective buyer and limits the role of features to simply supporting and evidencing the presence of confirmed benefits. This combination of a specific feature and its meaningful benefit statement are referred to as a **selling point**. As the following illustrates, selling

---

EXHIBIT 7.2   Features/Potential Benefits/Confirmed Benefits

Salesperson in golf shop selling Titleist golf balls to a weekend golfer		Confirmed Benefit?	Explanation
Feature:	Solid 1.58″ diameter core		
Potential Benefit:	Higher initial velocity and launch angle.	No	The typical weekend golf customer would not immediately see how the benefit of higher velocity and launch angle will benefit him or her.
Feature:	Solid 1.58″ diameter core		
Potential Benefit:	Provides more distance on shots for the typical golfer and lowers your score.	Yes	Longer shots and lower scores are a primary interest of the typical weekend golfer. Customers can immediately understand the benefit to themselves.

Selling a new Frito-Lay snack to a regional supermarket chain		Confirmed Benefit?	Explanation
Feature:	Daily delivery		
Potential Benefit:	Retailer can reduce inventory costs	No	This prospective buyer considers inventory costs a regular cost of doing business. The potential benefit is not perceived as being important.
Feature:	Daily delivery		
Potential Benefit:	Assures product freshness, which will lead to high customer satisfaction.	Yes	Prospective customer places tremendous emphasis on customer satisfaction. Consequently, this potential benefit is confirmed as being valuable.

points should be phrased in a conversational tone and clearly describe the benefit in a manner that emphasizes its applicability and importance to the individual buyer.

- "This particular copier automatically selects the paper size that best matches your original document. Based on the experience of other customers using this model, it will speed up reproduction of your longer reports and reduce waste. Not only will this save you money in terms of reduced waste, but it will also increase the efficiency of your office staff, which you expressed as one of your major concerns."

- "The design of this particular golf club provides you with an expanded sweet-spot for maximum ball contact. This will not only increase the distance of your shots, but will also provide the improved accuracy you are looking for."

- "Our unique use of overnight express for merchandise delivery reduces your need for back-up inventory while eliminating the possibility for the out-of-stocks and disappointed customers that you mentioned were costing you business."

Extensive research by Learning International, a major sales training and consulting firm, concludes that stating features and potential benefits may result in successful sales calls or at least lead to a continuation of the sales dialogue on the next sales call. This same research, however, concluded that a far more promising way to achieve sales call success is to seek customer confirmation of potential benefits. According to Learning International, successful sales calls have approximately five times as many confirmed benefit statements as unsuccessful sales calls. The Learning International research strongly suggests that using feature statements and potential benefit statements will help a salesperson avoid failure but will not ensure success. These same conclusions were reached by a British-based consulting firm in a study of 5,000 sales calls involving high-technology products.[2]

The use of confirmed benefits is further explained in "Professional Selling in the 21st Century: Using Confirmed Benefits."[3] In selecting specific features and benefits to be stressed, salespeople should focus on any unique benefits not offered by the competition,

---

PROFESSIONAL SELLING IN THE 21ST CENTURY

Using Confirmed Benefits

Jamie Howard, vice president of Chicago-based Active Solutions, emphasizes selling benefits rather than features to advance the sale.

In today's competitive business environment it has become more difficult for sales professionals to separate their solutions from the competition. It is important to realize that what advances the sale to the next step is not always directly related to the features of the product, but instead to the value the benefits of the product creates.

The contract furniture industry is as competitive as any other industry. When a large corporation is in the market for new furniture, as many as five competitors will be asked to bid. In one high profile project last year, creating value through showing our solution's benefits was the only chance to win. The products being proposed had very similar features and our price was slightly higher. My team had to develop a strategic plan to create value for

what we were offering. When everything is perceived to be similar, features will not be the deciding factor in the client's decision. The majority of the time the client will make his or her decision based on other variables. In this case, our price was higher and the features were similar. We had to create value for our product by focusing on the benefits rather than the features. The benefits had to be tied to the buyer's needs, which we developed during the questioning phase of the sales cycle. By identifying the client's needs, we were able to present the benefits that created added value over the competition. The customer's perceived value of our solution separated us from the competition. Following months of strategic meetings, we won the high profile project—the largest in our company's history. The client acknowledged that understanding how our solution benefited them was the key in their decision-making process because we had solved a problem for them instead of just offering a product.

as long as the benefits are of interest to the prospective buyer. These might include product benefits along with non-product benefits such as delivery, financing, extraordinary customer service, or additional sales support available to the buyer.

ORDERING SELLING POINTS FOR EFFECTIVENESS

On the basis of benefits being more important and persuasive than features are to buyers, there is some logical support for establishing and explaining the benefit before identifying the feature in a selling point. Nevertheless, there is no significant and objective research that evidences this sequential order as being more effective. Many salespeople prefer to change the order around as they advance from one selling point to the next in order to keep the presentation conversational and more interesting. One selling point after another, each having features and benefits sequenced in the same order can quickly become mechanistic and monotonous to the prospective buyer.

Buying Motives

While the sequence of presenting features and benefits within a particular selling point is not critically important, the sequence in which the selling points themselves are presented is extremely important and can greatly impact the effectiveness of a presentation. The buyer's problems and needs will equate to **buying motives.** As previously discussed in Module 3, "Understanding Buyers," a perceived need or problem that the buyer considers important will result in a corresponding buying motive—a need-activated drive to search for and acquire a solution to resolve the need or problem. Corresponding to the relative importance of the underlying need, buying motives vary in importance and must be categorized by the salesperson as either **major buying motives** or **minor buying motives**.

Major Buying Motives

Major buying motives are the prospect's most important concerns and have the most influence on the ultimate purchase decision. Major buying motives should be the main focus of the features and benefits comprising the presentation. Consequently, the order of importance of the major buying motives should guide the sequencing of features and benefits in the salesperson's presentation with the most important being addressed first, second most important being addressed second, and so on.

Minor Buying Motives

Minor buying motives are less significant and thus secondary to the major buying motives. They are peripheral concerns that should not be dealt with until after the major buying motives are addressed. In reality, as they are peripheral to the major buying motives, many minor buying motives will be resolved by the same features and benefits associated with the major buying motives. Consequently, by the time a salesperson has presented the features and benefits related to the major buying motives, many of the minor buying motives would no longer be active influencers of the purchase decision. In these cases, many successful salespeople will mention a minor buying motive as they discuss, in more detail, the selling point associated with a major buying motive.

The SELL Sequence for Effective Presentations

A popular presentation model uses the **SELL Sequence** to guide salespeople through the successive presentation of features and benefits in gaining the prospective buyer's confirmation of the benefits.[4] As depicted in Figure 7.1, this model uses each letter of the word SELL to represent a presentation sequence that quite naturally leads to confirmed benefits and advances the sale forward toward the stage of gaining commitment: **S** = *Select and describe a feature;* **E** = *Explain what the feature does;* **L** = *Lead into a meaningful benefit;* and **L** = *Let the customer talk.*[5]

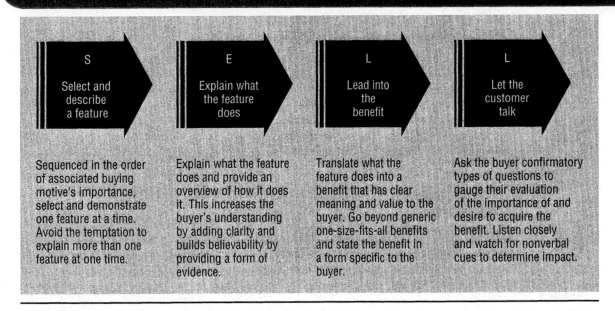

The SELL Sequence Model   FIGURE 7.1

S	E	L	L
Select and describe a feature	Explain what the feature does	Lead into the benefit	Let the customer talk
Sequenced in the order of associated buying motive's importance, select and demonstrate one feature at a time. Avoid the temptation to explain more than one feature at one time.	Explain what the feature does and provide an overview of how it does it. This increases the buyer's understanding by adding clarity and builds believability by providing a form of evidence.	Translate what the feature does into a benefit that has clear meaning and value to the buyer. Go beyond generic one-size-fits-all benefits and state the benefit in a form specific to the buyer.	Ask the buyer confirmatory types of questions to gauge their evaluation of the importance of and desire to acquire the benefit. Listen closely and watch for nonverbal cues to determine impact.

The Sell Sequence Model guides the salesperson through a natural and effective presentation of features and benefits that leads to confirmed benefits.

Select and Describe a Feature

It is important that the salesperson avoids the all too common problem of trying to show and explain more than one feature at a time. Rather than confusing the issue and risking the buyer missing an important point of information, top salespeople relate that they select, show, and demonstrate one feature at a time in order to do a thorough job of explaining what it does and the meaningful benefits provided to the buyer. Make the first shot your best shot. That is, select your best feature that corresponds to the buyer's most important major buying motive and work through the SELL model for that particular feature–benefit combination and elicit the buyer's benefit confirmation. Then, take the next best feature or change focus to the buyer's second most important buying motive and work through the same sequence.

Explain What the Feature Does

It is important that the buyer understands what the feature does—how it goes about producing the benefit. Different types of buyers (analytical communication styles versus expressives, for example) will desire and require different levels of detail. Nevertheless, all buyers require some form of evidence that the feature will in fact yield the promised benefit. In this way, this step is the bridge between the feature and the benefit that explains how the benefit results from the feature. A well-thought-out, succinct, and clear explanation supports the benefit and increases the prospective buyer's belief that the promised benefit will be received through the purchase of the proposed solution.

Lead into the Potential Benefit

In this step, information from the previous two steps—the feature and what it does—is translated into an outcome that is valuable to the prospective buyer. These outcomes should be very specific for a number of reasons. First, the beneficial outcome should be obviously linked back to the need it is purporting to address. For best results, do not rely on the buyer making the connection by himself or herself. Provide a reference back to the applicable need or problem being addressed. Second, generalized "one-size-fits-all" benefit statements do not carry the impact or generate the level of perceived customer value that a benefit specific to the buyer and his or her situation can provide. As illustrated previously in Exhibit 7.2, benefits that are specific to the buyer are more persuasive and have a higher likelihood of becoming confirmed benefits in the next step of this model.

Let the Customer Talk and Confirm the Benefit

It is in this step that the buyer confirms the benefit. Remember, only confirmed benefits—not features or potential benefits—have the power to persuade and advance the sale forward. Occasionally, the buyer will appreciate the benefit and have such a positive evaluation of its value that they will make a confirmatory statement on their own and without any questioning from the salesperson. However, the salesperson will usually find it necessary to ask the buyer a confirmatory type of question in order to gauge their evaluation of the importance of and desire to acquire the stated benefit.

Assessing Buyer Responses to the Feature–Benefit Presentation

The last "L" in the SELL Sequence Model calls attention to the importance of a salesperson continually assessing and evaluating the reactions and responses of prospective buyers. Inexperienced salespeople often rush through the entire presentation from beginning to end and never stop to invite feedback from the buyer. Feedback from the prospective buyer provides the salesperson with important information measuring the climate between the salesperson and the buyer, the buyer's level of interest in the product's features and benefits, whether the salesperson has successfully responded to the buyer's concerns, and how well the presentation is progressing toward the buyer making a purchase decision.

As detailed and discussed in Module 4, the observant salesperson can receive a great deal of continual feedback in the form of the buyer's nonverbal cues. In addition to observing nonverbal cues, high performing salespeople incorporate verbal probes at key points throughout the presentation in order to evaluate the buyer's interest and assess the progress of the selling presentation. These verbal probes are typically confirmatory forms of questions in search of simple "yes" or "no" responses from the buyer. Traditionally, these confirmatory questions have been referred to as **trial closes**. Recently, the phrases **check-backs** and **response-checks** have become a more popular and common name for this form of questions seeking feedback from the buyer. While feedback can be sought at any point of the presentation, response checks are commonly employed in two key points: (1) after a specific feature-benefit sequence in order to confirm the benefit and better assess the prospective buyer's level of interest and (2) following the response to an objection in order to evaluate the level to which the salesperson has handled the problem. Exhibit 7.3 provides an illustrative selection of response-check examples that salespeople indicate are typical of those they commonly use.

The effective use of response-checks offers a number of advantages. Probably the most evident is increased buyer involvement. Asking for buyer feedback helps to ensure that the presentation remains a two-way, collaborative exchange. The effective use of response-checks also helps the salesperson evaluate the level of the buyer's understanding and keeps the salesperson on the right track. If feedback indicates a lack of understanding—or even worse a lack of interest—on the part of a prospective buyer, the salesperson must make changes to the presentation and its component features and benefits so that they are better aligned with the needs and expectations of the buyer. On the other hand, positive feedback indicating a high level of understanding and interest on the part of the buyer would signal the salesperson to stay the course and advance the presentation toward gaining the buyer's purchase commitment. A series of positive response-checks indicates that the buyer is nearing the readiness stage for wrapping up the details and closing the sale. The more positive affirmations a salesperson receives in relation to his or her response-checks, the easier the final purchase decision becomes and the more confident the prospective buyer is in having made the appropriate decision.

Illustrative Examples of Response-Checks (Trial-Closes)   **EXHIBIT 7.3**

- "How does this sound to you?"
- "Does this make sense to you so far?"
- "Would this particular feature be useful to you in your current operations?"
- "What do you think?"
- "So this is something that would be valuable to you?"
- "Isn't that great?"
- "Do you like this color?"
- "From your comment, I'm guessing that this is a feature/benefit that you would like to have. Did I guess correctly?"
- "Does that answer your concern?"
- "Would this be an improvement over what you are doing right now?"
- "Is this what you had in mind?"

SALES AIDS FOR MAXIMIZING PRESENTATION EFFECTIVENESS

The benefit selling approach is designed to create a prospective buyer's awareness of the value provided by a proposed solution in line with his or her needs and problems, generate interest in learning more about the solution and its benefits, and stimulate the buyer's desire to obtain the benefits confirmed as being important. However, simply informing the prospect about the benefits and their value to the buyer is seldom sufficient to generate the level of interest and desire required to result in a purchase decision. To maximize the effectiveness of the sales presentation, salespeople utilize sales aids and tools that capture and hold the buyer's attention, boost the buyer's involvement and understanding, increase the believability of the claims, and build the buyer's retention of information (see Exhibit 7.4).

As illustrated in Figure 7.2, salespeople have a variety of different types of sales aids available for use in presentations. These various sales aids can be categorized into five categories of sales presentation tools: Verbal Support, Sales Call Setting, Visual Aids, Proof Providers, and Electronic Media.

Many times, these sales aids are provided by the selling organization. However, experienced salespeople are quick to comment that some of their most effective sales tools are those that they developed themselves for specific prospects and selling situations. A rapidly growing trend is the development and use of online libraries of sales aids and tools. These are typically developed by selling organizations for the exclusive use of their salespeople and access is restricted through the use of password authentication. Hewlett-Packard maintains an extensive online database and library of sales aids that include

Reasons for Using Presentation Tools and Sales Aids   **EXHIBIT 7.4**

- Capture prospective buyer's attention
- Generate interest in the recommended solution
- Make presentations more persuasive
- Increase the buyer's participation and involvement
- Provide the opportunity for collaboration and two-way communication
- Add clarity and enhance the prospect's understanding
- Provide supportive evidence and proof to enhance believability
- Augment the prospect's retention of information
- Enhance the professional image of the salesperson and selling organization

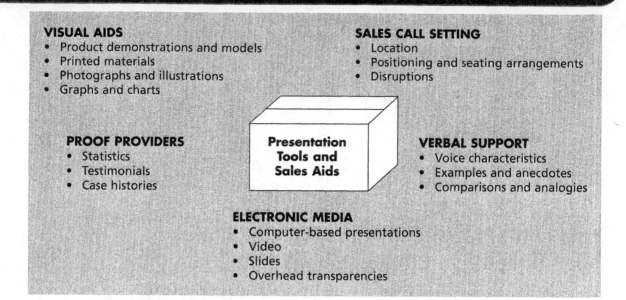

FIGURE 7.2 The Sales Presentation Toolbox

VISUAL AIDS
- Product demonstrations and models
- Printed materials
- Photographs and illustrations
- Graphs and charts

SALES CALL SETTING
- Location
- Positioning and seating arrangements
- Disruptions

PROOF PROVIDERS
- Statistics
- Testimonials
- Case histories

Presentation Tools and Sales Aids

VERBAL SUPPORT
- Voice characteristics
- Examples and anecdotes
- Comparisons and analogies

ELECTRONIC MEDIA
- Computer-based presentations
- Video
- Slides
- Overhead transparencies

To maximize presentation effectiveness, salespeople should carefully select and incorporate presentation tools and sales aids from those available in the Sales Presentation Toolbox.

product brochures and specification sheets, graphics, proposal templates, competitive comparisons, and an archive of PowerPoint presentations. Content can be downloaded and printed as is or customized to better fit a specific need. Equipped with a handheld or laptop computer and portable color printer, a salesperson can produce professional quality sales aids or a full-color proposal in a matter of minutes.

Not all sales presentation tools are suitable for all products, selling situations, or buyers. Nor should a salesperson feel the need to use each and every tool in any given presentation. A salesperson should think through and visualize the presentation he or she is developing. Based on what the salesperson envisions, he or she should consider several questions to arrive at a decision on what tools to incorporate:

- "How might the presentation be made stronger?"
- "What presentation tools would help to capture and hold the buyer's attention?"
- "What sales aids could aid the buyer's understanding and retention?"
- "Which sales aids would better evidence and build the buyer's believability of the benefits and value offered by this solution?"

Verbal Support

Among the five categories of presentation tools, the elements comprising the **verbal support** group are immediately available to the salesperson. More important, they are very effective in holding the prospective buyer's attention, building interest, and increasing both understanding and retention of information. Primary components of the verbal support group are **voice characteristics, examples and anecdotes,** and **comparisons and analogies.**

Voice Characteristics

As emphasized in "Professional Selling in the 21st Century: Energizing the Presentation,"[6] a salesperson can know his or her product inside and out and have the presentation down pat, but if there is no energy and passion in his or her voice, the potential for making the

PROFESSIONAL SELLING IN THE 21ST CENTURY

Energizing the Presentation

David Jacoby, sales instructor for CDW Corporation emphasizes the importance of energizing your sales presentation through effective use of voice characteristics, nonverbal communication, and mentally painting pictures of solutions and benefits in the buyers mind.

When presenting, your voice says it all—literally. This is especially true in telesales, where the entire sales cycle takes place over the phone. Our research underscores that in a face-to-face conversation, vocalization accounts for 38 percent of a customer's comprehension, while in a phone conversation it accounts for 86 percent. Assuming one has successfully identified all of the confirmed needs through the ADAPT questioning process, it is up to the salesperson to present the solution in a way that prompts the customer to take action. Vocalization can keep the customer's attention and create impact through speaking rates and pause duration, pitch and frequency, and intensity and volume. While presenting, maintain control of your vocalization through self-monitoring. At various intervals ask yourself, "If I were on the other end of the phone, would I be intently listening or daydreaming about my next meeting?" It will be hard at first, but try to see your presentation from your customer's perspective to make it more effective. By developing vocal skills and adding them to your sales arsenal, you will be able to create and maintain customer interest. Remember, your voice says it all.

sale will be seriously impaired. Voice coach Jeffrey Jacobi emphasizes that, "Your voice and how you use it determine how people respond to you. The sound of your voice relays to people whether you are confident, likable, boring, unpleasant, honest, or even dishonest."[7] Voice quality can be used to bring excitement and drama to the presentation by doing three things: varying the pitch, fluctuating the speed, and altering the volume.

Varying and changing pitch on key words adds emphasis and increases impact. It is analogous to putting different colors and hues into your voice. The increased intensity and vividness grabs attention, holds interest, and helps the buyer remember what is said. Fluctuating the speed of speech can add emphasis and guide the buyer's attention to selected points of the presentation. Important details—especially quantitative information—should be provided at a slower, more careful pace. Less critical information can be presented at a faster pace in order to grab the buyer's attention and redirect their interest. Changes in volume can be used to add emphasis to an important phrase or topic while a softer volume—almost a whisper—can build intrigue and pull the prospect into the conversation. Altering of volume from loud to soft can better grab and hold the buyer's interest while simultaneously adding clarity and emphasis to increase understanding.

Examples and Anecdotes

An example is a brief description of a specific instance used to illustrate features and benefits. Examples may be either real or hypothetical and are used to further explain and emphasize a topic of interest. Anecdotes are a type of example that is provided in the form of a story describing a specific incident or occurrence. While a salesperson's use of examples and anecdotes bring clarity into the presentation in order to improve the buyer's understanding and retention, they also contribute proof and believability of benefit claims.

A production equipment salesperson might further explain the purpose of an infrared guidance control by using the following example:

> . . . for example, if the feedstock coming off the main paper roll gets out of line by as little as 1/16 of an inch, the infrared guidance control will sense it

and automatically make the correct adjustments. This prevents a paper jam from shutting down your package printing line and costing lost time and wasted product.

Similarly, a Snap On tool salesperson might use the following anecdote as an explanation of the Snap On lifetime guarantee:

> . . . for instance, one of your mechanics uses this ratchet handle as a substitute hammer to drive a retaining pin into an axle and damages the ratchet mechanism. Snap On will replace the broken tool at no charge, even though the damage was caused by misuse.

Comparisons and Analogies

A comparison is a statement that points out and illustrates the similarities between two points. An analogy is a special and useful form of comparison that explains one thing in terms of another. Analogies are useful for explaining something complex by allowing the buyer to better visualize it in terms of something familiar that is easier to understand. Comparisons add interest and clarity while improving the retention of information. The substantiation of claims that is provided through comparisons and analogies is also effective in providing proof to the claims of benefit and value.

A salesperson wishing to add emphasis and meaning to his or her verbal description of the Honda S2000's performance capabilities might use a direct comparison to the performance capabilities of a competitive model the prospective buyer might also be considering:

> You have the performance specifications on both cars, and as you can see . . . the 6 second 0 to 60 performance of the S2000 outperforms the Audi TT by a good 10 percent. Isn't that the kind of performance you are looking for?

A salesperson for Newell-Rubbermaid might illustrate the benefits of setting up an end-of-aisle display of special occasion containers by using the following comparison to the store manager's sales goals for the product category:

> . . . sales data from stores similar to yours indicate that adding an end-of-aisle display for these seasonal containers will increase their sales by 35 to 40 percent during the fourth quarter holiday season. This would certainly help you achieve—and possibly exceed—the store's goal of a 20 percent increase for this general product category.

A BMW salesperson presenting to an Air Force pilot the option of an in-car global positioning system map and tracking system might use the following analogy:

> . . . having the onboard map and tracking system is like having a friendly flight controller with you on every trip. You will always know exactly where you are and what route you should travel to reach your destination. You will never get lost or be delayed because you took the wrong turn.

Sales Call Setting

Many times the salesperson has little or no control over the setting in which the sales call and presentation will take place. Nevertheless the setting can influence results and salespeople should consider the two primary elements of sales settings—**location, positioning** and **seating arrangements**, and **disruptions**—as they address the following questions:

- Will the atmosphere be supportive and nonthreatening?
- Where would the prospect feel more open to ideas and willing to listen?
- What location will minimize potential distractions?

Location

Where the sales presentation takes place can have a strong positive or negative influence on its success. The commonly accepted rule of thumb that you should strive to conduct a sales presentation on one's own turf as opposed to that of the buyer has not been well supported in today's climate of consultative, trust-based selling. In fact, most sales presentations take place in the prospect's own office. If the prospective buyer has a private office and interruptions can be controlled, it will usually be the best location. The familiar surroundings put the buyer at ease. As the guest, the salesperson is duly treated with respect. In those instances where interruptions cannot be controlled or the prospect has a reputation for being highly domineering, meeting offsite at a neutral location is often more productive. The offsite meeting could be at a related third-party's facilities or perhaps a lunch meeting where the salesperson assumes the psychological role of host.

Positioning and Seating Arrangements

Although most sales calls are made while seated with the prospective buyer at a desk or table, many sales calls are actually made standing up. For instance, a detail representative for pharmaceutical companies such as Pfizer or Merck often makes sales calls while walking down the hall with the doctor as he or she moves from one patient's examining room to another. An agriculture chemical salesperson for Dow or Growmark might find himself or herself making a presentation to a farmer out in the demonstration field next to the application equipment.

Whether sitting or standing, the salesperson should be aware of interpersonal communication and behavior concepts such as proxemics that were discussed in Module 4. If standing, collaborative communication can be facilitated by the salesperson positioning himself or herself two to four feet from the buyer and at an angle rather than straight across from the buyer. Standing too close and straight across from the buyer can be unconsciously as well as consciously perceived as threatening. If the presentation is going to be made from a seated position, read the prospective buyer's nonverbal cues as to what seat to take and when to be seated. As with standing, seating yourself directly across from the buyer can be seen as threatening or intimidating. If the office is arranged so that the only seat available is in front of the desk and directly across from the buyer, make the most of it by sitting at a bit of an angle. Not only will this take the edge off any unconscious intimidation, but also it is less formal and will make it easier to show and demonstrate visual aids. The ideal seating arrangement is around a small table or at the side of the prospective buyer's desk where the salesperson can direct the buyer's attention and effectively share visual aids and other presentation tools while being able to observe the buyer's nonverbal cues and feedback.

Disruptions

Interruptions and disruptions are any occurrences that distract the buyer's attention away from the presentation. Some, such as something related to the buyer's job or home life are not directly controllable by the salesperson. However, many distractions and interruptions can be directly controlled or at least influenced by the salesperson. For instance, requesting that the prospect have his or her assistant hold all routine calls can minimize routine phone interruptions. Asking prior to beginning the presentation whether others will be joining the meeting can prevent having to start over when a latecomer unexpectedly strolls into the room. Is there activity going on outside the office window that might momentarily distract the buyer's concentration? If so, it might be possible to position yourself so the buyer's line of sight is redirected away from the window. These are but a few examples of how the salesperson can minimize distractions. However, to be successful in doing so the salesperson must be observant of the surroundings and proactively influence sources of potential disruptions. Even the best-prepared salespeople will occasionally encounter a disruption that must be handled effectively. As detailed in Exhibit 7.5, when that happens, the salesperson must quickly read the verbal and nonverbal cues and decide whether to tactfully regain the prospect's attention or to make an appointment to return at a better time.

EXHIBIT 7.5   How to Handle Disruptions

- Be patient and observe the situation. Look and listen for verbal and nonverbal cues. Some disruptions are momentary distractions while others demand the prospect's attention and may take some time.

If Disruption Is Momentary in Nature and Controllable	If Disruption Requires More of Buyer's Attention and Is Not Controllable
- Redirect the customer's attention to the presentation by calling an interesting detail to his or her attention or asking a question - Restate the selling points of interest that were being discussed just prior to the disruption - Make sure you are covering details that the customer perceives as being important; if not, change to a different selling point that would be of more importance to the buyer - Incorporate the use of sales aids to increase the buyer's involvement and participation in the presentation	- Suggest that it might be better to continue the presentation at a time more convenient for the buyer - Set and confirm a specific day and time to return - Be slightly early for the next appointment - Briefly summarize where you were in the previous appointment - Restate and gain the buyer's reconfirmation of the features and benefits that had already been covered prior to the disruption - Continue the selling presentation making sure to cover details the customer perceives as being important; if not, change to a different selling point that would be of more importance to the buyer

Proof Providers

As discussed earlier in this module, confirmed benefits answer the buyer's question, "What's in it for me?" In a similar fashion, proof providers such as **statistics**, **testimonials**, and **case histories** can be utilized to preempt the buyer from asking, "Can you prove it?" or "Who says so?" Claims of benefits and value produced and provided to the buyer need to be backed up with evidence to highlight their believability.

Statistics

Facts and statistics lend believability to claims of value and benefit. When available, statistics from authoritative, third-party sources carry the highest credibility. Among others, third-party sources include independent testing organizations and labs (e.g., Consumer Reports, Underwriters Laboratory), professional organizations (e.g., American Dental Association, Risk and Insurance Management Society), research companies (e.g., Booze-Allen & Hamilton, The Industry Standard, PricewaterhouseCoopers), institutions (e.g., Sandia, MIT), and various governmental entities (e.g., Census Bureau, state licensing bureaus, Department of Commerce). Statistics prepared by the selling organization as well as the salesperson can also be useful in providing evidence for claims. Facts and statistics are most powerful when they fairly represent all sides to the story and are presented in printed form rather than simply stated orally. Not only does the printed word carry more credibility, but also it is convenient and can be left as a reminder to aid the prospect's retention of information.

Testimonials

Testimonials are similar to facts and statistics, but in the form of statements from satisfied users of the selling organization's products and services. Supportive statements from current users are excellent methods to build trust and confidence. They predispose the prospective buyer to accept what the salesperson says about the benefits and value offered by a recommended solution and reduce the prospect's perceived risk in making a purchase decision. As shown in "An Ethical Dilemma," the power of testimonials sometimes tempts salespeople to misuse them.

Written testimonials are especially effective when they are on the recommending user's letterhead and signed. However, testimonials that list customers, trade publications, trade associations, and independent rating organizations along with one-sentence comments in a presentation can also be effective. For instance:

- "The American Dental Association has endorsed the new Laserlite drilling system as being safe and painless for the patient."
- "In January, *Fortune* magazine recognized CDW as the top-rated technology vendor on the basis of services provided to the buying customer."
- "The *RIMS Quality Scorecard* rated Arthur J. Gallagher & Co. as the highest rated insurance broker in North America in terms of value and service provided to its clients."

AN ETHICAL DILEMMA

Jane Rafael is an account manager for International Supply and Uniform (ISU), a major provider of work wear and uniforms to companies, institutions, and individuals throughout North America. During her recent sales presentation to the Dallas-based Waits Manufacturing Corp., Jane was well into the presentation of her proposed weekly uniform supply program when the buyer asked about the quality of the uniforms. Jane responded that J. D. Powers (a well-known organization rating product and service quality) had recently rated them one of the highest quality providers of work uniforms. This appeared to satisfy the buyer and the sale was closed. Upon leaving the buyer's office, the sales assistant working with Jane that day asked about the J. D. Powers rating, commenting "I can't believe I missed something that important. Where can I get a copy of it?" Jane replied, "Actually, J. D. Powers has never rated uniform suppliers that I know of. The buyer was ready to make the commitment and just needed some kind of quality reference to help him make the decision. Don't worry about it. Nobody ever checks things like that. Besides, our quality is excellent. There will be no problems." What are the dangers in how Jane uses references and testimonials? How might the sales assistant help Jane change this habit?

Testimonials are used extensively across industry and product/service types. To maximize their effectiveness testimonials should be matched according to relevance and recognition to the prospective buyer. It is critical that the organization or person providing the supporting testimony be known or recognized by the prospect, above reproach, and in a position of respect.

Case Histories

Case histories are basically a testimonial in story or anecdotal form. Their added length allows more detail to be presented in order to further clarify an issue or better itemize the proof for a given statement. Case histories can also break the monotony of a long presentation. Like their counterpart testimonials, case histories should only be used when they clearly illustrate a particular point and are appropriate for the prospective buyer. Unrelated or tangential stories not only distract the customer but can be a source of irritation that works against credibility building. Case histories should be short and to the point lasting no more than a minute. They should support the presentation rather than becoming the center of attention.

Visual Aids

Visual aids allow the salesperson to involve one or more of the buyer's senses in the presentation and help to illustrate features and benefits. Visual aids add clarity and dramatization to impact the effectiveness of a sales presentation and advance the sale toward a purchase commitment. Among the variety of visual aids available to a salesperson, **product demonstrations and models, printed materials, photographs and illustrations**, along with **charts and graphs** have proven to be very effective in adding impact to and reinforcing the sales presentation.

Product Demonstrations and Models

The product itself is the most effective sales aid because it provides the prospective buyer with an opportunity for hands-on experience. When the actual product does not lend itself to being demonstrated, models can be used to represent and illustrate key features and benefits of the larger product. The value of an actual product demonstration is applicable to all types of products and services. For example, Boeing salespeople use scale models to give the buyer a detailed and realistic feel for the aircraft, which cannot be tucked into the salesperson's briefcase. As the sale progresses, the prospective buyer's team will be given actual hands-on experience with the real product. Simmons and Sealy, leading manufacturers of quality sleep products require that their registered dealers have demonstration models of mattress sets on display and available for customers to try out. Major vendors of office furniture will set up an actual model office so that the prospective client can experience its actual use. Pharmaceutical companies provide doctors with actual samples of the product for trial use with selected patients.

As detailed in Exhibit 7.6, the salesperson should make sure the product being demonstrated is typical of what is being recommended. Furthermore, it should be checked to assure that it is in good working order prior to the demonstration and that setup and removal do not detract from the presentation. The last thing the salesperson wants is to have to apologize for poor appearance or inadequate performance.

Printed Materials

Printed materials include such items as brochures, pamphlets, catalogs, articles, reprints, reports, testimonial letters, and guarantees. Well-designed printed materials can help the salesperson communicate, explain, and emphasize key points of the selling organization and products. They are designed to summarize important features and benefits and can be effectively used not only during the presentation but left behind as reminder pieces for the buyer after the salesperson has left. During subsequent phone calls with the buyer, the salesperson can review important topics and point out information to the buyer that is included in the printed material. When printed materials are left with a buyer, the salesperson's name and contact information should be clearly printed on the material or an attached business card. Exhibit 7.7 provides salespeople with a number of tips for preparing printed materials and visuals.

As with all sales aids, when using printed materials with a prospective buyer, they should be placed directly in front of the buyer. If anyone must read upside down, it should be the salesperson and not the buyer. To draw the buyer's attention to a certain section of the printed material, the salesperson can highlight the selected areas with a marker prior to the presentation. Then, during the presentation the salesperson can use a pen or pointer to direct the buyer's attention to the specific section that is relevant to the feature or benefit under discussion.

EXHIBIT 7.6   Guidelines for Product Demonstrations in the Presentation

- Assure the appearance of the product is neat and clean
- Check for problem-free operation
- Be confident and able to skillfully demonstrate the product
- Practice using the product prior to the demonstration
- Anticipate problems and have back-up or replacement parts on hand
- Setup and knockdown should be easy and quick

Tips for Preparing Printed Materials and Visuals   **EXHIBIT 7.7**

- Printed materials and visuals should be kept simple
- When possible, use phrases and let the buyer's mind complete the sentences
- Use the same layout and format throughout to tie the presentation together
- Check for typographical and spelling errors
- Use colors sparingly and for functional rather than decorative purposes
- Leave plenty of white space; don't crowd the page too full
- Each visual should present only one idea
- Target using a maximum of seven words per line and seven lines per visual
- Where possible use graphics (charts and graphs) rather than tables
- Use bullet points to emphasize key points
- Never read the presentation directly from the visual
- Clearly label each visual with titles and headings to guide the prospective buyer

Photographs and Illustrations

Photographs and illustrations are easy to produce and relatively inexpensive. Using images allows the salesperson to present a realistic portrayal of the product or service. Many products cannot be taken into a prospective buyer's office because of their size. A well-detailed image can give the prospect an idea of the product's appearance and size. Line drawings and diagrams can show the most important details of a product. Images are most effective when they illustrate and simplify a more complex product or feature and make it easy to communicate information about size, shape, construction, and use.

Charts and Graphs

Charts and graphs are useful in showing trends and illustrating relationships. As such they can show the prospect what the problem is costing them or how a solution might work. Charts and graphs often illustrate relationships in terms of bars, lines, circles, or squares. For example, a salesperson for an office equipment vendor might get the cost figures associated with their use of an outside copy center for the previous two years. This information could then be used in a comparative bar graph to better illustrate the savings possible if they had their own copier. Salespeople for a leading medical technology company use a chart format to compare the features and benefits of their product versus the competitors' equipment the buyer is considering. The chart format succinctly and effectively supports statements of superiority made during the presentation.

Electronic Media

Salespeople today can customize graphic presentations using their laptops and hand-held computers, VCRs and DVDs, and slide and overhead projectors. Customizing and enriching presentations by using electronic multimedia can be done inexpensively and in a fairly short period of time. Microsoft PowerPoint, for example, allows the salesperson to quickly build a complete, high-impact graphic presentation customized for an individual prospect. The availability of technologies such as **computer-based presentations, video, slides,** and **overhead transparencies** leaves the salesperson with no reason to deliver a "canned presentation."

Computer-Based Presentations

The computing power of today's laptops and even handheld computers combined with presentation software such as PowerPoint allows the salesperson to create powerful multimedia presentations. Pictures of products, video testimonials of satisfied customers, as well as product demonstrations and competitive comparisons can all be included in a PowerPoint presentation. Editing with computer-based artwork and different fonts further enhances the presentation. Exhibit 7.8 provides some tips for preparing

EXHIBIT 7.8   PowerPoint Tips

- **Avoid Needless Animation.** Occasional animation can be used for emphasis, but don't overdo it as it gets annoying.
- **Get a Fresh Background.** Acquire a background that is not a stock template in PowerPoint and incorporate your company's logo and visual branding into the design.
- **Cut Down on the Number of Slides.** Ten slides should be the limit for a 30-minute presentation. Too much slide flipping detracts from the message.
- **Run Spell Check.** Grammatical errors and typos suggest that your company pays little attention to detail.

PowerPoint slides.[8] Once completed, the PowerPoint software produces notes that can be used as convenient handouts during the presentation.

Video

The rapidly shrinking size of video players and monitors combined with the ability to replay digitized video from a compact disk or DVD direct to a laptop or hand-held computer screen have further advanced the popularity and effectiveness of video in presentations. Unlike slides, pictures, and printed materials, video has the advantage of both sound and action. The product can be shown in action, for example, the prospect can be taken on a virtual tour of the selling organization and see the product being produced or he or she can simultaneously see and hear a personal message from the president of the selling organization as well as testimonials from satisfied customers.

Slides

Many companies produce relatively inexpensive slides for their salespeople to use in presentations. GlaxoSmithKline uses before-and-after slides to depict the effectiveness of a topical cream it sells. The first slide shows an affected area of the skin, and the next slide shows the cleared skin after three days of treatment. The slides also indicate that 93 percent of the patients on this cream clear up after just three days. Slide shows can easily be changed depending on the audience and have become more sophisticated through the use of multiple projectors and the addition of soundtracks.

Overhead Transparencies

The proliferation of computers and the availability of small, lightweight, and powerful projectors have practically eliminated the use of transparencies and overhead projectors. However, transparencies and overhead projectors are still widely used when more sophisticated methods are not available. Transparencies are easy to make and inexpensive to produce. Last minute changes can be made on a copying machine and color printers can produce full-color transparencies for greater impact. Because of their ease of production and low cost, many salespeople carry transparencies and a portable projector as a backup to their more sophisticated computer presentations.

Using Tools and Sales Aids in the Presentation

Practice! Practice! Practice! Rehearsal of the presentation is the final key to making effective sales presentations. Understand what features are relevant and what benefits are meaningful to the prospective buyer in terms of value to be realized. Be confident in developing and using multiple sales aids to add impact to the presentation itself. As the following further details, using the **SPES Sequence** can facilitate the effectiveness of presentation tools and sales aids: **S** = *State selling point and introduce the sales aid;* **P** = *Present the sales aid;* **E** = *Explain the sales aid;* **S** = *Summarize.*[9]

State the Selling Point and Introduce the Sales Aid

This means stating the full selling point including the feature and potential benefit and then introducing the sales aid. For instance, "To demonstrate this benefit, I'd like you to take a look at this video" or "This graph summarizes the increased performance you will experience with the Honda S2000." This prepares the buyer for the visual aid and informs him or her that attention is required.

Present the Sales Aid

This involves presenting the sales aid to the customer and allowing a few moments for examination and familiarization before saying anything. For example, when using printed materials, place the material directly in front of the customer and allow it to be reviewed momentarily in silence. Allow the customer to review the sales aid and satisfy their natural curiosity before using it.

Explain the Sales Aid

No matter how carefully a sales aid is prepared, it will not be completely obvious. The customer will not necessarily understand the significance unless the salesperson provides a brief explanation. Don't rely on a chart or graph to fully illustrate the points being supported. Similarly, a product demonstration might be enjoyed by the prospect while they totally miss the information or experience supporting the presentation. The salesperson should point out the material information and explain how it supports his or her points.

Summarize

When finished explaining the significance of the sales aid, summarize its contribution and support and remove the sales aid. If not removed, its presence can distract the prospective buyer's attention from subsequent feature and benefit points.

GROUP SALES PRESENTATIONS

Sales presentations to groups are fairly commonplace in business-to-business selling. For example, retail chains often employ buying committees when considering the addition of new products for their stores. Hospitals use cross-functional teams comprising medical and administrative personnel to choose vendors such as food service providers. The decision of which advertising agency will be chosen is usually made by a group of marketing and upper-management people. Corporations often depend on representatives from several departments to make purchase decisions that affect all employees, such as the choice of insurance providers.

Delivering sales presentations to groups presents special challenges and opportunities. In addition to the basic fundamentals of planning and delivering sales presentations to individual buyers, there are additional strategies and tactics that can enhance sales presentations to groups.

When selling to groups, salespeople can expect tough questions and should prepare accordingly. While buyer questions are part of most sales presentations whether to individuals or groups, they are particularly crucial when there are multiple buyers. Most buying groups are assembled to tap the individual expertise and interests of the group members. For example, a buying committee for a company's computer information system could include technical specialists; finance and accounting personnel; and representatives from production operations, logistics, management, and marketing. All of these individuals are experts and demand in-depth information in order to make a decision. In some situations, this calls for a sales team to adequately address all questions, while in some cases, an individual salesperson has the cross-functional expertise required to make the sale.

When selling to a group, salespeople should take every opportunity to **pre-sell** individual group members prior to the group presentation. Pre-selling to individual buyers or sub-groups of buyers takes place before a major sales presentation to the entire group.

Buying procedures in a given company may or may not allow pre-selling. If it is an option, the salesperson should definitely work with the individuals comprising the buying group prior to presenting to the group as a whole. By doing so, the salesperson can better determine individual and group interests and motives and possibly build a positive foundation for the group presentation. Pre-selling can also reveal the roles of the individuals in the buying center as discussed in Module 3. Knowing who the decision maker is, along with the other roles such as users and influencers, is crucial for success in group sales presentations. In the following discussion, we will focus on two key areas: tactical suggestions for group presentations, and handling questions in group settings.

Sales Tactics for Selling to Groups

Assuming that the salesperson or sales team has planned a comprehensive presentation and done as much pre-selling as possible, there are some specific sales tactics that can enhance presentations to groups. Sales tactics for group presentations fall into three general categories: arrival tactics, eye contact, and communications tips during presentation delivery.

Arrival Tactics

Try to arrive at the location for the presentation before the buying group arrives. This provides an opportunity to set up and check audio-visual equipment, prepare collateral material for distribution to the group, and become familiar and comfortable with the surroundings. It also sets the stage for the salesperson to personally greet individuals from the buying team as they enter the room. In a symbolic way, it also signals territorial command, or that the salesperson is in charge of the meeting. Though the control of the presentation meeting is typically shared with the buying group, arriving first sends a message that the salesperson is prepared to start promptly at the appointed time, thus showing respect for the buyer's time.

From the very beginning, the salesperson is hoping to connect with each individual in the group, rather than connecting only at the group level. By arriving first, the salesperson may have the opportunity to talk briefly with each individual. If nothing more, a friendly greeting, handshake, and introduction can help establish rapport with individuals in the group. When not allowed to arrive first, salespeople should attempt individual introductions when joining the group. If that is not practical, salespeople must try and engage each individual through eye contact and, if appropriate, introductory remarks early in the presentation that recognizes the individual interests of those present. For example, a salesperson for a food service company might begin a presentation to a hospital with the following:

> Thank you for the opportunity to discuss our food service programs with you today. In planning for our meeting, I recognize that the dietary group is most concerned about the impact of any proposed change on the quality of patient care. Linda (the head dietitician), I believe we have a program that will actually enhance the quality of care that your patients receive. John (the head of finance), we will also propose an efficient, cost-effective alternative . . .

Opening remarks such as these, when kept brief, can be most effective in building involvement with all individuals in a small group.

Eye Contact

For both small and large groups, establishing periodic eye contact with individuals is important. With small groups, this is easily accomplished. With larger groups, especially formal presentations where the salesperson is standing and the group is sitting, there may be a tendency to use the so-called overhead approach. This method calls for looking just over the heads of the group, with the idea that those seated furthest from the presenter will feel included as part of the group. This method should be avoided. It might be fine for formal speech to a large audience in a convention hall, but is far too impersonal for groups of 10 to 25 individuals. Also avoid a rapid scanning from side-to-side. This gives the appearance of nervousness and is ineffective in connecting with individual group members. The most effective eye contact is to try and connect with each individual or small sub-groups for only a few seconds, moving through the entire group over the course of the presentation. Professional entertainers often use this method to connect with audience members, and salespeople can do the same.

Communications Tips

When selling to groups, it's essential to make all members of the group feel that their opinions are valuable. It is also important to avoid being caught in the middle of disagreements between members of the buying group. For example, if one member likes the salesperson's proposal and another thinks it is too expensive, any resolution of this disagreement must be handled carefully. While the salesperson may present information that resolves the issue, in some cases, disagreements among group buying members may be resolved outside the meetings. It is to the salesperson's advantage if disagreements can be handled during the presentation, as it keeps the sales process moving while unresolved issues can stall the sales process. As an example of how salespeople can play a peacemaker role, consider this exchange:

Buyer A: "I really like this system and think we should install it as soon as possible."

Buyer B: "I like it too, but it's way too expensive. Is there a less expensive alternative?"

Buyer A: "Sure, but they won't do the job."

Salesperson: (directed to Buyer B) "Could I add something here? I believe we have a cost-effective system, and that our lease-to-purchase plan reduces the capital expenditure and allows a favorable payback period. Could we take another look at the numbers?"

The point is that salespeople must be diplomatic as a participant in discussions that might develop between members of the buying group. This sometimes means remaining silent while the discussion comes to a resolution, and sometimes it means playing an active role. There are no hard and fast rules in this area, and salespeople must simply use their best judgment to guide their actions.

In delivering group presentations, it is important to maintain contact with group members. Thus, reading or over-relying on densely worded slides should be avoided. Think of slides and other audio-visual aids as support tools, not as a "roll-and-scroll" presentation to be read to the group. Contact with the group can also be enhanced by natural movement. Too much pacing about can be detrimental to holding the group's attention, just as remaining tethered to a laptop can detract from group communication. When possible, salespeople should stand to the left of visual aids, as people read right-to-left. When standing to the left, it is easier to direct attention to the visual aids while momentarily deflecting attention away from the speaker. In this way, the salesperson becomes an unobtrusive narrator and the visual aid has maximum impact.

Body language can add or detract to sales effectiveness in the group setting. In general, posture should reflect an energetic, relaxed person. Conventional wisdom dictates that presenters should avoid contact with their own bodies while presenting. Salespeople who stuff their hands in their pockets, scratch their heads, or cross their arms are creating distractions to their own messages.

Handling Questions in Group Presentations

Just as is the case with sales presentations to individuals, questions from buyers in a group are an important part of the buyer–seller interaction that leads to a purchase decision. Salespeople should recognize that questions fill information gaps, thus allowing buyers to make better decisions. In a group setting, questions can also add a dramatic element, making the presentation more interesting for those in attendance. To the extent possible, salespeople should anticipate group questions, then decide whether to address the question before it arises, or wait and address the question should it arise during the presentation.

To effectively handle questions that arise during the presentation, salespeople should listen carefully and maintain eye contact with the person asking the question. Generally, it is a good idea to repeat or restate the question. Questions should be answered as succinctly and convincingly as possible.

By listening carefully to the question, salespeople should show proper respect to the person asking the question. At the same time, they are helping direct the attention of the group to the question. As the question is posed, it is important for the salesperson to maintain eye contact with the person asking the question. Again, this demonstrates respect for the person and for his or her right to ask questions. This may require some practice, as salespeople may be tempted to glance at sales materials or perhaps their watch when the attention is shifted to the person asking the question. To do so could insult the questioner who may feel slighted by the lack of attention.

In many cases, it is a good idea to repeat or, in some cases, restate the question. This will ensure that everyone understands the question. It also signals a shift from the individual back to the group. Additionally, it allows the salesperson to state the key issue in the question succinctly. This is often important because not all questions are well-formulated and are sometimes accompanied by superfluous information. Consider this dialogue:

Buyer: "You know, I have been thinking about the feasibility of matching our Brand X computers with Brand Y printers. Not too long ago, matching multiple brands would have been a disaster. Are you telling me now that Brand X computers are totally compatible with Brand Y printers?"

Seller: "The question is: Are your computers compatible with our printers? Yes they are—with no special installation requirements."

When restating questions, salespeople must be careful to accurately capture the essence of the buyer's concern. Otherwise, they could be perceived as avoiding the question or trying to manipulate the buyer by putting words in his or her mouth. Therefore, when in doubt, it is a good practice when restating a question to seek buyer confirmation that the restated question is an accurate representation of the original question. For example, salespeople might say, "Ms. Jackson, as I understand the question, you are concerned about the effectiveness of our seasonal sales promotion programs. Is that correct?"

When answering questions, there are three guidelines. First, salespeople should not attempt to answer a question until they and the group members clearly understand the question. Second, salespeople should not attempt to answer questions they are not prepared to answer. It is far better to make a note and tell the group you will get back to them with the answer than to speculate or give a weak answer. Third, try to answer questions as directly as possible. Politicians are often accused of not answering the questions posed during press conferences, but rather steering the answer toward what they wish to talk about. Salespeople will quickly lose credibility if they take a long time to get to the point in their answer. To answer convincingly, start with a "yes" or "no," then explain the exceptions to the general case. For example, say, "Yes, that is generally the case. There are some exceptions, including . . ." This is preferred to answering, "Well that depends . . ." then explaining all of the special circumstances only to conclude with "but, generally, yes, that is the case."

When answering questions, it is important to address the entire group rather than the individual who asked the question. Otherwise, salespeople may lose the attention of other group members. When salespeople conclude their answers, they have the option of going back to the person who asked the question, continuing their presentation, or taking a question from another group member. Salespeople can rely on their common sense and experience to decide what is appropriate in a given situation.

In larger groups, it is particularly important to avoid getting locked into a question-and-answer dialogue with one person if other people are showing an interest in asking questions. Indeed, it is important to take all questions, but it is also important to spread the opportunity to ask questions around the room, coming back to those who have multiple questions until all questions are answered. If one person is a dominant force within the buying group, other group members will typically defer their questions until that person has asked all of their questions at different points in the presentation.

When selling to a group, salespeople should have a clear objective for their presentation. To get the group to take the desired action, salespeople must make a convincing case, motivate the group to take action, and make it easy for the group to take the desired action. Some of the methods for handling buyer objections and earning a commitment as discussed in Module 8 will prove useful for accomplishing these tasks.

In some cases, the group will wish to deliberate and let the salesperson know of their decision at a later time. This is not uncommon, because the group may need a frank discussion without outsiders to reach a final decision. Should this occur, salespeople should be certain the group has all the information they need or offer to provide the needed information promptly and offer to follow-up within a specified time period.

The process for planning and delivering a group presentation is much the same as it is for sales presentations to individuals. By paying attention to the special considerations in this section, salespeople can build on their experience with sales presentations to individuals and deliver effective sales presentations to groups.

SUMMARY

1. **Describe the difference between features, potential benefits, and confirmed benefits and the role they play in benefits selling.** Any given product or service is comprised of multiple features that produce different benefits. Features are defined as a characteristic of a product or service that provides value. Features answer the question, "What is it?" A benefit is the value provided by a feature and addresses the buyer's question, "What's in it for me?" Not all benefits will be valued at the same level by all buyers, thus the categorization of potential benefits versus confirmed benefits. A potential benefit describes a general form of value that is assumed to be of importance but not yet acknowledged as such by the buyer. Once the prospective buyer acknowledges the importance of a benefit to his or her buying situation, it is a confirmed benefit. Because confirmed benefits represent customer value that is provided by the proposed solution, some sales programs refer to the confirmed benefit as the value proposition. Confirmed benefits are important because buyers do not purchase features. Rather, they purchase value that is provided in the form of confirmed benefits.

2. **Construct complete selling points using feature and benefit statements.** Selling points are the foundation of benefit selling. In benefit selling, the salesperson describes the benefits as they relate to specific needs of the prospective buyer and uses a description of the feature to support and evidence the presence of confirmed benefits. This combination of a specific feature and its meaningful benefit statement are referred to as a selling point. Selling points are most effective when they are phrased in a conversational tone and clearly describe the benefit in a manner that emphasizes its applicability and importance to the individual buyer.

3. **Explain the four steps of the SELL Sequence.** The SELL Sequence is a popular presentation model that guides salespeople through the successive presentation of features and benefits in gaining the prospective buyer's confirmation of the benefits.

This model uses each letter of the word SELL to represent a presentation sequence that is designed to lead to confirmed benefits and advance the sale forward toward the stage of gaining commitment. The sequence steps are: **S** = *Select and describe a feature;* **E** = *Explain what the feature does;* **L** = *Lead into a meaningful benefit;* and **L** = *Let the customer talk.*

4. **Discuss the advantages of using response-checks in the selling presentation.** Response-checks are confirmatory probes used by the salesperson to gather feedback from the buyer. Effective use of response-checks offers a number of advantages including increasing buyer involvement and ensuring that the presentation remains a two-way, collaborative exchange. Response-checks also help the salesperson evaluate the level of the buyer's understanding and keep the salesperson on the right track. If feedback indicates a lack of understanding or lack of interest on the part of a prospective buyer, the salesperson must make changes to the presentation and its features and benefits so that they are better aligned with the needs and expectations of the buyer. On the other hand, positive feedback indicating a high level of understanding and interest on the part of the buyer would signal the salesperson to stay the course and advance the presentation toward gaining the buyer's purchase commitment. A series of positive response-checks indicates that the buyer is nearing the readiness stage for wrapping up the details and closing the sale.

5. **List and explain the different forms of presentation tools and sales aids that can increase the impact of a presentation.** To maximize the effectiveness of the sales presentation, salespeople utilize sales aids and tools that capture and hold the buyer's attention, boost the buyer's involvement and understanding, increase the believability of the claims, and build the buyer's retention of information. Salespeople have a variety of different types of sales aids available for use in presentations. These various sales aids can be categorized into five categories of sales presentation tools: Verbal Support (*voice characteristics, examples and anecdotes, comparisons and analogies*), Sales Call Setting (*location, positioning and seating arrangements, disruptions*), Visual Aids (*product demonstrations and models, printed materials, photographs and illustrations, graphs and charts*), Proof Providers (*statistics, testimonials, case histories*), and Electronic Media (*computer-based presentations, videos, slides, overhead transparencies*).

6. **Delineate the four steps of the SPES process for effectively utilizing sales aids in presentations.** The SPES Sequence provides the salesperson with guidelines for effectively incorporating sales aids into a selling presentation. Each letter stands for a specific set of actions to be undertaken by the salesperson: **S** = *State selling point and introduce the sales aid;* **P** = *Present the sales aid;* **E** = *Explain the sales aid;* **S** = *Summarize.*

   - *State the Selling Point and Introduce the Sales Aid.* State the full selling point and then introduce the sales aid. For instance, "This graph summarizes the increased performance you will experience with the Honda S2000." This prepares the buyer for the visual aid and informs him or her that attention is required.

   - *Present the Sales Aid.* Present the sales aid to the customer and allow a few moments for examination and familiarization before saying anything. For example, when using printed materials, place the material directly in front of the customer and allow it to be reviewed momentarily. This allows the customer to review the sales aid and satisfy his or her natural curiosity before using it.

   - *Explain the Sales Aid.* No matter how carefully a sales aid is prepared, it will not be completely obvious. The customer will not necessarily understand the significance unless the salesperson provides a brief explanation. The salesperson should point out the material information and explain how it supports his or her points.

   - *Summarize.* When finished explaining the significance of the sales aid, summarize its contribution and support and remove the sales aid. If not removed, its presence can distract the prospective buyer's attention from subsequent feature and benefit points.

7. **Explain some of the special considerations in making sales presentations to groups.** Making a sales presentation to a group requires all of the preparation and selling skills necessary in selling to individuals. In addition, salespeople should expect especially tough questions when selling to a group of buyers because individuals in a group are typically experts in their specialty area, and the individual interests of buyers in a group can be quite varied. When possible, salespeople should pre-sell individuals or sub-groups prior to making a group presentation. It is important for salespeople to try to establish an individual connection with group members and to pay particular attention to handling questions from the group.

UNDERSTANDING PROFESSIONAL SELLING TERMS

sales presentation	sales call setting
SPIN	location
ADAPT	positioning and seating arrangements
benefit selling	disruptions
FAB	proof providers
features	statistics
potential benefits	testimonials
confirmed benefits	case histories
value proposition	visual aids
selling point	product demonstrations and models
buying motives	printed materials
major buying motives	photographs and illustrations
minor buying motives	charts and graphs
SELL Sequence	electronic media
trial closes	computer-based presentations
check-backs	video
response-checks	slides
verbal support	overhead transparencies
voice characteristics	SPES Sequence
examples and anecdotes	pre-sell
comparisons and analogies	

DEVELOPING PROFESSIONAL SELLING KNOWLEDGE

1. How do the questioning sequences SPIN and ADAPT relate to benefits selling?

2. What are the relationships and differences between features, potential benefits, and confirmed benefits? How should they be used in effective presentations?

3. How might the concepts of major buying motives and minor buying motives influence the order in which a salesperson should present features and benefits to a buyer?

4. What is the SELL Sequence and how might it impact the effectiveness of a salesperson's presentation?

5. What are response-checks and how do they advance the selling process forward toward the commitment stage?

6. What are the different sales presentation tools and how can they be used to enhance persuasive power of the presentation?

7. Why and how is selling to a group different from selling to an individual? What impact do these differences have on a salesperson's presentation?

8. What is the purpose of pre-selling buyers or sub-groups of buyers prior to the major presentation to the group?

9. What advantages might a salesperson gain by arriving early for a group presentation?

10. What is the best way for a salesperson to handle questions from the audience in a group presentation?

BUILDING PROFESSIONAL SELLING SKILLS

1. Visit one retail store in each of the following categories: bedding, sporting goods, and computers. Take notes on the different presentation tools and sales aids, if any, that you observed or experienced being used in selling a product. What presentation tools and sales aids would you have used in making each of the three presentations? Why?

2. Develop a list of presentation tools and sales aids that you might use in a job interview to enhance the presentation of your skills and capabilities. Describe how you would go about using each of your listed items.

3. Assume the role of a computer salesperson for the CanDo Computer Company selling to a small company wanting to equip their field sales force of five salespeople with laptop computers.

   a. Develop and explain the SELL Sequence you would use for four different feature–benefit combinations.
   b. Describe what presentation tools and sales aids you might use to enhance your presentation.

ROLE PLAY

Situation: Read item 3.

Characters: Yourself—salesperson for the CanDo Computer Company; the buyer—director of purchasing for MidWest Supply

Scene: *Location*—The office of the Director of Purchasing for MidWest Supply. *Action*—As described, MidWest Supply is considering equipping their five-person salesforce with laptop computers. You are there to present your line of laptops, gain a sale, and begin a long-term relationship with MidWest Supply.

Role play the SELL Sequences you would use for four different feature–benefit combinations and demonstrate how you might use the presentation tools and sales aids you feel would be effective in adding power to your presentation.

Upon completion of the role play, address the following questions:

3a. How well would the demonstrated SELL Sequences move the sale forward?

3b. What other ways could these SELL Sequences be presented that might be more effective?

3c. How well did the presentation tools and sales aids portrayed positively impact the selling presentation? In what ways did they impact the presentation (e.g., attention, clarification, retention, proof, etc.)?

3d. What other sales aids might have been used effectively?

4. Jane Gilmore is a salesperson for Nike athletic shoes. She is meeting with Sarah Franklin, head buyer for The Athlete's Foot a regional chain of athletic shoe stores headquartered in St. Louis—with the objective of selling several new models to the 12-store chain. Jane has put a great deal of preparation into her sales call including a bound set of printed materials consisting of product brochures, competitive charts, and forecasts of financial performance. The sales aids must have been very effective. Jane opened the binder and placed it in front of the buyer so that Jane could point out several of the supporting materials during her presentation. However, shortly

after beginning her presentation, the buyer picked the binder up and began browsing through it before Jane ever had an opportunity to use any of the material in her presentation.

    a. What should Jane do now?

    b. What could Jane have done differently that might have prevented this interruption from happening?

ROLE PLAY

Situation:	Read item 4.
Characters:	Jane Gilmore—salesperson for Nike athletic shoes; Sarah Franklin—head buyer for The Athlete's Foot
Scene:	*Location*—The office of Sarah Franklin at the headquarters of The Athlete's Foot. *Action*—As described, Jane is presenting a new line of athletic shoes for consideration by The Athlete's Foot as stocking items in each of their stores. Jane had intended to use a binder of printed sales materials to reinforce several points in her presentation. However, shortly after getting started with her presentation, the buyer has picked up the binder and begun to browse through it.

Role play how you might regain control over the presentation and refocus the buyer's attention on the presentation instead of the binder of materials.

Role play how you could have used the binder in a different way so as to minimize or even prevent the buyer from taking control of the materials.

Upon completion of the role play, address the following questions:

4a. How well do you think the demonstrated method for regaining control over the presentation would work in reality?

4b. What other actions might Jane employ that could also be effective?

4c. In what other ways could Jane have better prevented Sarah from taking control of the sales aids and losing her focus and participation in the presentation?

5. Epson, a leading manufacturer of presentation equipment and materials, sponsors a Web site exclusively dedicated to the improvement of individual presentations. Among the more interesting links at the site are What's New, Basics, Tutorials, Resources, and The Presenters Club.

- **What's New** is an ever-changing series of articles and graphics explaining the latest developments in research, equipment, and software. It's a great source for keeping up to date on major product introductions from all companies, not just Epson.

- **Basics** offers free online tips for planning and delivering presentations, including the use of visual aids.

- **Tutorials** guide the user through the use of PowerPoint and projectors, including running a projector from a laptop computer.

- **Resources** presents the user with a large and ever-growing stock of innovative PowerPoint templates, clip art, and sound clips. The entire library of interesting elements is available for downloading into presentations at no charge.

- **The Presenters Club** is a "members only" part of the Web site and contains some of the really neat content that can make you look and feel like a real pro! Possibly the greatest feature of The Presenters Club is that membership is also free of charge. All you need to do is complete and submit the short registration form and you are in.

Go the presentersonline Web site at http://www.presentersonline.com.

- Take time to look around and familiarize yourself with this site. It has a great deal of content that can give you a competitive advantage in classes as well as in your work after graduation.

- Click on "Basics."

- Scroll down and take in the different categories of online training, such as Delivery, Content, and Visuals. These are offered at no charge and each of the topic areas is short and can be completed in a few minutes. Note that the displayed items are a selection of the larger library archive that is also available to you.

- Browse through the training topics available and locate three subjects that are of some interest to you—something you might enjoy and benefit from knowing.

- One at a time, click on each of your selected three topics.

- Read through and study the materials offered. Take notes and build your understanding and skills.

Write a summary reaction paper that identifies each of the three subjects you selected to study. Under each subject, briefly explain what you learned and how you might use the knowledge and abilities gained.

MAKING PROFESSIONAL SELLING DECISIONS

Case 7.1: Texas Paint & Coatings (TPC)
Background

Texas Paint & Coatings (TPC) is a producer of specialty paints and coatings for industrial and agricultural equipment manufacturers. In business for over 25 years, TPC has established a strong reputation as a competitive supplier of high-quality acrylic and resin-based coatings. Working with the NASA Space Research Center in Houston, TPC is rolling out a breakthrough self-priming paint product that offers several significant benefits to equipment manufacturers. By totally eliminating the need for any form of a primer coat, the new product can cut application time in half and eliminates about one-third of the material cost involved in the typical paint process. The self-priming paint can be directly applied to any clean metal surface using either a low-pressure spray or roller. An additional benefit is its flash-drying characteristic, which means it dries and cures after only 3 to 5 minutes exposure to room temperature air. In just 5 minutes after application it is fully cured, rock hard, and highly scratch, chemical, and fade resistant.

Current Situation

Richard Henry is an account manager for TPC and has been working to establish John Deere's Fort Worth, Texas, facility as an account. With the previous line of traditional paint products, he had been successful in gaining about 10 percent of the plant's annual paint requirements. However, that seemed to be the limit. Even with the great relationship he has established with Tim Dickerson, head paint and coating buyer for Deere's Fort Worth construction equipment plant, Richard has not been able to gain additional share of the plant's paint requirements.

Richard sees the self-priming product as his path to capturing a majority share of the plant's paint needs. The cost and time savings will certainly be a major item of interest. But first, he must convince Tim that the new paint meets and even exceeds the performance specifications. As he is looking through the information he has in his database, he sees that there is a wealth of NASA test data and competitive information that will document the performance of the new coating, but he is pondering how he might organize and present it in a way that will be most effective. He is also trying to think of an effective demonstration he might provide that will give Tim a hands-on experience with the paint's superior performance.

Questions

1. Work up examples of what Richard's SELL Sequences might look like.
2. What different presentation tools and sales aids might Richard use to enhance his presentation of the new self-priming paint?
3. Once he has established the superior performance of the new paint, what should Richard do?

ROLE PLAY

Situation:	Read Case 7.1.
Characters:	Richard Henry—salesperson for Texas Paint and Coatings; Tim Dickerson—head paint and coating buyer for John Deere–Fort Worth
Scene:	*Location*—The office of Tim Dickerson at John Deere–Fort Worth. *Action*—As described, Richard is presenting a revolutionary new self-priming paint. While cost savings will be important, his first concern is to establish that the new paint exceeds all performance requirements.

Role play how Richard might incorporate different presentation tools and sales aids to make his presentation to Tim more effective.

Role play how Richard might collaborate with Tim to illustrate the possible cost savings provided by the new paint.

Upon completion of the role play, address the following questions:

1. What other tools and sales aids might prove useful in demonstrating the performance of the new paint?
2. What information will Richard need in order to substantiate the possible cost savings to Tim? Where and how might he get that information?

Case 7.2: All Risk Insurance and National Networks
Background

The All Risk Insurance Company has 3,200 sales agents spread across five regions that cover the United States. They are moving toward the development of a national network that would tie each of the agent offices together with the regional offices and corporate headquarters. The improved communication capability will allow all company personnel to have full access to customer records and form the core of a comprehensive customer relationship management system that is to be rolled out in 18 months.

Current Situation

Jim Roberts is a network account specialist for National Networks, a specialist in large corporate network solutions, and has been working with the technology-buying group at All Risk Insurance for several months now. Jim has worked through several meetings with the buying group members and has a meeting scheduled for next Wednesday to present his recommendations and demonstrate why they should select National Networks as the supplier for this sizable project. The final decision will be made by Joyce Fields (director of information systems), John Harris (comptroller and CFO), Mike Davis (director of agent services), and Dianne Sheffield (director for customer services). Jim also knows that there is one other competitor who will also be making a presentation in hopes of landing the project. The equipment being proposed by both vendors is virtually identical due to the detailed specifications that All Risk Insurance had included in the RFP. Prices are also likely to be pretty similar. The decision will most likely come down to the services each competitor includes in their proposals. Based on the information Jim has collected from different sources, he has come up with a comparison of customer services offered by National Networks and the competitor. (see table at the bottom of page)

Questions

1. Develop complete SELL Sequences for each of National Networks' feature–benefit sets.
2. For each of the features and benefits, describe several presentation tools and sales aids that Jim might use to enhance his presentation.

3. What recommendations might you have for Jim as he prepares to present to the group of buyers at All Risk?

ROLE PLAY

Situation: Read Case 7.2.

Characters: Jim Roberts—salesperson for National Networks; Joyce Fields—director of information systems for All Risk Insurance; John Harris—comptroller and CFO for All Risk Insurance; Mike Davis—director of agent services for All Risk Insurance; Dianne Sheffield—director for customer services for All Risk Insurance

Scene: *Location*—A conference room at All Risk Insurance. *Action*—As described, Jim Roberts is presenting the National Network proposal for a corporate computer network linking All Risk's corporate offices with each of its five regional offices and 3,200 sales agents out in the field.

Role play Jim's presentation of the SELL Sequence for each of the feature–benefit sets incorporating presentation tools and sales aids suitable for use in the group presentation.

Upon completion of the role play, address the following questions:

1. What other presentation tools and sales aids might prove useful to Jim in presenting his proposed solution to the All Risk buying team?
2. How might Jim employ other tactics for selling to a group that could increase the effectiveness of his presentation and advance the sale to the point of gaining an order?

Features	Capability of National	Capability of Competitor	Benefits
Service and repair centers	175 affiliated service and repair centers across the United States	21 affiliated service and repair centers across the United States	Ensures fast and reliable repairs for hardware and software
Installation and testing	Installation and testing done by National Network employees	Installation and testing outsourced to several different companies	Knowledge that all installations will be done the right way
Customer call center	24 hour, 7 days per week and staffed by National Network employees	24 hour, 7 days per week and staffed by an outsource commercial provider	Knowledgeable staff always available to assist All Risk employees with problems

ADDRESSING CONCERNS AND EARNING COMMITMENT

ADDRESSING CONCERNS

"If you ask the right questions, the client will pave the way to the close."

When I started with Merrill Lynch Private Client in 1987, I served what could be defined as an apprenticeship to a very successful vice president who continues to be a great mentor. Over 15 years with Merrill Lynch, I worked my way up to the title of vice president and senior financial advisor. When I first started to work for Merrill Lynch, I thought the titles of "consultant" and "advisor" implied that clients did not need to be persuaded or "sold" on ideas that were truly good for them. I quickly discovered that in a relationship where a bad decision could mean financial destruction, my real job was addressing concerns and earning commitments, every day and all day long.

After graduation from college with a major in marketing, I was familiar and comfortable with the consultative sales process that was somewhat new to many people in the late 1980s. To Merrill Lynch's credit, they were following that type of process with their clients versus accosting the prospect with the "stock of the day" pressure tactics associated with the industry.

I would often repeat a saying to myself and others around me. It was simply, "If you ask prospects or clients enough questions, they will pave the way to the close." So, I did ask questions . . . usually ones involving deep thought and genuine concern. We would often map out some pretty sophisticated solutions. Armed with so much information, I constantly had to resist the urge to give long monologues. When I asked questions, listened, then answered accurately and concisely (resisting the urge to give long dissertations to try to impress the client), I usually was able to overcome any concern.

One of the best relationships I had over my entire career with ML also helped me realize that one needs to ask the right questions and sometimes they are pretty simple. I was trying to transfer a multimillion corporate retirement plan relationship to ML that would be one of significance. I knew corporations hated to go through this tedious process of retirement plan evaluation. So once you got the opportunity with a prospect, you wanted to close because if serviced well by a provider, a retirement plan may never leave or go through that process again.

With my partner, I assembled what I thought was the best set of retirement benefits ever amassed through our office. It was constructed from textbook dialogue of terrific questions involving every important component to the plan. For weeks, I would call on the client to address the complicated issues and we would conclude each conversation with mutual enthusiasm. Why were they not signing the papers! I kept racking my brain over what complex retirement plan feature I was not addressing. The president of the company answered and he agreed we had long ago extinguished any doubt or concern about the retirement plan and that they really wanted to come over to our firm. I wanted to grab the "old school" sales bat and beat a transfer out of the corporate prospect. Then, out of frustration I simply asked, "Why have you not signed the papers!?" When asked the simple question, he disclosed that the current retirement plan provided also had their banking business and, as president of the company, he did not want to make a decision that might jeopardize that very important business concern. The papers were signed the very next day when we told him that essentially, it would be illegal for a bank to hold a retirement plan "hostage" against a banking relationship. We reminded him that the bank would in no way want to close out business accounts that were profitable for the bank, and that moving the retirement

Objectives

After completing this module, you should be able to

1 Explain why it is important to anticipate and overcome buyer concerns and resistance.

2 Understand why prospects raise objections.

3 Describe the five major types of sales resistance.

4 Explain how the LAARC method can be used to overcome buyer objections.

5 Describe the traditional methods for responding to buyer objections.

6 List and explain the earning commitment techniques that enhance relationship building.

plan would probably improve their banking service because of the bank's concern over losing it to the recently created full-service business banking accounts created by my firm.

I still believe if you ask enough questions, the client will pave the way to the close. However, I have qualified that by reminding myself that the right questions to ask are sometimes the simplest.

Source: Interview with John Marcum, July 15, 2004.

An objection or sales resistance is anything the buyer says or does that slows down or stops the buying process. The salesperson's job is to uncover these objections and answer them to the prospect's or client's satisfaction. It is very difficult for a salesperson to earn commitment if there is doubt or concern on the buyer's part. Thus, the salesperson must uncover and overcome any and all objections. In doing so, the salesperson strengthens the long-term relationship and moves the sales process closer to commitment.

A brief discussion follows on why it is important for salespeople to anticipate and negotiate buyer concern. Following a discussion of why prospects raise objections, this module covers the five major types of objections. Next, different approaches to handling sales resistance are explained. Finally, techniques to earn commitment are reviewed.

ANTICIPATE AND NEGOTIATE CONCERNS AND RESISTANCE

Over the years, many salesforces were taught that **sales resistance** was bad and would likely slow down or stop the selling process. Salespeople were also told that if they received resistance, then they had not done a good job explaining their product or service.

These notions have changed over the years to where objections now are viewed as opportunities to sell. Salespeople should be grateful for objections and always treat them as questions. The buyer is just asking for more information. It is the salesperson's job to produce the correct information to help buyers understand their concern. Inexperienced salespeople need to learn that sales resistance is a normal, natural part of any sales conversation. The prospect that does not question price, service, warranty, and delivery concerns is probably not interested.

Although many salespeople fear sales resistance from their prospects or customers, it should be viewed as a normal part of the sales process. At a minimum, the salesperson now has the prospect involved. The salesperson can now start to determine customer interest and measure the buyer's understanding of the problem. In some situations, a salesperson cannot overcome resistance (for example, delivery dates don't match; technology does not fit). Under these circumstances, the successful salesperson gracefully ends the sales call while leaving open the option for further business.[1] Finally, if the sales resistance is handled correctly, the outcome can lead to customer acceptance.

Reasons Why Prospects Raise Objections

There are many reasons why prospects will raise objections.

1. The prospect wants to avoid the sales interview. Some prospects do not want to create any more work for themselves than they already have. Granting a sales interview takes time, and buyers already have a busy schedule handling normal day-to-day tasks. Buyers may want to avoid the salesperson because they view his or her call as an interruption in their day. Most buyers do not have the time to see every salesperson that knocks on their door.

2. The salesperson has failed to prospect and qualify properly. Sometimes, poor prospects slip through the screening process. The prospect may have misunderstood the salesperson's intentions when asked for the interview. The salesperson should attempt to qualify the prospect during the sales call. For example, a computer software company used telemarketing to qualify prospects. Leads were turned over to the salesforce for

in-person visits. The major product line was an inventory control package that costs $20,000. The salesperson asked the owner of the company if she had a budget for this project. The owner answered $5,000. The salesperson gave the owner the names of a couple of inexpensive software companies, thanked the owner for her time, and moved on. The owner was not about to spend $20,000 and said so early in the sales conversation. This resistance actually helped the salesperson. What if this resistance had stayed hidden for four to six weeks while the salesperson continued to call on the owner? Both the salesperson's and owner's time would have been wasted.

3. Objecting is a matter of custom. Many purchasing agents have a motto never to buy on the first call with a salesperson. Trust has not yet been developed, and a thorough understanding of the salesperson, his or her company, and the products has not been accomplished. The buyer will need most of this information to make a decision. Many buyers may say no during the first few calls to test the salesperson's persistence.

4. The prospect resists change. Many buyers like the way they are presently doing business. Thus, buyers will tell the salesperson that they are satisfied with what they have now. Many prospects simply resist change because they dislike making decisions. Prospects may fear the consequences of deciding and dread disturbing the status quo. A purchase usually involves dismissing the present supplier and handling all the arrangements (price, terms, delivery, and product specifications) to smoothly move the new supplier in. Once a buyer is comfortable with his or her suppliers, he or she will generally avoid new salespeople until a major need arises.

5. The prospect fails to recognize a need. The prospect may be unaware of a need, uninformed about the product or service, or content with the present situation. In any case, the lack of need creates no motivation to change suppliers. Many purchasing agents were content with their overnight mail service and were slow to recognize the fax machine as a viable solution to getting information to their customers quickly. The poor quality of the reproduced document turned away many buyers. Only when the need for the information outweighed the aesthetics of the document did buyers readily embrace the fax machine.

6. Prospect lacks information. Ultimately, all sales resistance comes back to the fact that the prospect simply lacks the information he or she needs to comfortably make a decision. The salesperson must view this as an opportunity to put the right information in front of the buyer. If the salesperson diagnoses correctly and presents the right information, then the resistance problem can be more easily overcome. Exhibit 8.1 summarizes why prospects raise objections and lists strategies for dealing with them.

Why Prospects Raise Objections and Strategies for Dealing with Them   **EXHIBIT 8.1**

Buyer wants to avoid the sales interview
   Strategy: set appointments to become part of the buyer's daily routine
Salesperson has failed to prospect and qualify properly
   Strategy: ask questions to verify prospect's interest
Buyer won't buy on the first sales call
   Strategy: regular calls on the prospect lets the prospect know the salesperson is serious about the relationship
Prospect does not want to change the present way of doing business
   Strategy: salesperson must help the prospect understand there is a better solution than the one the prospect is presently using
Prospect has failed to recognize a need
   Strategy: salesperson must show evidence that sparks the prospect's interest
Prospect lacks information on a new product or on the salesperson's company
   Strategy: salesperson must continually work to add value by providing useful information

Types of Objections

Although there appears to be an infinite number of objections, most fall into five or six categories. Buyers use delay techniques to avoid taking immediate action. Comments such as "Give me a couple of weeks to think it over" can save the buyer the discomfort of saying no at the end of a presentation. "Your price is too high" or "I have no money" are easy ways for purchasing agents not to buy a salesperson's offering. Price is probably the most often cited objection but usually is not the most important issue. It is obvious that buyers do not buy merely on price; if this were true, then the lowest price supplier would get all the business and eventually be the only supplier left selling the product. "No need at this time" is another typical objection. The buyer may not be in the market to purchase at this point in time.

It is not unusual for salespeople to encounter product objections. Most buyers have fears associated with buying a product. The buyer may be afraid that the product's reliability will not perform up to the standards the salesperson said it would. Not only do the salespeople have to demonstrate that their product will perform at the level they say it will, they must also show how it stacks up to the competition. A competitor introducing a new technology (e.g., e-commerce) may change the way a salesperson competes on a particular product line (e.g., office products).

Many buyers are constantly assessing their supplier on service (e.g., delivery, follow-up, warranties, guarantees, repairs, installation, and training). If the service is good and department heads are not complaining, the buyer is likely to stay with the status quo. Service is one variable that companies and salespeople can use to differentiate their product. Enterprise Rent-a-Car will deliver cars to the home of the renter and has made this an issue in its advertising. A salesperson for a wholesale distributor may make the point to a prospect that their fresh fruit, fish, and meat can be delivered daily when their competitors only deliver three times per week.

Many buyers will feel intense loyalty to their present suppliers and use this as a reason not to change. Buyers may be equally committed to the salesperson from whom they are presently buying. As a nonsupplier to the company, the salesperson must continue to call on the buyer and look for opportunities to build trust with the prospect. The salesperson may want to investigate whether the buyer has had any previous bad experience with his or her company that is causing the buyer not to do business with that company. Some salespeople and their buyers will not hit it off. The salesperson has to recognize these feelings and move on if several calls do not result in an eventual sale.

At first glance, an inexperienced salesperson may be overwhelmed with the thought of how they will handle all the different types of objections buyers will raise. It does not take long, however, for a salesperson to learn that most objections fall into just a few categories. When preparing to buy a product or service, a prospect generally obtains information in five areas: need, product or service features, company or source, price, and timing of the buy. Objections could come from any of these areas, as shown in Exhibit 8.2. A more detailed look at each of these areas follows.

Need Objections

Without a need, prospects have little or no reason to talk to a salesperson. If the prospect has been qualified properly, the salesperson believes the prospect has a need for the product. Many buyers have been conditioned to say automatically, "I don't need your product" (i.e., **need objection**). This may be the result of the buyer being out of budget or not having the time to look at your product or proposal. Other buyers may respond, "We are getting along just fine without your product. No one in my company is asking for your product. Call back in a few months and maybe something will change."

The salesperson has a tough challenge ahead if the buyer sincerely believes they have no need. It is the salesperson's job to establish a need in the buyer's mind; if the salesperson cannot do this, then logically, an objection can be expected.

Types of Objections	EXHIBIT 8.2
No Need	Buyer has recently purchased or does not see a need for the product category "I'm not interested at this time."
Product or Service Objection	Buyer may be afraid of product reliability "I'm not sure the quality of your product meets our needs." Buyer may be afraid of late deliveries, slow repairs, etc. "I'm happy with my present supplier's service."
Company Objection	Buyer is intensely loyal to the present supplier "I am happy with my present supplier."
Price Is Too High	Buyer has a limited budget "We have been buying from another supplier who meets our budget constraints."
Time/Delaying	Buyer needs time to think it over "Get back with me in a couple of weeks."

Many prospects do not know they have a specific need for a product until a situation occurs that makes them aware of it (i.e., engineering calls and needs a special software package). Therefore, objections to the need require the salesperson to stimulate the need awareness of the prospect with relevant information—features and benefits that peak the prospect's interest. Exhibit 8.3 summarizes a number of the no-need objections.

Product or Service Objections

Often the product or service lacks something the buyer wants and the salesperson can't deliver. A competitive advantage for Ontario Systems, a large software firm, is they have a 24-hour 800 service available to all of their customers. Their number one competitor offers only 8:00 AM–8:00 PM call-in phone service. For those clients that run three shifts and need 24-hour service, their choice is easy: they buy from Ontario.

Other prospect objections could be simply emotional—the prospect doesn't like the way the product looks or feels (i.e., **product or service objection**). Still others have a problem with the products' performance characteristics (i.e., I need a copier that has color and staples in the bin). The salesperson also must do an adequate job of fact-finding and qualifying. Many of these issues can be resolved by knowing what the prospect is looking for.

Objections toward the product center around understanding the fit between the product and the customer's needs. The salesperson's job is to learn what product features are important to the buyer and sell to those features. Products are bundles of benefits that customers seek to fit their needs. Tying the benefits to the customer's needs helps the prospect bridge the gap from no-need to need. Exhibit 8.4 summarizes a number of product or service objections.

Possible Need Objections	EXHIBIT 8.3
I have all I can use (all stocked up). I don't need any. The equipment I have is still good. I'm satisfied with the company we use now. We have no room for your line.	

EXHIBIT 8.4 Possible Product or Service Objections

I don't like the design, color, or style.
A maintenance agreement should be included.
Performance of the product is unsatisfactory (i.e., copier too slow).
Packaging is too bulky.
The product is incompatible with the present system (i.e., we prefer Apple over IBM).
The specifications don't match what we have now.
How do I know if you'll meet our delivery requirements?
The product is poor quality.

Company or Source Objections

Marty Reist is a manufacturer's representative for a small company in the sporting goods industry. He has to go against the big boys daily. Sales representatives from Nike, Titleist, and Reebok probably don't have to work really hard to get past the gatekeepers. Marty, on the other hand, must justify his existence every day. "I've never heard of your company" (i.e., **company or source objection**) is something Marty must overcome.

Other buyers may be happy with their present supplier. It is not unusual for buyer/seller relationships to last 10 to 15 years and even longer. Robert Carroll, a former sales representative from Monsanto Agricultural Division heard the following quote from many of his farmers and farm co-ops, "I'm perfectly happy with Monsanto, my crops look good. I've been buying from them for years, and they have always treated me right." This is one of the hardest objections to overcome, especially if the prospect feels genuine loyalty to his or her present supplier.

Professional salespeople never criticize their competitors. The salesperson can point out any superior features they might have. They can also ask for a single order and ask for an evaluation against their present supplier.

Another form of source objection is a negative attitude a buyer might have about the salesperson's company or the poor presentation of a previous salesperson. A buyer might remember a late or damaged order the company did not properly handle. A former salesperson may have made promises to the buyer and did not follow through on them. The salesperson must investigate any and all source objections. The salesperson may uncover source problems that can be overcome with time. Exhibit 8.5 outlines typical company or source objections.

Price Objections

Most sales experts agree that price is the most common form of buyer resistance. This objection has the prospect saying they can't afford the product, the price is too high, or the product is not in their budget at this time (i.e., **price objection**). This objection may be a request for the salesperson to justify to the prospect how they can afford

---
EXHIBIT 8.5 Company or Source Objections

Your company is too small to meet my needs.
I've never heard of your company.
Your company is too big; I'll get lost in the shuffle.
Your company is pretty new; how do I know you'll be around to take care of me in the future?
Your company was recently in the newspaper. Are you having problems?

Price Objections   EXHIBIT 8.6

We can't afford it.
I can't afford to spend that much right now.
That's 30 percent higher than your competitor's comparable model.
We have a better offer from your competitor.
I need something a lot cheaper.
Your price is not different enough to change suppliers.

the product or how they can work it into their budget. Most salespeople feel the price objection is an attempt by the buyer to get the salesperson to lower their price. The salesperson must address the price objection by citing how the benefits (value) outweigh the cost. Many companies never sell as the low-cost option. Stryker Medical sells hospital beds and stretchers to hospitals and emergency rooms. They are never the lowest cost. Stryker's salespeople almost always hear the price objection. First, they have to educate their prospects and customers that their products last 25 to 50 percent longer than their competitors. They can demonstrate with evidence their product will still be around 5 to 10 years after their competitor's has been discarded. If one of their stretchers is $1,500 more than their competitors, they must break down the price over the entire life of the stretcher. They can actually show a savings over time. By providing the right information, Stryker can show value over their competitor's offering.

Price objections probably occur more frequently than any other type. Price objections may be used to cover the real reason for a reluctance to buy. Probing and asking questions are the salesperson's tools to get to the real reasons for a buyer's objection. Exhibit 8.6 summarizes a number of price objections.

Time Objections

The **time objection**, or as some salespeople call it, the stalling objection, is used by buyers to put off the decision to buy until a later date. Many inexperienced salespeople hear this technique and believe the prospect is going to buy in the future, but just not today. Some buyers use this technique to get rid of salespeople so that the buyer does not have to formally reject the salesperson and his or her sales proposal. Sometimes proposals are very complex and the buyer does need time to think them over. The salesperson must be sensitive to this and not push too hard to get an answer until the buyer has had adequate time to make a decision. It is acceptable for the salesperson to review the reasons to act now or soon. Waiting can have consequences (i.e., prices rise, new tax begins the first of the year, etc.) and the buyer should be made aware of these. Exhibit 8.7 illustrates possible time objections.

Time Objections   EXHIBIT 8.7

I need time to think it over.
Ask me again next month when you stop by.
I'm not ready to buy yet.
I haven't made up my mind.
I don't want to commit myself until I've had a chance to talk to engineering (i.e., any other department).

Using LAARC: A Process for Negotiating Buyer Resistance

The term **LAARC** is an acronym for listen, acknowledge, assess, respond, and confirm and describes an effective process for salespeople to follow to overcome sales resistance:

- *Listen:* Salespeople should listen to what their buyers are saying. The ever-present temptation to anticipate what buyers are going to say and cut them off with a premature response should be avoided. Learning to listen is important—it is more than just being polite or professional. Buyers are trying to tell the salesperson something that they consider important.

- *Acknowledge:* As buyers complete their statements, salespeople should acknowledge that they received the message and that they appreciate and can understand the concern. Salespeople should not jump in with an instantaneous defensive response. Before responding, salespeople need a better understanding about what their buyers are saying. By politely pausing and then simply acknowledging their statement, salespeople set themselves up to be a reasonable person—a professional who appreciates other people's opinions. It also buys salespeople precious moments for composing themself and thinking of questions for the next step.

- *Assess:* This step is similar to assessment in the ADAPT process of questioning. This step in dealing with buyer resistance calls for salespeople to ask assessment questions to gain a better understanding of exactly what their buyers are saying and why they are saying it. Equipped with this information and understanding, salespeople are better able to make a meaningful response to the buyer's resistance.

- *Respond:* Based on his or her understanding of what and why the buyer is resisting, the salesperson can respond to the buyer's resistance. Structuring a response typically follows the method that is most appropriate for the situation. The more traditional methods for response include putting off the objection until a more logical time in the presentation, switching focus, using offsetting strategies, using denial, building value, and providing proof. "An Ethical Dilemma" presents the problem of when a trainer and a salesperson have different views on how to respond to an objection.

- *Confirm:* After responding, the salesperson should ask confirmatory questions—response checks to make sure that the buyer's concerns have been adequately met. Once this is confirmed, the presentation can proceed. In fact, experience indicates that this form of buyer confirmation is often a sufficient buying signal to warrant the salesperson's attempt to gain a commitment.

AN ETHICAL DILEMMA

Chuck McShurley has been selling for only a few months. He has heard about the importance of relationship building and is concerned with one of his company's sales trainers. The trainer, Ernie, has stated that a good salesperson should have a pat answer for every objection. Ernie went on to state during training that these answers to objections should be memorized and ready to use each and every time the objection occurs. Chuck feels that each objection may have subtle differences and one pat answer is probably not going to work in all cases. During a recent role play, Chuck did not use his memorized answer to the objection, but a better one he came up with during the role play. Ernie gave him a low score on the role play for not following instructions. What should Chuck do during his next role play when he gets an objection?

	Objection Response Techniques **EXHIBIT 8.8**
Technique	**How It Works**
Forestall	Take care of the objection before the prospect brings it up.
Direct Denial	A rather harsh response that the prospect is wrong.
Indirect Denial	Softening the blow when correcting a prospect or customer's information.
Translation or Boomerang	Turn a reason not to buy into a reason to buy.
Compensation	Counterbalance the objection with an offsetting benefit.
Question	Ask the buyer assessment questions to gain a better understanding of what they are objecting to.
Third-Party Reinforcement	Use the opinion or data from a third-party source to help overcome the objection and reinforce the salesperson's points.

[handwritten annotations: "slide"; "unbiased"; "testimonials – studies – surveys."]

Methods for Responding to Objections

A brief summary of traditional methods for responding to objections follows. Exhibit 8.8 summarizes how each technique works.

Forestalling

When salespeople hear an objection arising repeatedly, they may decide to include an answer to the objection within their sales presentation before voiced by the prospect (i.e., **forestalling**). Marty Reist of MPRS Sales, Inc., often tells his prospects he realizes he's not Nike, Titleist, or Reebok, but his size has not kept him from providing outstanding service to his customers. Marty can add a third-party testimonial to back up his statements and put his prospect's mind at ease. This technique should only be used when there is a high probability that the prospect will indeed raise the objection.

Direct Denial

When using the **direct denial** technique to handle sales resistance, the salesperson is directly telling the customer they are mistaken. Prospects may have incorrect facts or may not understand the information they have.

The prospect might say the following:

> Prospect: I hear you don't offer service agreements on any of your products.

The salesperson knowing this is not true cannot soft pedal their answer. In this situation the prospect is clearly incorrect and the direct denial is the best solution.

> Salesperson: I'm sorry, that is not correct. We offer three- and five-year service contracts, and our warranty is also five years.

The important part of using the direct denial is to not humiliate or anger the prospect. The direct denial should be used sparingly, but it may be easier to use when the salesperson has a good feel for the relationship they have with the buyer.

Indirect Denial

Sometimes it is best not to take an objection head on. The indirect approach takes on the objection, but with a softer more tactful approach. With the **indirect denial**, the salesperson never tells the prospect directly that they are wrong. The best way to utilize this method is to think of it as offering sympathy with the prospect's view and still managing to correct the invalid objection of the buyer. An example follows:

> Prospect: I heard your emergency room beds are $4,000 higher than your competitor's.
>
> Salesperson: Many of our customers had a similar notion that our beds are much more expensive. The actual cost is only $1,200 higher. I have testimonials from other hospitals stating our beds last up to five years longer. You actually save money.

The salesperson here tries to soften the blow with the opening sentence. Then the salesperson must correct the misconception. Techniques can be combined as the salesperson adds information from a third party to add credibility to his or her statement.

Translation or Boomerang

The **translation** or **boomerang** method converts the objection into a reason the prospect should buy. What the salesperson is trying to do is to take a reason not to buy and turn it into a reason to buy. Our friend, Marty Reist of MPRS Sales, Inc., offers the following advice. Marty states:

> Whenever I hear the objection "I don't think your company is large enough to meet our service needs," I immediately come back with "That is exactly the reason you should do business with us. We are big enough to meet your service needs. In fact, you will be calling an 800 number with a larger company and you won't know who you'll get to help you. With our company, anytime you have a problem, question, or concern, you'll call me and talk to a familiar voice."

Another example using the price objection might go like this:

> Buyer: "Your price appears to be high."
>
> Salesperson: "Our high price is an advantage for you; the premium sector of the market not only gives you the highest margin, but it is the most stable sector of the market.

The goal of the translation or boomerang method is to turn an apparent deficiency into an asset or reason to buy.

Compensation

There may be a time when a salesperson has to admit that their product does have the disadvantage that the prospect has noticed. The **compensation** technique is an attempt to show the prospect that a benefit or advantage compensates for an objection. For example, a higher product price is justified by benefits such as better service, faster delivery, or higher performance.

A buyer may use the objection that your company's lead time is 14 days compared to 10 days for your leading competitor. The salesperson's response could be: "Yes, our required lead time is 14 days, but we ship our orders completely assembled. This practically eliminates extra handling in your warehouse. My competitor's product will require assembly by your warehouse workers." With the compensation method the objection is not denied at all—it is acknowledged, then balanced by compensating features, advantages, and benefits.

Questioning or Assessing

Another potentially effective way to handle buyer resistance is to convert the objection into a question. This technique calls for the salesperson to ask **questions** or **assess** to gain a better understanding of the exact nature of the buyer's objections.

You Can't Be Afraid of Sales Resistance

John Huff, a Shering-Plough sales representative states, "You can't be afraid of sales resistance. I had a trainer once who said a salesperson has not done his or her job properly if there is sales resistance. From my experiences in the field, I don't necessarily agree with this. Some of my doctors are so busy with patients that they can't keep up on every medication and the changes that take place day to day. That's where I come in; it's my job to get the doctor the correct information so he or she can make an informed decision. It's not easy to overcome every prospect's objection, but I know now if prospects question price, delivery of samples, the ability of the product to get the job done, etc. at the very least they're showing interest and I've got a chance to win them over."

Sometimes it is difficult for the salesperson to know the exact problem. This technique is good for clarifying the real objection. This technique can also be effective in resolving the objection if the prospect is shooting from the hip and does not have a strong reason for the objection. John Huff, in "Professional Selling in the 21st Century: You Can't Be Afraid of Sales Resistance," describes the importance of providing the correct information when sales resistance is encountered. Exhibit 8.9 illustrates the question method as a tool to overcome sales resistance.

Third-Party Reinforcement

The **third-party reinforcement** technique uses the opinion or research of a third person or company to help overcome and reinforce the salesperson's sales points. A wide range of proof statements can be used by salespeople today. Consumer reports, government reports, and independent testing agencies can all be used to back up a salesperson's statement. Secondary data like this or experience data from a reliable third party could be all that is needed to turn around a skeptical prospect. A salesperson must remember this technique will only work if the buyer believes in the third-party source the salesperson is using.

Once the salesperson has answered all the buyer's questions and has resolved resistance issues that have come up during the presentation, the salesperson should summarize all the pertinent buying signals.

Questioning (Assessing) to Overcome Sales Resistance	EXHIBIT 8.9

Example 1
Buyer: I'm not sure I am ready to act at this time.
Salesperson: Can you tell me what is causing your hesitation?

Example 2
Buyer: Your price seems to be a little high.
Salesperson: Can you tell me what price you had in mind? Have other suppliers quoted you a lower price?

Example 3
Buyer: Your delivery schedule does not work for us.
Salesperson: Who are you comparing me to? Can you please tell me what delivery schedule will work for your company?

SUMMARIZING SOLUTIONS TO CONFIRM BENEFITS

The mark of a good salesperson is the ability to listen and exactly determine the customer's needs. It is not unusual for salespeople to incorporate the outstanding benefits of their product into the sales presentation. A salesperson can identify many potential benefits for each product and feature. However, it does not make sense for a salesperson to talk about potential benefits that the buyer may not need. The salesperson must determine the confirmed benefits and make these the focal point of the sales summary before asking for the business. A salesperson must be alert to the one, two, or three benefits that generate the most excitement to the buyer. The confirmed benefits that are of greatest interest to the buyer deserve the greatest emphasis. These benefits should be summarized in such a way that the buyer sees a direct connection in what he or she has been telling the salesperson over the course of the selling cycle and the proposal being offered to meet his or her needs. Once this is done, it is time to ask for the business.

SECURING COMMITMENT AND CLOSING

Ultimately, a large part of most salespeople's performance evaluation is based on their ability to gain customer commitment, often called closing sales. Because of this close relationship between compensation and getting orders, traditional selling has tended to overemphasize the importance of gaining commitment. In fact, there are those who think that just about any salesperson can find a new prospect, open a sale, or take an order. These same people infer it takes a trained, motivated, and skilled professional to close a sale. They go on to say that the close is the keystone to a salesperson's success, and a good salesperson will have mastered many new ways to close the sale. This outmoded emphasis on closing skills is typical of transaction selling techniques that stress making the sales call at all cost.

Another popular but outdated suggestion to salespeople is to "close early and often." This is particularly bad advice if the prospect is not prepared to make a decision, responds negatively to a premature attempt to consummate the sale, and then (following the principles of cognitive consistency) proceeds to reinforce the prior negative position as the salesperson plugs away, firing one closing salvo after another at the beleaguered prospect. Research tells us that it will take several sales calls to make an initial sale, so it is somewhat bewildering to still encounter such tired old battle cries as "the ABCs of selling, which stand for Always Be Closing."

Manipulative closing gimmicks are less likely to be effective as professional buyers grow weary with the cat-and-mouse approach to selling that is still practiced by a surprising number of salespeople. It is also surprising to find many salespeople who view their customers as combatants over whom victory is sought. Once the sale is made by salespeople who have adversarial, me-against-you attitudes, the customer is likely to be neglected as the salesperson rides off into the sunset in search of yet another battle with yet another lowly customer.

One time-honored thought that does retain contemporary relevance is that "nobody likes to be sold, but everybody likes to buy." In other words, salespeople should facilitate decision making by pointing out a suggested course of action but should allow the prospect plenty of mental space within which a rational decision can be reached. Taken to its logical conclusion, this means that it may be acceptable to make a sales call without asking for the order. Salespeople must be cognizant, however, of their responsibility to advance the relationship toward a profitable sale, lest they become the most dreaded of all types of salespeople—the paid conversationalist.

It has already been mentioned that the salesperson has taken on the expanded roles of business consultant and relationship manager, which is not consistent with pressuring customers until they give in and say yes. Fortunately, things have changed to the point that today's professional salesperson attempts to gain commitment when the buyer is ready to buy. The salesperson should evaluate each presentation and attempt to determine the causes of its success or failure with the customer. The difference between closing and earning commitment is that commitment is more than just securing an order. Commitment insinuates the beginning of a long-term relationship.

Guidelines for Earning Commitment

Earning commitment or gaining commitment is the culmination of the selling process. However, it should not be viewed as a formal stage that only comes at the end of the presentation. Many salespeople fail to recognize early buyer commitment by focusing on their presentation and not the comments being made by the buyer. **Commitment signals** are favorable statements that may be made by the buyer, such as:

> I like that size.
> That will get the job done.
> The price is lower than I thought it would be.
> I didn't realize you delivered every day.

These statements should be considered green lights that allow the salesperson to move the process forward. They also may come in the form of trial commitments.

Throughout the presentation it is appropriate to determine a prospect's reaction to a particular feature or product. At this time, a trial commitment is a question designed to determine a prospect's reaction without forcing the prospect to make a final yes or no buying decision. The trial commitment is an effort to elicit how far along the prospect is in his or her decision making. Confirmation on the prospect's part on key features helps the salesperson determine how ready the prospect is to buy.

Open-ended questions are a good way to test prospect readiness. A salesperson might ask during his or her presentation, "What do you think of our computer's larger memory capacity?" The answer to this will help direct the salesperson to his or her next sales points. However, many statements made by buyers should be considered red lights, a formal objection. The salesperson must consider each of these objections and work to overcome them. Red light statements might include:

> I'm not sure that will work.
> The price is higher than I thought it would be.
> Your delivery schedule does not work for us.
> I don't see the advantage of going with your proposal.

Red light statements are commitment caution signals and must be resolved to the buyer's satisfaction before asking for a commitment. Closing early and often and having a closing quota for each sales call are traditional methods that are not liked by buyers. The salesperson should put himself or herself in the buyer's shoes and think about how

---

PROFESSIONAL SELLING IN THE 21ST CENTURY

Using Fewer Earning Commitment Techniques Makes Sales Representatives More Successful!

Dave Wheat, sales manager for TransWestern Publishing, has changed his selling style over the past 20 years. Dave states, "I remember coming out of college and going to basic sales training. The focus back then was to learn a lot of closing techniques and use them all if you could. I remember our sales trainer claiming the best salespeople were the best closers. This never set quite right with me, as I noticed early on that my prospects and customers appeared uncomfortable when I spent a lot of time closing. I quickly learned that I didn't need to close all of the time or use all my closing techniques. Basically, I've reduced my list to three. I use a summary close, a success-story close (customers like to know if you've done this before), and I use a direct close. For over 10 years now this is all I use and it has worked for me."

he or she would like to be hammered with many closes throughout a sales presentation, particularly if a few red lights are introduced. Many times, the best method for earning commitment is to simply ask for the business. If the prospect has been qualified properly and a number of confirmed benefits have been uncovered, then the natural next step is to ask for the business. When does the salesperson ask for the business? When the buyer is ready to buy. The example in "Professional Selling in the 21st Century: Using Fewer Earning Commitment Techniques Makes Sales Representatives More Successful" describes Dave Wheat's views on how to earn commitment.

Techniques to Earn Commitment

Some sales trainers will try to teach their salesforces literally hundreds of commitment techniques. One trainer recommended to his salesforce that the salespeople learn two new commitment techniques per week. Then at the end of the year, they would have more than 100 commitment techniques ready to use. Relationship managers today do not need many commitment techniques. A few good ones will suffice. Five techniques that are conducive to relationship building follow:

1. **Ask for the Order/Direct Commitment.**
   It is not unusual for inexperienced salespeople to lose an order simply by not asking the customer to buy. Professional buyers report that an amazing number of salespeople fear rejection. When the buyer is ready to buy, the salesperson must be prepared to ask for the buyer's commitment. The **direct commitment** is a straightforward request for an order. A salesperson ought to be confident if he or she has covered all the necessary features and benefits of the product and matched these with the buyer's needs. At this time, the salesperson cannot be afraid to ask "Tom, can we set up an office visit for next week?" or "Mary, I'd like to have your business, if we can get the order signed today, delivery can take place early next week." Many buyers appreciate the direct approach. There is no confusion as to what the salesperson wants the buyer to do.

2. **Legitimate Choice/Alternative Choice.**
   The **legitimate choice** asks the prospect to select from two or more choices. For example, will the HP 400 or the HP 600 be the one you want? An investment broker might ask his or her prospect, "Do you feel your budget would allow you to invest $1,000 a month or would $500 a month be better? The theory behind this technique suggests buyers do not like to be told what to do but do like making a decision over limited choices.

3. **Summary Commitment.**
   A very effective way to gain agreement is to summarize all the major benefits the buyer has confirmed over the course of the sales calls. Salespeople should keep track of all the important points covered in previous calls so they can emphasize them again in summary form.
   In using the **summary commitment** technique, a computer salesperson might say:

   Of course, Tom, this is an important decision, so to make the best possible choice, let's go over the major concepts we've discussed. We have agreed that Thompson Computers will provide some definite advantages. First, our system will lower your computing costs; second, our system will last longer and has a better warranty, thus saving you money; and finally, your data processing people will be happier because our faster system will reduce their workload. They'll get to go home earlier each evening.

   The summary commitment is a valuable technique in that it reminds prospects of all the major benefits that have been mentioned in previous sales calls.

4. **The T-Account or the Balance Sheet Commitment.**
   The **T-account commitment** or **balance sheet commitment** is essentially a summary commitment on paper. With the T-account commitment, the sales representative

T-Account Close EXHIBIT 8.10	
Reasons to Buy	**Reasons Not to Buy**
• Daily delivery schedule meets our needs • Warranty agreement is longer than the one I have now (5 years versus 3 years) • You provide a training program • Your service department is located in our city	• Because of extra services • Your price *is too high*

takes out a sheet of paper and draws a large "T" across it. On the left-hand side, the salesperson and buyer brainstorm the reasons to buy. Here, the salesperson will list with the buyer all the positive selling points (benefits) they discussed throughout the selling process. Once this is completed, the salesperson asks the buyer for any reasons that he or she would not want to purchase. Visually, the left-hand side should help the buyer make his or her decision as seen in Exhibit 8.10. This will not work if the weight of the reason not to buy outweighs the reasons to buy. In the example in Exhibit 8.10, the buyer wants to act, but does not have the money at this time.

5. **Success Story Commitment.**

   Every company has many satisfied customers. These customers started out having problems, and the sales representative helped solve these problems by recommending the product or products that matched the customer's needs. Buyers are thankful and grateful when the salesperson helps solve problems. When the salesperson relates a story about how one of his or her customers had a similar problem and solved it by using the salesperson's product, a reluctant buyer can be reassured that the salesperson has done this before successfully. If the salesperson decides to use the customer's name and company, then the salesperson must be sure to get permission to do so. A **success story commitment** may go something like this:

   > Tom, thanks for sharing your copier problems with me. I had another customer you might know, Betty Brown, who had the same problem over at Thompson Electronics. We installed the CP 2000 and eliminated the problem completely. Please feel free to give Betty a call. She is very happy with our solution.

   Some companies will use the success story commitment by actually taking the prospect to a satisfied customer. The salesperson may leave the prospect alone with the satisfied customer so the two can talk confidentially. A satisfied customer can help a salesperson earn commitment by answering questions a reluctant prospect needs answered before they can purchase. A summary of relationship-building earning commitment techniques can be found in Exhibit 8.11.

Probe to Earn Commitment

Every attempt to earn commitment will not be successful. Successful salespeople cannot be afraid to ask a prospect why he or she is hesitating to make a decision. It is the salesperson's job to uncover the reason why the prospect is hesitating by asking a series of

Techniques to Earn Commitment   EXHIBIT 8.11
1. Direct Commitment—Simply ask for the order. 2. Legitimate Choice/Alternative Choice—Give the prospect a limited number of choices 3. Summary Commitment—Summarize all the confirmed benefits that have been agreed to 4. T-Account/Balance Sheet Commitment—Summary close on paper 5. Success Story Commitment—Salesperson tells a story of a business that successfully solved a   problem by buying his or her product

questions that get at the key issues. For instance, a buyer may state that he or she is not ready to sign an order. The salesperson must ask, "Mary, there must be a reason why you are reluctant to do business with me and my company. Do you mind if I ask what it is?" The salesperson must then listen and respond accordingly. A salesperson cannot be afraid to ask why a prospect is reluctant to purchase.

Traditional Methods

Sales trainers across the nation teach hundreds of techniques to earn commitment. Exhibit 8.12 is a summary of the traditional commitment techniques. The vast majority of these are not conducive to building a strong buyer–seller relationship. As prospects become more sophisticated, most will be turned off by these techniques and they will be ineffective. "An Ethical Dilemma" asks the question, "How many earning commitment techniques should a good salesperson have ready to use on a sales call?"

Research has clearly shown that buyers are open to consultative techniques of handling objections (for example, questioning and assessing, direct denial with facts, and so on) and earning commitment (for example, asking for the order in a straightforward manner, summarizing key benefits). On the other hand, buyers have stated that standard persuasive (traditional) tactics that have been used for years are unacceptable. They now view traditional techniques of handling objections (for example, forestalling, postponing) and earning commitment (for example, standing room only, fear) as overly aggressive and unprofessional.[2]

EXHIBIT 8.12 Traditional Commitment Method

Method	How to Use It
Standing-Room-Only Close	This close puts a time limit on the client in an attempt to hurry the decision to close. "These prices are only good until tomorrow."
Assumptive Close	The salesperson assumes that an agreement has been reached. The salesperson places the order form in front of the buyer and hands him or her a pen.
Fear or Emotional Close	The salesperson tells a story of something bad happening if the purchase is not made. "If you don't purchase this insurance and you die, your wife will have to sell the house and live on the street."
Continuous Yes Close	This close uses the principle that saying yes gets to be a habit. The salesperson asks a number of questions, each formulated so that the prospect answers yes.
Minor-Points Close	Seeks agreement on relatively minor (trivial) issues associated with the full order. "Do you prefer cash or charge?"

AN ETHICAL DILEMMA

Brooke Scherry just returned from a sales training seminar where she was told a good salesperson should learn two new closing techniques a week and at the end of the year they would have over 100 closing techniques at their disposal. The company Brooke works for leans toward closing when it is appropriate. How many earning commitment techniques should a good salesperson have ready to use on a sales call? What advice do you have for Brooke about closing too often as opposed to when it is appropriate?

SUMMARY

1. **Explain why it is important to anticipate and overcome buyer concerns and resistance.** During the early years of selling, salespeople looked at sales resistance as a negative that was a likely indication that their buyer was not going to buy. This notion has changed over the years and now objections are viewed as opportunities to sell. Salespeople should be grateful for objections and always treat them as indications that the prospect needs more information, and if the salesperson provides the correct information, they are moving closer to gaining the sale.

2. **Understand why prospects raise objections.** Some prospects are happy with their present suppliers and want to avoid the sales interview. In other instances, the salesperson has failed to properly qualify the prospect. A prospect who has recently purchased a product is probably not in the market for another. Sometimes, prospects simply lack information on the salesperson's product category and they are uncomfortable making a decision.

3. **Describe the five major types of sales resistance.** Typically, objections include: "I don't need your product," "Your product is not a good fit," "I don't know your company," "Your price is too high," "This is a bad time to buy."

4. **Explain how the LAARC method can be used to overcome buyer objections.** LAARC allows the salesperson to carefully listen to what the buyer is saying. It allows the salesperson to better understand the buyer's objections. After this careful analysis, the salesperson can then respond. The buyer feels the salesperson is responding to his or her specific concern rather than giving a prepared answer.

5. **Describe the traditional methods for responding to buyer objections.** Salespeople have a number of traditional techniques at their disposal to handle resistance. Some of the more popular techniques include: forestalling, answering the objection before the prospect brings it up; direct denial; indirect denial, softens the answer; translation or boomerang, turn a reason not to buy into a reason to buy; compensation, offset the objection with superior benefits; question, use questions to uncover buyer's concerns; and third-party reinforcements, use the opinion or research of others to substantiate claims.

6. **List and explain the earning commitment techniques that enhance relationship building.** Many techniques can be used to earn commitment. Most are gimmicky in nature and reinforce the notion of traditional selling. Successful relationship-building techniques include the summary commitment, the success story commitment, and the direct commitment or ask for the order.

UNDERSTANDING PROFESSIONAL SELLING TERMS

sales resistance	third-party reinforcement
need objection	commitment signals
product or service objection	direct commitment
company or source objection	alternative choice
price objection	legitimate choice
time objection	summary commitment
LAARC	T-account or balance sheet commitment
forestalling	success story commitment
direct denial	standing-room-only close
indirect denial	assumptive close
translation or boomerang	fear or emotional close
compensation	continuous yes close
questions or assess	minor-points close

DEVELOPING PROFESSIONAL SELLING KNOWLEDGE

1. Why is it important for a salesperson to anticipate a buyer's concerns and objections?

2. Is one type of sales resistance (i.e., need, price) more difficult to handle than another (i.e., source, product, time)?

3. Should the direct denial method ever be used?

4. Some trainers have been heard to say, "If a salesperson gets sales resistance, then he or she has not done a very good job during the sales presentation." Do you agree with this?

5. Under what circumstances does a salesperson want sales resistance?

6. Are there ever going to be situations where the salesperson can't overcome sales resistance?

7. Some trainers and sales experts think that closing is the most important stage of the sales process. Do you feel this way?

8. Why should salespeople have many closing techniques ready to use during a sales call? Explain.

9. Can the LAARC method be used for all types of sales resistance? Explain.

10. What is the best method to handle sales resistance?

BUILDING PROFESSIONAL SELLING SKILLS

1. Explain why each of the following statements would be considered a signal commitment.

   a) The prospect makes a positive statement.
   b) A worried look is replaced by a happy look.
   c) The prospect starts playing with a pen or the order form.
   d) The prospect looks at the product with a favorable expression.
   e) The prospect touches the product.
   f) The prospect is using or trying out the product.
   g) The prospect's tone of voice changes or his or her body relaxes.
   h) The prospect questions price, usage, or delivery.

2. Using the following list, address each of the indicated buyer objections by using the LAARC process. The Listen step is implicit and omitted from the written responses. Take time to write out your answers. Responses will be used in class discussion.

   a) Your price is too high.
      Acknowledge
      Assess
      Respond
      Confirm
   b) I like what I see, but I need to talk with my boss before I do anything.
      Acknowledge
      Assess
      Respond
      Confirm
   c) I just don't think we need it; we already use your competitor's products and they work alright.
      Acknowledge
      Assess
      Respond
      Confirm
   d) I'm just not sure our employees can adapt to the new technology.
      Acknowledge
      Assess
      Respond
      Confirm

e) The last time we bought from your company we had problems with product reliability.
Acknowledge
Assess
Respond
Confirm

3. **Situation:**   Read the Ethical Dilemma on page 222.

   Characters: Chuck McShurley, sales representative; Ernie, sales trainer

   Scene 1:   *Location*—Sales training classroom. *Action*—The trainer tells the class they need one pat answer.

   Write out an answer to the following objections, no need, no money. Use your answers to these objections as written. How did they work? Have the buyer respond negatively to your answers. What next?

   Scene 2:   *Location*—Sales training classroom. *Action*—The trainer wants the class to continue the role play once the buyer answers negatively to the memorized response.

ROLE PLAY

   Role play how Chuck should respond once the buyer disagrees with Chuck's attempt to handle the objection.

   Upon completion of the role plays, address the following questions:

   3a. What are the potential problems for Chuck if he disagrees with his sales trainer?
   3b. Is it ever alright to tell a prospect or customer you don't know the answer?

4. **Situation:**   Read the Ethical Dilemma on page 230.

   Characters: Brooke Sherry, sales representative; buyer

   Scene: *Location*—Buyer's office. *Action*—Brooke has begun her sales presentation.

ROLE PLAY

   Role play Brooke trying 3 to 5 closes during her presentation.

   Upon completion of the role play, address the following questions:

   4a. Were you comfortable using 3 to 5 closes during your presentation?
   4b. What risks does the salesperson run by closing several times during his or her presentation?

5. The ability to handle sales resistance and earn commitment are two crucial areas that have much to do with a salesperson's success.

   Assignment 1
   Go to your favorite search engine and type in "sales, how to close," "sales, how to handle sales resistance," "sales, how to handle objections."

   What did you find?

   Write a short report to your boss that you want to lead a sales meeting and cover each of these topics. Write up some of the things you want to talk about that will help your salesforce.

   Assignment 2
   Type in: "**http://www.davekahle.com/close.htm.**"

   What does he mean that you have to "open" before you "close"?

   Assignment 3
   Type in: "**www.summitconsulting.com/articles.**" Next, scroll down to "overcoming objections." Click on "Overcoming Sales Resistance Areas." Read the article "Consulting Tips from the Million Dollar Consultant: Overcoming Sales Resistance Areas." Which of these four areas do you think are most difficult to overcome? Does the article leave out any areas?

MAKING PROFESSIONAL SELLING DECISIONS

Case 8.1: Thompson Engineering

Tyler Houston sells for Thompson Engineering. He has been calling on Hudson Distributors for close to two years. Over the course of 15 calls, he has sold them nothing to date. He thinks that he is extremely close to getting an order. Tyler knows that Hudson is happy with its present supplier, but he is aware that they have received some late deliveries. Tom Harris, Hudson's senior buyer, has given every indication that he likes Tyler's products and Tyler.

During Tyler's most recent call, Tom told him that he'd have to have a couple of weeks to go over Tyler's proposal. Tom really didn't have any major objections during the presentation. Tyler knows his price, quality, and service are equal to or exceed Hudson's present supplier.

Questions

1. Tom told Tyler that he needed a couple of weeks to think about his proposal. How should Tyler handle this?
2. What should Tyler have done during the sales presentation when Tom told him that he needed to think it over?
3. What techniques should Tyler have used to overcome the forestalling tactic?

Situation:	Read Case 8.1	**ROLE PLAY**
Characters:	Tyler Houston, sales representative; Tom Harris, senior buyer	
Scene 1:	*Location*—Tom's office. *Action*—Tom has just stated he needs a couple of weeks to go over Tyler's proposal.	

Role play how Tyler should respond to Tom's needing two weeks to think it over.

Scene 2:	*Location*—Tom's office. *Action*—Tyler is summarizing his product's advantages (i.e., price, quality, service).

Role play Tom's summary and his asking for the order.

Upon completion of the role plays, address the following questions:

1. Why do buyers hesitate and ask for more time to think over proposals?
2. How hard should Tyler press to get Tom to act now?

Case 8.2: Data Computers

Steve Thomas sells for Data Computers. Steve has recently completed his training seminars and has been back in the field for three months. He has been anxious to try out the selling processes his company uses. He is equally excited about the techniques he has been taught on how to handle sales resistance and earn commitment. His trainers were very impressed with his ability to use the T-account method to earn commitment. Steve feels this technique is very pragmatic and visually shows his prospects why they should use his products. He has been surprised at how ineffective this technique has been on recent sales calls. He is beginning to wonder if he should try some other earning commitment techniques.

Here is a copy of Steve's notes from a prospect he has been working on.

Steve's Notes:

Client: Anderson Printing, Bob Martin, purchasing agent

Prospect looks good—looks like a good fit

Potential to earn business B+/A−

Present equipment—4 years old

Fact-finding call on 9/1, buyer went to local college, 2 kids

9/15 Took engineers in and looked at his present system. Basically it is ready to be replaced. Purchased in 1999.

9/22 Made major proposal to Bob Martin, couldn't get engineers to attend. They had all-day meetings. Gave proposal to Bob and made appointment to come back in two days to review proposal.

9/24 Overall good meeting, I used the T-account method with Bob, the results are shown on the following page.

Steve is afraid he is going to lose the order. He didn't leave Bob with a good feeling.

1. Look over the notes from each one of Steve's sales calls. Can you make any recommendations on what Steve might have done differently?
2. Steve and Bob came up with five reasons to buy and two reasons not to act. What is holding Bob back?

Reasons To Act	Reasons Not To Act
1. New system's faster, saves time and energy	1. Still thinks the price is high even with the cost savings
2. Can have immediate delivery, does not have to wait	2. Needs to talk over decision with engineers
3. Really likes the cost savings	
4. Can save up to $100 per month in operating cost	
5. Quality looks great	

ROLE PLAY

Situation: Read Case 8.2

Characters: Steve Thomas, sales representative; Bob Martin, service buyer

Scene 1:   *Location*—Bob's office. *Action*— Steve is going to review the proposal with Bob.

Role play the T-account earning commitment with Bob.

Scene 2:   *Location*—Bob's office. *Action*— Steve has just asked for the order after the T-account earning commitment technique has been used.

Role play Bob telling Steve he needs time to think it over and Steve's response.

Upon completion of the role plays, address the following questions:

1. Can you find any fault in Steve's logic that there are more reasons to act than not to act?
2. What are the problems with relying on one earning commitment technique?

EXPERIENTIAL EXERCISE

2.1

Ethics Scale

Objective

You will develop an understanding of the multitude of ethical situations that exist.

THE EXERCISE ASSIGNMENT

How ethical is each of the following situations? Be prepared to defend your answer. Please circle your response for each situation.

1. The salesperson seeks confidential information about competitors by questioning suppliers.

   very ethical   ethical   neither   unethical   very unethical

2. The salesperson seeks information from the purchaser on competitors' quotations for the purpose of submitting another quotation.

   very ethical   ethical   neither   unethical   very unethical

3. The buyer gives the salesperson information on competitors' quotations, then allows him or her to requote.

   very ethical   ethical   neither   unethical   very unethical

4. The buyer exaggerates the seriousness of a problem to a salesperson in order to get a better price or some other concession.

   very ethical   ethical   neither   unethical   very unethical

Source: Adapted from Trawick, I. F., J. E. Swan, G. W. McGee, and D. R. Rink, *Journal of The Academy of Marketing Science*, 1991, Vol. 19, No. 1, p. 17–23; Dubinsky, A. J. and T. N. Ingram, "Correlates of Salespeople Ethical Conflict: An Exploratory Investigation," *Journal of Business Ethics*, 3, 1984, p. 343–353; Dubinsky, A. J. and I. M. Gwin, "Business Ethics: Buyers and Sellers," *Journal of Purchasing and Materials Management*, Winter 1981, Vol. 17, p. 9–16.

5. To obtain a lower price or other concession, the buyer *falsely* informs an existing supplier that the company may use another source.

very ethical   **ethical**   **neither**   **unethical**   **very unethical**

6. The buyer solicits quotations from new sources, when a marked preference for existing suppliers is the norm, merely to fill a quota for bids.

very ethical   **ethical**   **neither**   **unethical**   **very unethical**

7. The salesperson attempts to get the buyer to divulge competitors' bids in low-bid buying situations.

very ethical   **ethical**   **neither**   **unethical**   **very unethical**

8. The salesperson exaggerates how quickly orders will be delivered to get a sale.

very ethical   **ethical**   **neither**   **unethical**   **very unethical**

9. The salesperson lets it be known that he or she has information about a competitor if purchasing agent is interested.

very ethical   **ethical**   **neither**   **unethical**   **very unethical**

10. The salesperson hints that, if order is placed, the price might be lower on the next order, when it is not so.

very ethical   **ethical**   **neither**   **unethical**   **very unethical**

11. The salesperson stresses only positive aspects of the product, omitting possible problems the purchasing firm might have with it.

very ethical   **ethical**   **neither**   **unethical**   **very unethical**

12. The buyer allows such factors as race, sex, ethnic group affiliation, and religious persuasion to affect salesperson selection.

very ethical   **ethical**   **neither**   **unethical**   **very unethical**

13. The buyer discriminates against a vendor whose salespeople use "backdoor" selling instead of going through purchasing department.

very ethical   **ethical**   **neither**   **unethical**   **very unethical**

14. The buyer discriminates on the basis of nepotism. (Nepotism is used here in a broad sense to cover all preferential treatment extended to suppliers who are relatives or friends, or are recommended by higher management.)

very ethical   **ethical**   **neither**   **unethical**   **very unethical**

15. In a shortage situation, the salesperson allocates product shipments to purchasing agents the seller personally likes.

very ethical   **ethical**   **neither**   **unethical**   **very unethical**

16. In order to obtain a lower price or other concession, the buyer informs an existing supplier that the company may use a second source.

very ethical   **ethical**   **neither**   **unethical**   **very unethical**

17. In a reciprocal buying situation, salesperson hints that unless an order is forthcoming, the prospect's sales to the selling firm might suffer.

very ethical   **ethical**   **neither**   **unethical**   **very unethical**

18. The salesperson attempts to use the economic power of the firm to obtain concessions from the buyer.

very ethical   **ethical**   **neither**   **unethical**   **very unethical**

19. The salesperson has less competitive prices or other terms for buyers who depend on the firm as the sole source of supply.

    very ethical   ethical   neither   unethical   very unethical

20. The buyer accepts from a supplier gifts such as sales promotion prizes and "purchase volume incentives."

    very ethical   ethical   neither   unethical   very unethical

21. The buyer accepts trips, meals, or other free entertainment.

    very ethical   ethical   neither   unethical   very unethical

22. The salesperson gives a purchaser who was one of the best customers a gift worth $50 or more at Christmas or other occasions.

    very ethical   ethical   neither   unethical   very unethical

23. The salesperson gives a potential customer a gift worth $50 or more at Christmas or other occasions.

    very ethical   ethical   neither   unethical   very unethical

24. The salesperson grants price concessions to purchasing agents of companies in which the salesperson owns stock.

    very ethical   ethical   neither   unethical   very unethical

25. The salesperson attempts to sell to a purchasing agent a product that has little or no value to buyer's company.

    very ethical   ethical   neither   unethical   very unethical

Building Relationships after the Sale

Objective

You will discover the importance of follow-up activities in building relationships.

THE EXERCISE ASSIGNMENT

Not many years ago salespeople often thought their jobs were complete once the order was signed. Today, for a business to survive, repeat business is critical. A greater emphasis has been placed on the follow-up stage of the selling process. Continued building of the relationship should be your goal well after the sale.

1. Show appreciation after the sale. How might you accomplish this?

   _____

   _____

   _____

2. Monitor delivery and installation. Why is this important?

   _____

   _____

   _____

3. Learn the names of the switchboard operator, receptionists, office manager, users of the product, etc. How might you accomplish this and why is it important?

   _____

   _____

   _____

4. Keep all of your promises. How might you accomplish this and why is this important?

_____

_____

_____

5. Find ways to add value to your product or service. How might you accomplish this and why is it important?

_____

_____

_____

6. What should you try to accomplish during follow-up calls?

_____

_____

_____

Comparing the Traditional Selling Process with the Process of Trust-Based Relationship Selling

Objective

To assist the student in acquiring a richer understanding of the differences between the traditional process of selling and the process inherent to trust-based relationship selling.

THE EXERCISE ASSIGNMENT

Study and discuss the activities comprising the traditional task-focused selling process and the trust-based relationship selling process (See Exhibit 1.2 on p. 8). As you study these two processes, compare and contrast their component activities, their emphasis, and focus. Then complete the following study questions:

1. Compare and contrast these two processes of selling. How are they similar? How do they differ?

   _____

   _____

   _____

   _____

   _____

   _____

   _____

   _____

2. What is the primary focus of each of the two processes?

_____

_____

_____

_____

_____

_____

_____

_____

_____

3. Why has the evolution toward trust-based relationship selling taken place? What has caused (is causing) this shift from one process to another?

_____

_____

_____

_____

_____

_____

_____

_____

_____

_____

4. What advantages are offered to the seller by trust-based relationship selling?

_____

_____

_____

_____

_____

_____

_____

_____

_____

To the buyer?

_____

_____

_____

_____

_____

5. What inherent disadvantages to the seller result from trust-based relationship selling?

_____

_____

_____

_____

_____

_____

_____

_____

To the buyer?

_____

_____

_____

_____

_____

_____

3.1

Gathering Information about the Buyer

Objective:

You will understand why collecting information about your prospect is important.

THE EXERCISE ASSIGNMENT

The more you know about your buyer, the better chance you have to sell. Over time you should be able to accumulate knowledge about your prospect. The information you will need varies with the kind of product you are selling. As a rule, you should definitely know a few basic things about your customers. A salesperson can learn a great deal about a customer over time by collecting bits and pieces of information, sorting them out, and developing a personalized, custom presentation for the customer.

The following information is helpful in preparing this personalized presentation.

1. The prospect's name, with correct spelling and correct pronunciation. Why is it important to know the correct spelling and pronunciation of your prospect's name?

   _____

   _____

   _____

2. The prospect's correct title. Why is it important to know the correct title of your prospect?

   _____

   _____

   _____

3. The prospect's hobbies. Why is it important to know your prospect's hobbies?

_____

_____

_____

4. The prospect's friends. Why is it important to know the names of your prospect's friends?

_____

_____

_____

5. The prospect's status in the community. Why is it important to know the prospect's status in the community?

_____

_____

_____

6. Things not to talk about with the prospect. Why is it important to know certain topics not to talk about with the prospect?

_____

_____

_____

7. The prospect's children. Why is it important to know the names and ages of your prospect's children?

_____

_____

_____

8. The prospect's favorite teams. Why is it important to know your prospect's favorite sports teams?

_____

_____

_____

9. Harvey Mackay in _Swim with the Sharks Without Being Eaten Alive_ has his salesforce collect information on 66 items that profile their customers. Some of these include:

(1) Does the customer smoke?
(2) What is spouse's education?
(3) Graduated from what university?
(4) Members of which clubs or service clubs?
(5) Their vacation habits?
(6) The make and model of car they drive?

Why is this type of information important to the salesperson?

_____

_____

_____

_____

_____

POINTS FOR DISCUSSION

1. How can this information improve the communication process with the buyer?

_____

_____

_____

_____

2. How do you collect this information?

_____

_____

_____

_____

3. How long should it take you to collect this information?

_____

_____

_____

_____

4. What other types of information would be valuable to have?

_____

_____

_____

_____

Key Questions During the Buying Process

Objective:

You will be able to understand the importance of good, effective questioning.

THE EXERCISE ASSIGNMENT

During the buying process, the salesperson must always be gathering pertinent information. Answers to the following questions will help the salesperson identify the key individuals in a buying center and devise a strategy to penetrate the buying process. These questions should be asked of the various individuals the salesperson meets within a company.

1. Who, besides you, will be making the decision to buy? Explain why this question is important. _____

_____

_____

2. What problems do you foresee in changing suppliers? Explain why this question is important. _____

_____

_____

3. What will you need to do to win the support of the others? Explain why this question is important. _____

_____

_____

4. When do you plan to make the purchase decision? Explain why this question is important. _____

   _____

   _____

5. What sense of urgency do you feel about this buying decision? Explain why this question is important. _____

   _____

   _____

6. Other important questions? _____

   _____

   Why? _____

Triggering the Buying Process— Needs Awareness

Objective:

You will be able to determine both external and internal stimuli of the buying process needs recognition stage.

THE EXERCISE ASSIGNMENT

One of the most simple, yet far-reaching insights into buying behavior is that it is actually a *process*. There is a logical sequence of stages that collectively result in product and vendor choices. The salesperson is most concerned with *who* triggers stage one and *how* it becomes activated. As described earlier in Module 3, the eight sequential stages comprising the organizational buyer's decision process are as follows:

Stage 1. Anticipation or recognition of a problem (need) and a general solution

Stage 2. Determination of characteristics and quantity of needed item

Stage 3. Description of characteristics and quantity of needed item

Stage 4. Search for and qualification of potential source

Stage 5. Acquisition and analysis of proposal

Stage 6. Evaluation of proposals and selection of supplier(s)

Stage 7. Selection of order routine

Stage 8. Performance feedback and evaluation

The buying process begins when someone realizes a problem can be solved or an opportunity can be met by purchasing a product or service. This needs recognition can be initiated by either internal or external stimuli.

Assume that you are a salesperson for Sharp Business Equipment. An existing account, Performance Services International, has expressed interest in updating its office and communications equipment. With the understanding that needs can be initiated by internal as well as external cues and stimuli, you have been working with the central purchasing office to develop better recognition and understanding of the company's needs and potential solutions.

Use the following worksheet to identify internal and external stimuli or cues that might arouse anticipation or recognition of a problem or need and initiate the buying process.

Internal Stimuli:

E
X   *Accounting department requests FAX machine.* How might this source be triggered?
A   *Salesperson meets with and works with different members of the accounting department*
M
P   *and demonstrates the usefulness and benefits of a FAX.*
L
E   _____

1. _____. How might this source be triggered?

   _____

   _____

   _____

2. _____. How might this source be triggered?

   _____

   _____

   _____

3. _____. How might this source be triggered?

   _____

   _____

   _____

4. _____. How might this source be triggered?

   _____

   _____

   _____

External Stimuli:

E

X   *Data processing department sees ad in trade publication.* How might this source be

A

M   triggered? *Understanding that members of the data processing department are*

P

L   *exploring the benefits of using a FAX machine, salesperson leaves several trade*

E   *publications in the office for them to read.*

1. _____. How might this source be triggered?

_____

_____

_____

2. _____. How might this source be triggered?

_____

_____

_____

3. _____. How might this source be triggered?

_____

_____

_____

4. _____. How might this source be triggered?

_____

_____

_____

4.1

Activating the ADAPT Process for Developing and Confirming Customer Needs

Objective

You will further develop your understanding and ability to apply the ADAPT process of needs development.

THE EXERCISE ASSIGNMENT

Congratulations!! You have recently joined Addvance Frozen Foods as their salesperson in the Midwestern Territory. A food processor specializing in providing the meat entrees for large institutions such as prisons and hospitals, Addvance is recognized as one of the industry leaders. This reputation not only includes market share, but also extends to leadership in innovative products and customer relations.

You have been working for several weeks to gain access to Jane Cummings, the foods buyer for the State of Illinois Prison System. With several other major food processors (including Kraft and General Foods) located in Chicago, the competition in this region has been great. As a result, Addvance has never been able to get any of its product line into the Illinois system. Nevertheless, Addvance has recently introduced and started shipping an innovative turkey-based line of products that averages 18 percent higher protein and 23 percent lower fat content than anything marketed by the competition. The higher protein level per serving is extremely important to such institutions as prisons, as it allows them to meet nutrition requirements with smaller servings of meat entrees and thus creates an opportunity for cost reduction. In addition to these tangible benefits, the product line's average selling price of $2.10 per pound is $0.22 a pound lower than Kraft's competing products and $0.20 under those of General Foods. Documenting the higher protein level and lower fat content certainly got Jane's attention. However, it was the combination of increased protein and lower price that got you the appointment to talk with Jane and members of her buying group in person.

As part of preparing for your sales call, you are compiling a set of anticipated questions that might assist you in better understanding Jane's current situation and confirming her needs. Information gained through this sort of effective questioning has proven valuable to you in the past as it helps you better respond to the customer's needs. Following the ADAPT model of questioning, develop a series of effective Assessment, Discovery, Activation, Projection, and Transition questions that you might use in the sales call with Jane Cummings.

Please use the following workbook pages to develop your questions:

Assessment Questions

1. _____

2. _____

3. _____

4. _____

5. _____

6. _____

Discovery Questions

1. _____

2. _____

3. _____

4. _____

5. _____

6. _____

Activation Questions

1. _____

2. _____

3. _____

4. _____

5. _____

6. _____

Projection Questions

1. _____

2. _____

3. _____

4. _____

5. _____

6. _____

Transition Questions

1. _____

2. _____

3. _____

4. _____

5. _____

6. _____

Role Plays for ADAPTive Questioning

Objective

You will continue building your listening skills and self-confidence in ADAPTive questioning through the use of in-class, mini–role plays.

INTRODUCTION

In this role play exercise, the instructor will be the prospect and students will take turns asking each type of question. As the role play progresses, it should become easier for you to understand the ADAPT process and what is required to make it effective.

THE COMPANY YOU REPRESENT

Students assume the role of salesperson for Sonoco. Founded in 1899 as the Southern Novelty Company, Sonoco Products Corporation is headquartered in Hartsville, South Carolina. This past year, it employed 17,000 people in 24 countries and ranked 22nd on the *Fortune* 500 list. For that same year, the company earned $117.5 million on nearly $2 billion in sales. The company specializes in producing many different types of packaging, from composite cans that hold orange juice, noodles, and tennis balls to labels that cover dozens of products in the health care and medical industry. Textile companies worldwide use the company's paper and plastic cones and tubes. The company also produces industrial containers, caulking tubes, recyclable plastic grocery bags, and even paper lids on the glasses travelers find at hotels.

YOUR PRODUCT

Sonoco produces both chipboard and corrugated partitions that are custom designed to fit the customer's packaging needs. The partitions are designed so that all cells within the box have the same size, which means that the product fits snugly throughout the box, minimizing chances for breakage and scratching. The company also manufactures machinery for inserting products into boxes. The following chart summarizes the features and advantages of Sonoco's packaging products:

Feature	Advantage
Custom designed and manufactured	Packaging will fit snugly around any size or shape product
Broad range of surface finishes, including water and starch finished, wax impregnated, and polyethylene coated	Allows versatility in shipping; not necessary to shop from several manufacturers to meet different packaging requirements
Automatic product insertion machinery available	Provides smooth product insertion without damage to glass or labeling
Easy-grip edges	Keeps partitions from falling out of cartons during manual or automatic decasing
Uses recyclable cardboard	Meets demand for environmental awareness
Durable, solid fibers	Helps withstand abrupt shocks
Clean, uniform edges and surfaces	Product arrives clean, dustfree, and looking its best
Custom-designed graphics available for outside of package	Can enhance company image and make product easier to sell in self-service stores
Frequent delivery available	Reduces need for large inventory of empty packaging
Design of flutes provides stronger boxes with less weight	Provides maximum protection while reducing shipping costs

THE EXERCISE ASSIGNMENT

In this role play, it is assumed that the Lilly Fields Glass Co. has called Sonoco and expressed an interest in Sonoco's packaging. This lead has been turned over to you, and today you will make the initial call on the purchasing manager of the Lilly Fields Glass Co., a manufacturer of water glasses, water pitchers, cocktail glasses, and glass beer steins. Its products are all currently sold to bars and restaurants.

Your task in this call is to first use **Assessment** questions to find out more about the Lilly Fields Glass Co. For example, are they considering any changes in their target market? Then, using **Discovery** questions, **Activation** questions, **Projection** questions, and **Transition** questions, explore (a) the prospect's problems; (b) the consequences of these problems; and (c) what solving these problems might mean to the purchasing manager. However, *you will not present solutions during this role play.*

To assist you in preparing for this call, here are examples of the kinds of problems your prospect might be having:

- Lilly Fields may need equipment to automatically insert glass products into shipping containers.
- Lilly Fields may need packaging with nonstandard specifications.
- Lilly Fields may need different materials incorporated into the same package.

- Lilly Fields may not know how to go about designing packaging.
- Lilly Fields may have been having a lot of damage in shipping.
- Lilly Fields may be spending a lot for extra warehouse space to store packaging.
- The purchasing manager may also have personal needs beyond those of the firm.

Based on the features and advantages explained earlier, you should be able to think of other problems that might be solved by using your product.

Prepare for the call by listing the potential consequences you might want to explore during the call. Use the **Salesperson's Preparation Form** provided for your use on the following pages to list questions you could use during the role play. At this point, don't be too concerned about the quality of the questions; it is more important that you focus on getting practice asking each kind of question. As you go through the next several role plays, you will learn more about what provides quality to each kind of question.

Remember that the purpose of the role play is to practice ADAPT questioning. Do not "pitch" to the prospect. Focus instead on getting information about his or her problems, needs, and concerns.

You will also be asked to summarize what you have heard and check that the prospect agrees with your summary. If you were going to propose a solution, you would want to be certain that you had properly interpreted the prospect's concerns.

SALESPERSON'S PREPARATION FORM

Assessment Questions

1. _____
2. _____
3. _____
4. _____
5. _____
6. _____

Discovery Questions

1. _____
2. _____
3. _____
4. _____
5. _____
6. _____

Activation Questions

1. _____
2. _____

3. _____

4. _____

5. _____

6. _____

Projection Questions

1. _____

2. _____

3. _____

4. _____

5. _____

6. _____

Transition Questions

1. _____

2. _____

3. _____

4. _____

5. _____

6. _____

Effective Questioning

Objective

You will understand the importance of asking effective questions.

INTRODUCTION

There are two ways to dominate or control a sales conversation. A salesperson can talk all the time, or the salesperson can be in control by asking good, effective questions. Effective questioning offers the salesperson the following advantages:

1. Questions establish an atmosphere of control.
2. Questions help you determine how cooperative your customer will be.
3. Questions get you valuable information about your customer's needs, desires, and problems.
4. Questions help you identify your customer's style and opinions as well as his or her current understanding and awareness of needs and of your product or service.
5. Questions help you avoid rejection.
6. Questions build trust and rapport.
7. Questions save you time.
8. Questions keep you from talking too much.
9. Questions get the customer involved.
10. Questions get and maintain the customer's attention.
11. Questions make your customer think.
12. Questions and subsequent answers, if you listen attentively, create a willingness on the part of the customer to listen to you when it is your turn to talk.
13. Intelligent questions make you look competent and knowledgeable.

A salesperson can use open-ended and closed-ended questions for effective questioning.

Open-ended and Closed-ended Questions

Open-ended Questions—Open-ended questions, also called nondirective questions, are designed to let the customer respond freely. That is, the customer is not limited to one- or two-word answers, and is encouraged to disclose personal and/or business information. These questions are typically used to probe the customer for descriptive information that allows the salesperson to better understand the specific needs of the customer.

Closed-ended Questions—Closed-ended questions, also called directive questions, are designed to limit the customer's response to one or two words. Although the most common form is the yes/no question, closed-ended questions can come in many forms—provided the response is limited to one or two words. For instance, "How many . . .", and "How often . . ." are examples of closed-ended questions. These questions are typically used to confirm or clarify information gleaned from responses to open-ended questions.

THE EXERCISE ASSIGNMENT

Used in combination, open- and closed-ended questions help the salesperson uncover and confirm customer needs, dissatisfactions, and opportunities. Let's look now at how these questions are used in the ADAPT process.

1. Observe a salesperson during an introductory call with a new prospect. What open-ended questions did the salesperson use?

   a. _____

   b. _____

   c. _____

   d. _____

   e. _____

   What types of information were gathered using open-ended questions? After the sales call, ask the salesperson how he or she will use this information.

   _____

   _____

   _____

   _____

   _____

   _____

   _____

2. What closed-ended questions did the salesperson use?

   a. _____

   b. _____

   c. _____

   d. _____

   e. _____

What types of information were gathered using closed-ended questions?
After the sales call, ask the salesperson how he or she will use this information.

_____

_____

_____

_____

_____

_____

EXPERIENTIAL EXERCISE

4.4

Thank-you Letters

Objective

You will increase your awareness of the important, effective, and efficient role played by thank-you letters in customer follow-up while gaining practice in writing thank-you letters.

THE EXERCISE ASSIGNMENT

Visualize yourself as a salesperson for Montgomery Paper Products, one of the top three firms in business supplies, paper, and paper products. Today has been a very hectic day, but one that you feel has been productive nevertheless. You have just returned to your office from calling on John Tracy, the head buyer for Worldwide Systems, Inc.

Worldwide currently sources all their paper needs from Acme Office Products. However, Acme has failed to keep Worldwide current on several technological advances. The fact that Montgomery Paper Products is the innovator and pioneer for several of these technological advances gives you an advantage in the marketplace. You have been using the potential benefits this new technology would produce for Worldwide as leverage to gain access to a portion of Worldwide's business.

Although John recognizes the benefits of changing to your line of products, he still has some reservations regarding your products being compatible with his existing equipment. You have been chipping away at this account for several months now. In fact, today's call is the sixth time you have met with John and other interested parties over at Worldwide. Even though they continue to express interest and ask that you keep them informed, they still have not committed to a purchase. Nevertheless, you sense they are moving closer.

Part One:

Using the following worksheet, compose a thank-you letter to John Tracy for his consideration in visiting with you today. You never know—a small act of professionalism might just be the one event that gets you the sale. Besides, the letter gives you an opportunity to get your name and product benefits in front of him one more time.

MONTGOMERY PAPER PRODUCTS

1800 Eastport Road   Chicago, IL 63984   (715) 756-8333

Part Two:

Visualize the same scenario, except that you did get the order you were after. Not only that, John indicated that if you and Montgomery Paper Products carry through and do what you say you will do, there is strong potential for added business. How would your thank-you letter differ from that in the earlier scenario? Compose this new letter in the space below:

MONTGOMERY PAPER PRODUCTS
1800 Eastport Road   Chicago, IL 63984   (715) 756-8333

Part Three:

Now for the hard one. Suppose the scenario is changed and Montgomery Paper is the primary supplier for Worldwide. You still service the account and John is the buyer. You still call on John, but you also spend a lot of time working with the people in the office and shop who actually use your products. In fact, relations are so good that most of the ordering is automatic. How would this letter look? Compose it in the space below:

MONTGOMERY PAPER PRODUCTS
1800 Eastport Road   Chicago, IL 63984   (715) 756-8333

Assessing the Effectiveness of Different Customer Contact Methods

Objective

You will develop your understanding of the various methods for making customer contact and how each method's effectiveness varies according to desired outcomes.

THE EXERCISE ASSIGNMENT

The effectiveness of the various methods available for salespeople to make contact with prospects and customers will vary according to what the salesperson hopes to accomplish. This exercise requires that you consider certain outcomes that a salesperson might desire and designate which contact method(s) might be the most effective. To encourage your thoughtful consideration of each method's strengths and weaknesses, the exercise also requires you to explain why you made your selections.

EVALUATING THE EFFECTIVENESS OF CUSTOMER CONTACT METHODS

For each of the following desired outcomes, indicate which customer contact method would be the best to use. Indicate your choice by entering the letter(s) corresponding to the chosen contact method(s):

In Person (P)   E-mail (E)
Form Letter (F)   Personalized Letter (L)
Telephone (T)   World Wide Web (W)

After you have made your selection, briefly explain why you believe this to be the optimal choice. This information will be used for class discussion.

Method

Creating awareness of product or company. _____

Why: _____

_____ _____

_____

Introducing yourself. _____

Why? _____

_____

_____

Getting an initial appointment. _____

Why? _____

_____

_____

Confirming an appointment. _____

Why? _____

_____

_____

Getting acquainted. _____

Why? _____

_____

_____

Discovering customer needs. _____

Why? _____

_____

_____

_____

Method

Determining customer buying motives.   _____

Why?   _____

_____

_____

_____

Determining influencers and decision makers in the buying organization.   _____

Why?   _____

_____

_____

_____

Assessing the Lifetime Value of a Customer

Objective

The lifeline of an organization is repeat business, obtained by keeping present customers happy. In this exercise you will calculate the value of a customer over a five-year period.

THE LIFETIME VALUE OF A CUSTOMER

Identify a salesperson with whom you can establish a rapport and working relationship that allows you to accompany or shadow the salesperson for a day. Note the various behaviors and activities the salesperson performs that have some relationship (good and bad) to the development and maintenance of buyer–seller relationships.

With the assistance of the salesperson, select one customer and calculate the lifetime value of that customer.

In a short report, present the relationship activities (good and bad) you observed during the shadowing opportunity, along with the lifetime value calculation. The report must contain explanation and support for the value determined.

As noted earlier, the lifeline of organizations today is repeat business. Present customers have already developed trust with their salesperson and, with proper nurturing, should be easier to sell to over time.

In the grocery industry, the average customer spends $100 per week for 50 weeks each year. The value of this customer each year is $5,000 and over five years, $25,000.

In the consumer goods industry, an average order from a small grocery store (independent grocer) is $1,000 per week. The value of this customer per year is $50,000 and over five years, $250,000.

THE EXERCISE ASSIGNMENT

1. Contact a salesperson and ask what an average customer would order per month. Calculate the value over five years for this customer.

_____

_____

_____

_____

_____

_____

_____

2. Discuss with the salesperson how much time it takes to develop this type of customer.

_____

_____

_____

_____

_____

_____

_____

_____

3. Discuss the implications of losing an active customer and how much time and effort it takes to replace a lost customer.

_____

_____

_____

_____

_____

_____

_____

4. Ask your salesperson the amount of effort it takes to get business from an existing account versus generating new business.

_____

_____

_____

_____

_____

_____

5.3

Prospecting Effectiveness

Objective

You will be able to identify several popular prospecting techniques and determine the effectiveness of the techniques.

THE EXERCISE ASSIGNMENT

Review the discussion of prospecting sources and methods on pp. 139–145. Select two methods from each category of external sources, internal sources, and personal contact sources and complete the following section.

List prospecting methods and record your opinion of its effectiveness.

External Sources

1. Prospecting method _____

   In your opinion, what is the strength or weakness of this prospecting method?

   _____

   _____

   _____

2. Prospecting method _____

   In your opinion, what is the strength or weakness of this prospecting method?

   _____

   _____

   _____

Internal Sources

1. Prospecting method _____

   In your opinion, what is the strength or weakness of this prospecting method?

   _____

   _____

   _____

2. Prospecting method _____

   In your opinion, what is the strength or weakness of this prospecting method?

   _____

   _____

   _____

Personal Contact Sources

1. Prospecting method _____

   In your opinion, what is the strength or weakness of this prospecting method?

   _____

   _____

   _____

2. Prospecting method _____

   In your opinion, what is the strength or weakness of this prospecting method?

   _____

   _____

   _____

Source: Adapted from Ingram, T. N. SMEI *Certification Study Guide,* The University of Memphis: SMEI Accreditation Institute, 1994.

Developing Feature and Benefit Statements for Your School

Objective

You will be able to develop feature and benefit statements for your school and apply them to relevant markets.

INTRODUCTION

Benefit statements describe a feature from a specific customer's point of view. They answer such customer questions as "How is this going to help *me* solve *my* problems?"

Any given feature may produce different benefits for different customers and no benefits for others. Therefore, it's important to develop benefit statements for specific markets. The more precisely you can express the benefit *in the language of the customer*, the more effective your statements will be. The following example will help you get started on this assignment.

Example

The following example will help you understand this exercise. First, choose three groups that represent target markets at your school (examples could be: Greeks, athletes, students with disabilities, faculty, staff, graduate students, general student population, freshmen, and so on).

1. Target Market (*for example, athletes*)
2. Target Market (*for example, students with disabilities*)
3. Target Market (*for example, graduate students*)

Next, select a feature of your school (an example might be a tutoring program available at your school).

1. Feature: *Tutoring program available to our students.*

Finally, develop a benefit statement for each of your target markets. Remember, any given feature may produce different benefits for one target group and no benefit for the others.

Target Market 1. *athletes* Benefit Statement: *Athletes spend time at practice and away games. The benefit of the tutoring program to athletes is they can use the program to catch up on their work and not fall behind.*

Target Market 2. *students with disabilities* Benefit Statement: *Students who are blind have readers available to read lessons to them. The benefit to the students is they do not have to pay for a reader.*

Target Market 3. *graduate students* Benefit Statement: *Graduate students are used as the tutors. The benefit to graduate students is they can supplement their income and feel good about helping others.*

THE EXERCISE ASSIGNMENT

Based on the example provided, develop additional features and benefit statements for your three target markets.

1. Feature: ————————————————————————————————
   Target Market 1: —————————— Benefit Statement: ——————
   ——————————————————————————————————————

   Target Market 2: —————————— Benefit Statement: ——————
   ——————————————————————————————————————

   Target Market 3: —————————— Benefit Statement: ——————
   ——————————————————————————————————————

2. Feature: ————————————————————————————————
   Target Market 1: —————————— Benefit Statement: ——————
   ——————————————————————————————————————

   Target Market 2: —————————— Benefit Statement: ——————
   ——————————————————————————————————————

   Target Market 3: —————————— Benefit Statement: ——————
   ——————————————————————————————————————

3. Feature: ————————————————————————————————
   Target Market 1: —————————— Benefit Statement: ——————
   ——————————————————————————————————————

   Target Market 2: —————————— Benefit Statement: ——————
   ——————————————————————————————————————

   Target Market 3: —————————— Benefit Statement: ——————
   ——————————————————————————————————————

4. Feature: ————————————————————————————————
   Target Market 1: —————————— Benefit Statement: ——————
   ——————————————————————————————————————

   Target Market 2: —————————— Benefit Statement: ——————
   ——————————————————————————————————————

Target Market 3: ——————————— Benefit Statement: ———————

——————————————————————————————

5. Feature: ———————————————————————————
   Target Market 1: ——————————— Benefit Statement: ———————

——————————————————————————————

   Target Market 2: ——————————— Benefit Statement: ———————

——————————————————————————————

   Target Market 3: ——————————— Benefit Statement: ———————

——————————————————————————————

6. Feature: ———————————————————————————
   Target Market 1: ——————————— Benefit Statement: ———————

——————————————————————————————

   Target Market 2: ——————————— Benefit Statement: ———————

——————————————————————————————

   Target Market 3: ——————————— Benefit Statement: ———————

——————————————————————————————

7. Feature: ———————————————————————————
   Target Market 1: ——————————— Benefit Statement: ———————

——————————————————————————————

   Target Market 2: ——————————— Benefit Statement: ———————

——————————————————————————————

   Target Market 3: ——————————— Benefit Statement: ———————

——————————————————————————————

8. Feature: ———————————————————————————
   Target Market 1: ——————————— Benefit Statement: ———————

——————————————————————————————

   Target Market 2: ——————————— Benefit Statement: ———————

——————————————————————————————

   Target Market 3: ——————————— Benefit Statement: ———————

——————————————————————————————

EXPERIENTIAL EXERCISE

6.2

Presentation Effectiveness—
Discussion Questions

Objective

You will be able to think through the presentation and to understand its key components.

THE EXERCISE ASSIGNMENT

Please respond to the following statements:

1. What is the main objective of a good presentation? _____
_____

2. How long should a good presentation be? _____
_____

3. Why are questions an important part of a presentation? _____
_____

4. When should you terminate a presentation? _____
_____

5. How should you terminate a sales call? _____
_____

Sales Call Planning Report

Objective

You will build your understanding of the importance of thorough strategic planning prior to calling on the customer by illustrating the integration of sales call objectives, features and benefits (FAB), and the ADAPT questioning process.

INTRODUCTION

Successful selling is based on thorough planning and preparation *before* the sales call and presentation. One of the most important areas of preparation pertains to understanding a product's features and how they might solve buyer needs. The link between product features and buyer needs is accomplished by converting a product's *FEATURES (what it is)* to *ADVANTAGES (what it does)*, and then translating these advantages into *BENEFITS that are relevant and meaningful to your buyer.*

Benefits are solutions to needs. It is important to realize that specific features may yield different benefits to different buyers. Thus, preparation includes imagining the variety of buyer needs that a feature might address and how to uncover potential benefits through questioning. Such preparation forces the salesperson to cognitively examine prospects in terms of:

1. product features that might give rise to buyer benefits
2. ADAPT questions to use in assessing the prospect's needs in relation to available product benefits
3. potential resistance in accepting and committing to the benefits as solutions to the prospect's problems and needs.

THE EXERCISE ASSIGNMENT

Unlike the other experiential exercises in this workbook in which the scenario was already set out for you, this exercise requires that you develop your own selling scenario, including (a) the product being sold, (b) the company you sell for, and (c) the prospect to whom you are selling. These product, company, and prospect profiles will then be used to anticipate the events and responses within a sales call in order to develop a detailed, strategic plan for making that call. All this will come together in a formal written report consisting of certain specific components.

We recommend that this assignment be done in groups of two students. You may exchange ideas, work through the various parts of the report together, and turn in one report. The assignment will be evaluated in terms of its preparation as well as its content. The report must be typed, be professional in appearance, and double spaced with one-inch margins. Headings, subheadings, and page numbers should be used to organize the report. A comb binder (available at Kinko's or PIP's) should be used rather than a plastic slip-on cover. The front cover should creatively, professionally, and neatly identify the specific product the report addresses, the members of the sales team, and the project due date. Inside, the report should consist of the following major sections:

Letter of Transmittal Assuming that your sales manager has requested a copy of your sales call plan, the first component of your report should be a letter of transmittal addressed to your sales manager (your instructor). Similar to an executive summary, this letter of transmittal references the manager's request, identifies your subject prospect along with the time and place of the sales call appointment, establishes the specific objectives you have set for this sales call, and provides a synopsis of the report's contents. This letter should be single-spaced and limited to one page.

Identification of Your Company This section profiles the company for which you sell. Actual companies may be used if you desire. This portion of the report develops detailed information, such as the name of the company, its size, and a brief history. Other information should also be included that might be relevant to a buyer. This information will facilitate the profile's use should it be used in a subsequent buyer–seller role play.

Identification of Your Product Choose a good or service that you would like to sell. (You might consider using a product from a company that you might want to go to work for, as this project can be quite beneficial to you in your job interviews.) All products are to be sold to another business or institution. Sales of products to individuals for their own use is not allowed. Experience indicates that the closer a product is to the retail marketplace, the harder it is to use, and the closer the product is to being industrial in nature, the better it seems to work. Your product choice should be in good taste and legal, and must not be in conflict with any school rules or policies.

The last portion of this section should be a chart of the product's general features, advantages, and benefits. To assist you in developing this information, an example of an FAB chart is included at the end of this exercise.

Profile of Competition Who are the major competitors? What are their strengths and weaknesses? How do competitive products compare to the FABs of your product? This section must develop and describe at least two competitors.

Profile of Prospect This section profiles both the buyer and the buyer's company. What is the name of the person you are calling on? What is his or her position and history with the firm? What is the company name and type of business? Where are they located? What information do we know before actually making a sales call? How is our product relevant to them? Is the use for resale or manufacture? What brands and suppliers are currently being used?

Expected Problems and Needs What types of customer problems might be discovered in working with this prospect? What advance information or intelligence do you have regarding problems or needs? In this section you should develop four potential problems relevant to both your prospect and your type of product. In the following section you will use these four potential problems as a guide to develop a series of ADAPT questions that would address these problems and ascertain corresponding needs.

Develop ADAPT Question Sequence As a major part of this section, you should develop and include a series of product and customer relevant questions that can be used to assess the needs of your prospects. These questions should follow the ADAPT questioning sequence (explained in Module 4, Questioning Skills). Workbook pages for developing ADAPT questions are included on pages 379–380. Keep in mind that the ADAPT sequence of questions is intended to help your prospect discover and solve a problem, as opposed to "pitching" a product.

Expected Objections and Resistance What forms of resistance are expected? This section should detail ten specific objections that you expect in making your presentation to this account. Classify each of these objections by type. For each objection, describe how you would respond. Classify each response by type. Note that you will need to read Module 8 in the text before completing this section.

Gaining Customer Commitment Describe and illustrate how you will gain customer commitment and finalize the sale. Your description should include a statement classifying the type of commitment-gaining method being used. Note that you will need to read Module 8 in the text before completing this section.

Customer Follow-Up This section discusses the follow-up activities that will be undertaken and provides a timetable for their implementation. Follow-up activities should be developed for both contingencies: (a) that you are successful in achieving the objectives set out for this sales call, and (b) that you are not successful in achieving the sales call objectives.

PROSPECT NEEDS	FEATURES	ADVANTAGES	BENEFITS

Your Name: _____

SALESPERSON'S PREPARATION FORM

Assessment Questions:

_____

_____

_____

_____

Discovery Questions:

_____

_____

_____

_____

_____

Activation Questions:

_____

_____

_____

_____

Projection Questions:

_____

_____

_____

_____

_____

Transition Questions:

_____

_____

_____

_____

_____

Helpful Hints for Sales Presentations

Objective

You will be able to understand some key issues that can make the sales presentation more effective.

THE EXERCISE ASSIGNMENT

Please respond to the following statements:

1. Use short, simple, uncomplicated words. Why? _____
_____
_____

2. Use words that create a visual image. Why? _____
_____
_____

3. Get the customers involved. Why? _____
_____
_____

4. Never argue with your customers. Why? _____
_____
_____

5. Work from appointments—this is the mark of a professional. Why? _____

_____

_____

_____

6. Plan each presentation. Have a specific objective. Why? _____

_____

_____

_____

7. Terminate the presentation as soon as you discover the prospect does not qualify. Why?

_____

_____

_____

8. Use *questions* to control the presentation. Why? _____

_____

_____

_____

9. Increase your effectiveness—practice, practice, practice! Why? _____

_____

_____

_____

Generating Buyer Involvement

Objective

You will increase your skill in generating the active involvement of the prospect in the presentation.

INTRODUCTION

Communication research suggests that both educational and persuasive communications are more effective when the buyer is actively involved in the presentation rather than being a passive observer. However, creating opportunities for buyer involvement often takes some thought and encouragement on the part of the salesperson.

THE EXERCISE ASSIGNMENT

Working in groups of three, consider yourselves in each of the four following selling situations. Brainstorm different techniques you could use to involve the customer for each selling situation. Using the space provided, identify five techniques you feel would be the most effective along with a brief discussion explaining why.

SITUATION 1: A retail salesperson for Mike's Bike Shop selling a new style, ultra-light racing bike to a racing fanatic.

Technique 1 _____

_____

Why? _____

_____

Technique 2 _____

_____

Why? _____

_____

Technique 3 _____

_____

Why? _____

_____

Technique 4 _____

_____

Why? _____

_____

Technique 5 _____

_____

Why? _____

_____

SITUATION 2: A manufacturer's representative selling a new line of ultra-light racing bicycles to the buyer for Mike's Bike Shop.

Technique 1 _____

_____

Why? _____

_____

Technique 2 _____

_____

Why? _____

_____

Technique 3 _____

_____

Why? _____

_____

Technique 4 _____

_____

Why? _____

_____

Technique 5 _____

_____

Why? _____

_____

SITUATION 3: An industrial–chemical salesperson selling corrosion and acid-proof polymer coatings to a manufacturer of acid dispensing equipment that is used in medical research labs.

Technique 1 _____

_____

Why? _____

_____

Technique 2 _____

_____

Why? _____

_____

Technique 3 _____

_____

Why? _____

_____

Technique 4 _____

_____

Why? _____

_____

Technique 5 _____

_____

Why? _____

_____

SITUATION 4: A salesperson for General Electric Jet Engine Division presenting a high-thrust, low-noise, fuel-efficient jet engine to the buying team at American Airlines to retrofit 150 of their 727-model aircraft.

Technique 1 _____

_____

Why? _____

_____

Technique 2 _____

_____

Why? _____

_____

Technique 3 _____

_____

Why? _____

_____

Technique 4 _____

_____

Why? _____

_____

Technique 5 _____

_____

Why? _____

_____

Why Salespeople Fail to Gain Commitment

Objective

You will be able to understand the issue of failure in gaining commitment.

THE EXERCISE ASSIGNMENT

One reason why sales are not completed is the salesperson makes no attempt to close the sale. Why, after investing all the time and effort in prospecting, qualifying, and making the presentation, would a salesperson not attempt to gain commitment? What are some other reasons why salespeople fail to gain commitment? Record your responses on the following lines.

1. _____

_____

2. _____

_____

3. _____

_____

4. _____

_____

5. _____

_____

6. _____

_____

Gaining Commitment— Caution Signals

Objective

You will be able to recognize gaining commitment caution signals.

INTRODUCTION

There are situations that do not warrant the salesperson attempting to gain customer commitment. It is risky to ask for the order when you are getting negative signals or when there is an indication that the prospect is uncomfortable about something. Trying to gain commitment following a negative indication without resolving the problem is being unresponsive to the prospect's need. Here are some situations where the salesperson should do something else before attempting to gain commitment.

THE EXERCISE ASSIGNMENT

Here are some situations where the salesperson should do something else before attempting to gain commitment. Examine each of the situations and explain why they should be viewed as a caution signal.

1. The prospect requests additional information on a technical product. Why would this be a buying caution signal?

_____

_____

_____

2. A rushed or inadequate presentation has been made. Why would this be a buying caution signal?

_____

_____

_____

3. The prospect is hostile or defensive and is not making an attempt to bargain. Why would this be a buying caution signal?

_____

_____

_____

4. The prospect raises an objection or asks for more information. Why would this be a buying caution signal?

_____

_____

_____

5. A significant interruption has disturbed the buying mood. Why would this be a buying caution signal?

_____

_____

_____

6. Gaining commitment on a minor point failed to reveal positive signs of interest. Why would this be a buying caution signal?

_____

_____

_____

Reasons for Sales Resistance

Objective

You will be able to understand the different reasons for sales resistance and how to overcome these barriers.

INTRODUCTION

There are two types of sales resistance: psychological and logical. Psychological resistance refers to an unwillingness to buy based on attitude, emotion, or prejudice. Such resistance is very subjective and varies from one prospect to another. Logical resistance or objections to the sales presentation refers to unwillingness to buy based on tangible considerations related to some aspect of the product.

THE EXERCISE ASSIGNMENT

Following are brief descriptions of the most common types of psychological and logical sales resistance. Write your suggestions for addressing these barriers in the space provided.

Psychological Barriers

1. Resistance to interference: Salesperson's call or visit is viewed as an interruption of what prospect is doing.

   Suggestions for salespeople to overcome this type of resistance:

   _____

   _____

   _____

2. Preference for established habits: Prospect finds comfort in present habits. A purchase usually involves a change in habits.

   Suggestions for salespeople to overcome this type of resistance:

   _____

   _____

   _____

3. Apathy toward product: Prospect feels no need for product, so is unwilling to spend money for it.

   Suggestions for salespeople to overcome this type of resistance:

   _____

   _____

   _____

4. Resistance to giving up something: Prospect views purchase as giving up money in exchange for product.

   Suggestions for salespeople to overcome this type of resistance:

   _____

   _____

   _____

5. Negative stereotype of salesperson: Prospect has feeling of contempt and suspicion toward all salespeople.

   Suggestions for salespeople to overcome this type of resistance:

   _____

   _____

   _____

6. Resistance to domination: Prospect has a need to feel in control of the situation.

   Suggestions for salespeople to overcome this type of resistance:

   _____

   _____

   _____

7. Preconceived ideas about product: Prospect's ideas and feelings, accurate or not, may close his or her mind to the purchase.

   Suggestions for salespeople to overcome this type of resistance:

   _____

   _____

   _____

8. Dislike of making decisions: Prospect may fear consequences of deciding and dread disturbing the status quo. May be due to lack of self-confidence.

Suggestions for salespeople to overcome this type of resistance:

_____

_____

_____

Logical Barriers

When a prospect raises an objection, he or she is signaling the feeling of conflict between buying and not buying the product. A pessimistic salesperson will feel discouraged by objections. The optimistic salesperson will welcome logical objections, realizing they indicate at least some desire to buy.

The specific causes of logical resistance vary from industry to industry, so only the broadest categories will be included here. Later in the session you will develop a list of the specific resistance you encounter in your interactions with prospects.

1. Price: Probably the most frequently cited objection.

Suggestions for salespeople to overcome this type of resistance:

_____

_____

_____

2. Delivery schedule: The importance of delivery time varies with the time-related priorities of the prospect.

Suggestions for salespeople to overcome this type of resistance:

_____

_____

_____

3. Specifications: Drawn up with input from the end user or by the technical experts.

Suggestions for salespeople to overcome this type of resistance:

_____

_____

_____

4. Inadequate warranty.

Suggestions for salespeople to overcome this type of resistance:

_____

_____

_____

5. Does not have feature a competitor has.

   Suggestions for salespeople to overcome this type of resistance:

   _____

   _____

   _____

6. Performance does not measure up to the competition.

   Suggestions for salespeople to overcome this type of resistance:

   _____

   _____

   _____

7. Other?

   Suggestions for salespeople to overcome this type of resistance:

   _____

   _____

   _____

EXPERIENTIAL
EXERCISE

8.4

Negotiating Buyer Resistance

Objective

You will develop your skills in recognizing and dealing with different forms of buyer resistance.

THE EXERCISE ASSIGNMENT

At the beginning of this exercise, your instructor will pass out cards to all members of the class. Each card contains a statement or comment that is commonly made by buyers to salespeople. These buyer statements illustrate a wide variety of the different forms of resistance. After reviewing the resistance statement appearing on the card, each member of the class will role play the part of a salesperson and demonstrate how they would handle the situation while negotiating the specific buyer resistance. Your role play should:

1. Be conducted within the LAARC framework for working through buyer resistance (as discussed in the introduction to Exercise 8.3)
2. Incorporate a variety of the strategies for responding to buyer resistance that have been discussed in class. Some of the more common strategies are listed below.

COMMONLY USED METHODS
FOR NEGOTIATING SALES RESISTANCE

I. Put-Off Strategies

II. Switching Focus Strategies
   a. Alternative Product
   b. Feel, Felt, Found
   c. Comparison and Contrast

III. Offsetting Strategies
   a. Compensation and Counter-Balance
   b. Boomerang

IV. Denial Strategies
   a. Indirect
   b. Direct

V. Handling Price Strategies
   a. Build Perceived Value
   b. Break Into Smaller Units
   c. Price-Value Comparisons
   d. Emphasize Uniqueness

VI. Proof Providing Strategies
   a. Case Histories
   b. Demonstrations
   c. Trial Usage

Source: Adapted from an exercise submitted by Jill S. Attaway, Michael A. Humphreys, Timothy A. Longfellow, and Michael R. Williams; Department of Marketing, Illinois State University, (1995).

9.1

Post-Presentation Follow-up: Analyzing a Sales Call

Objective

You will be able to analyze the sales call of a salesperson during a shadow call.

THE EXERCISE ASSIGNMENT

After you have shadowed a salesperson on a sales call, you will be able to evaluate the strengths and weaknesses of the call by responding to the following questions.

1. What might the salesperson have done better? _____

_____

_____

2. What did the salesperson say or do that they wish they had not? _____

_____

_____

3. Did the salesperson discuss topics that were not relevant to the sale? _____

_____

_____

_____

4. Did the salesperson venture into subjects that could have led to an argument?

_____

_____

_____

5. Did the salesperson's talk stray from the purpose at hand? _____

_____

_____

6. Did the salesperson talk too much? _____

_____

_____

7. Did the salesperson detect the prospect becoming weary when points were belabored?

_____

_____

_____

8. Did the salesperson interrupt or cut the customer off during the discussion? _____

_____

_____

_____

9. Was the presentation too one-sided? _____

_____

_____

10. How could the sale have been increased? _____

_____

_____

11. Could the salesperson's presentation have been more persuasive and the sales results better?

_____

_____

_____

12. Did the salesperson listen to what the customer had to say? _____

_____

_____

13. Did the salesperson present the product in terms of customer needs?

_____

_____

_____

14. As the salesperson talked, was he or she thinking of the customer?

_____

_____

_____

15. Were the suggested applications interesting to the customer? _____

_____

_____

_____

16. Whose real interest did the salesperson have in mind? _____

_____

_____

17. Will the salesperson be welcome on the next call to this customer?

_____

_____

_____

What to Do after Gaining Commitment

Objective

The salesperson has to complete a number of activities once the order has been signed. You will understand what activities must be completed after earning commitment.

THE EXERCISE ASSIGNMENT

You are a salesperson calling on your school's purchasing department and the buyer has just informed you that they have made the buying decision in your favor. What do you do now? Please respond to the following questions.

1. Confirm the customer's decision. How do you accomplish this?

_____

_____

_____

2. Show appreciation. How do you accomplish this?

_____

_____

_____

3. Cement the relationship. How do you accomplish this?

_____

_____

_____

4. Monitor delivery. How do you accomplish this?

_____

_____

_____

5. Monitor installation. How do you accomplish this?

_____

_____

_____

6. Keep your promises. How do you accomplish this?

_____

_____

_____

7. Handle complaints with sensitivity. How do you accomplish this?

_____

_____

_____

8. Respect the customer's time. How do you accomplish this?

_____

_____

_____

9. Provide information on the care and use of products. How do you accomplish this?

_____

_____

_____

10. List some specific follow-up actions that will cement the relationship between you and your customers.

_____

_____

_____

Enhancing Customer Relationships

Objective

You will be able to understand that building mutually satisfying relationships between buyers and sellers is essential for success in sales.

THE EXERCISE ASSIGNMENT

To build mutually satisfying relationships between buyers and sellers, professional salespeople must be competent in accomplishing five ongoing tasks:

1. Provide information. What does this mean and why is it important to building a relationship?

_____

_____

_____

_____

2. Reduce risk. What does this mean and why is it important to building a relationship?

_____

_____

_____

_____

3. Establish high standards and expectations. What does this mean and why is it important to building a relationship?

_____

_____

_____

_____

4. Anticipate and respond to customer problems and concerns. What does this mean and why is it important to building a relationship?

_____

_____

_____

_____

5. Monitor and improve customer satisfaction. What does this mean and why is it important to building a relationship?

_____

_____

_____

_____

10.1

Written Sales Proposals— Summarizing Quantitative Data

Objective:

You will master the skills of working in teams and present numbers and related data in clear, summarized formats for maximum clarity and persuasive impact.

INTRODUCTION

In this exercise, you will work in groups of two or three to develop a written sales proposal including quantitative product costs and client benefits, a clear synopsis of a timetable for installation, and a summary of the terms of a contract. This proposal has been requested by the client following four sales calls in which needs and expectations have been fully explored. The formal written proposal is to be mailed to the client along with a cover letter.

THE EXERCISE ASSIGNMENT

You are a salesperson for PRE-SELECT, Inc. (PSI). Headquartered in Chicago, PSI is the industry leader in pre-interview assessment and testing for the insurance industry. Focusing primarily on sales-related recruiting and selection, PSI's Interactive Employee Assessment System (IEAS) has been quite successful in lowering payroll costs by reducing sales agent turnover rates. Because of its highly recognized rate of success, PSI's customers include 13 of the top 20 insurance companies in the United States.

Although the system is continuously revised and updated, the basic program has been operating for six years. Using a personal computer in the field—usually at the branch office or agent's location—the IEAS consists of three computer-based components:

1. Pre-interview attitude and aptitude testing
2. Interactive simulations of critical work situations for use as part of the interview process
3. Periodic, post-hiring assessment for training focus

Salesperson Instructions

Ron Lovell, National Agency Director for Secure Future Insurance Company (SFIC), is interested in improving his company's recruiting and selection process for sales agents. SFIC is a national company with 150 agents across the United States. Although not ranked among the top 20 insurers, SFIC is a large and successful firm listed in the *Fortune* 1000. You have met with Ron on four previous occasions exploring problems, opportunities, and needs. During these meetings you discovered that SFIC's turnover rate among its sales agents approaches 42 percent. Compared to industry averages, that's not bad, but it does require hiring 375 new salespeople every year. SFIC's own estimate of hiring, training, and licensing costs is $7,500, for a total annual cost exceeding $2.8 million. Field experience indicates that, using PSI's computer-based system, turnover would fall to an average ranging from 15 to 20 percent, which offers considerable savings to SFIC.

You have been working up the figures for implementing the system at headquarters and in each of the 150 general offices. One-time hardware costs total $610,000. Although minimal training is required, installation and training would be priced out at $75,000 plus another $5,500 for chargeable travel expenses. Software licensing fees would total $135,000 per year. Sales tax on the hardware and software license would be computed at 6.5 percent. Finally, software maintenance fees run 15 percent of the annual licensing cost. According to the technical support department, this installation could be completed, with the full system operating in just over four months from the date of the order.

During your last call, you detailed the basics of the Interactive Employee Assessment System scaled to meet the needs of SFIC. Ron, along with the other officers attending the presentation, liked what he saw and requested that you put together a formal proposal. On your way out of the building, Ron mentioned that the proposal would have to be detailed enough to allow him to pass it through the capital budgeting department. This means detailing costs, projected savings, the payback period, and the installation-implementation schedule. As another positive indicator, Ron also asked that you arrange a follow-up meeting approximately two weeks after the proposal is received. Your task is to develop a follow-up letter and written sales proposal for his immediate attention.

Gaining Commitment with Buying Teams

Objective:

You will master the skills of working in teams and develop skills in gaining customer commitment.

INTRODUCTION

You will work in groups of three and brainstorm different methods for gaining the buyer's commitment in the following selling scenario. After reading the scenario, work in your groups to develop closes that could be applied. Use the worksheets to develop and illustrate each technique listed. Notice that the worksheets also call for you to explain why you feel this is a good technique. The examples each group develops will form the basis for a class discussion.

National Payroll Corporation (NPC) is the leading provider of electronic payroll processing. Their services include a full menu of payroll services, including accounting and record keeping, check writing, and the calculation and filing of all city, state, and federal payroll taxes. Their benefits offered to clients include not only lower costs than companies incur doing it all in-house, but also higher levels of accuracy and on-time filings of the ever-increasing number of tax forms.

As a salesperson for National Payroll Corporation, you have been calling on Acme Mechanical for about seven months now. Tony Fiona, the chief financial officer at Acme, likes what you have to offer and states that he is in favor of outsourcing the full payroll function to NPC. In fact, they have been close to signing several times, but it seems like some crisis always pops up at the last minute and diverts everyone's attention away from your proposition.

Tony has just called you at the office and requested that you come over to Acme this next week. He indicated that things looked pretty good right now. In fact, as a result of the crisis that left you sitting in the board room alone with an unsigned contract, the company has begun a major acquisition of one of its primary competitors. To handle all the auditing and accounting that the merger requires, Tony needs his full staff. At the same time, annual payroll tax reports are due in about three months and will require a large percentage of his staff's time.

Tony has presented the situation and available options to the various financial officers who would have to sign-off on the outsourcing decision. The response seemed favorable toward NPC's proposal. The only exceptions were two or three individuals who are reluctant to have an outsider handling delicate payroll information. Tony has set the meeting up so that all these individuals can be present. As Tony said right before he ended the phone conversation with you, "I've done everything I can to set it up for you. Now the ball is in your court. Get over here and see what you can do to tie this thing together. I have other fish to fry!"

THE EXERCISE ASSIGNMENT

With this scenario as the basis for your assumptions, use the following worksheet space to develop, explain, and illustrate with examples just how you would use different techniques to gain the commitment of the financial services buying team at Acme.

Method One:

_____

_____

_____

Method Two:

_____

_____

_____

Method Three:

_____

_____

Method Four:

Method Five:

Method Six:

Method Seven: